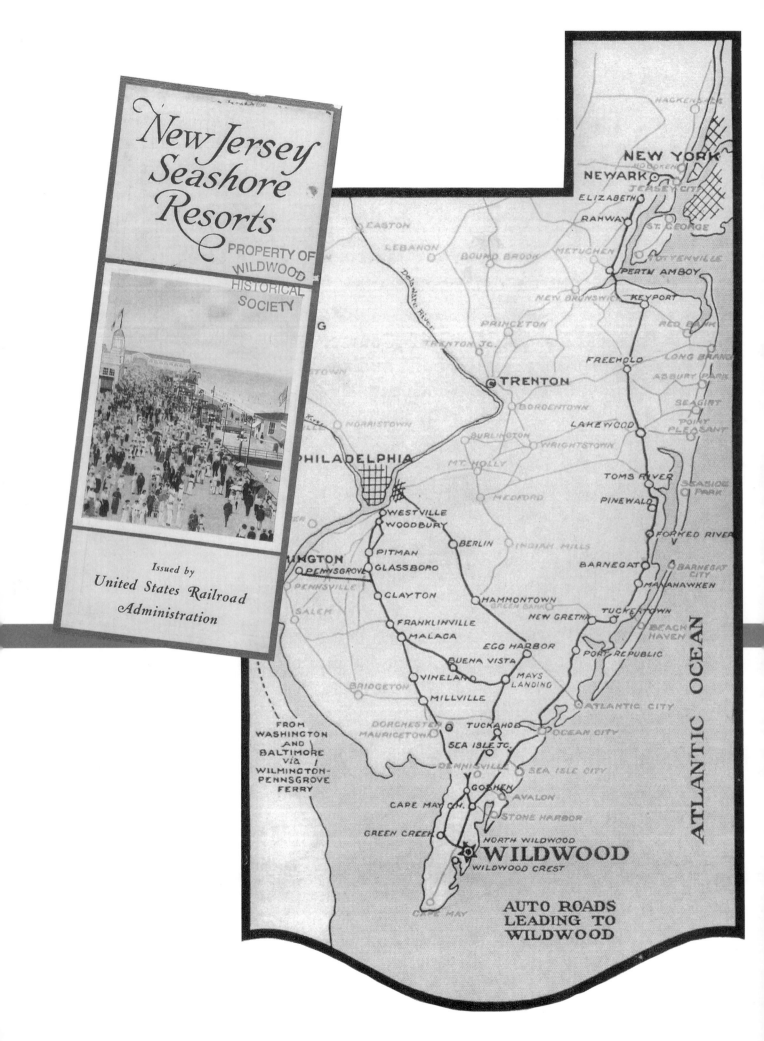

New Jersey Seashore Resorts

PROPERTY OF WILDWOOD HISTORICAL SOCIETY

Issued by
United States Railroad Administration

FROM
WASHINGTON
AND
BALTIMORE
via
WILMINGTON-
PENNSGROVE
FERRY

AUTO ROADS
LEADING TO
WILDWOOD

ATLANTIC OCEAN

NEW YORK
NEWARK
HACKENSACK
HOBOKEN
JERSEY CITY
ELIZABETH
RAHWAY
ST. GEORGE
METUCHEN
TOTTENVILLE
PERTH AMBOY
NEW BRUNSWICK
KEYPORT
PRINCETON
RED BANK
TRENTON JC.
FREEHOLD
LONG BRANCH
ASBURY PARK
TRENTON
BORDENTOWN
SEA GIRT
LAKEWOOD
POINT PLEASANT
EASTON
LEBANON
BOUND BROOK
BURLINGTON
WRIGHTSTOWN
NORRISTOWN
MT. HOLLY
TOMS RIVER
SEASIDE PARK
PHILADELPHIA
MEDFORD
PINEWALD
INDIAN MILLS
FORKED RIVER
WESTVILLE
WOODBURY
BERLIN
BARNEGAT
BARNEGAT CITY
PITMAN
GLASSBORO
MANAHAWKEN
PENNSGROVE
WASHINGTON
PENNSVILLE
CLAYTON
HAMMONTOWN
GREEN BANK
TUCKERTOWN
SALEM
FRANKLINVILLE
NEW GRETNA
BEACH HAVEN
MALAGA
EGG HARBOR
BUENA VISTA
PORT REPUBLIC
VINELAND
MAYS LANDING
BRIDGETON
MILLVILLE
ATLANTIC CITY
DORCHESTER
TUCKAHOE
MAURICETOWN
OCEAN CITY
SEA ISLE JC.
DENNISVILLE
SEA ISLE CITY
GOSHEN
AVALON
CAPE MAY C.H.
STONE HARBOR
GREEN CREEK
NORTH WILDWOOD
WILDWOOD
WILDWOOD CREST
CAPE MAY
Delaware River

BY THE SEA

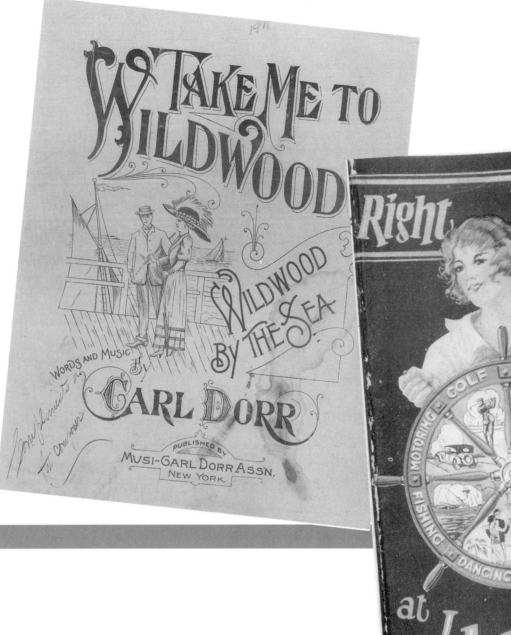
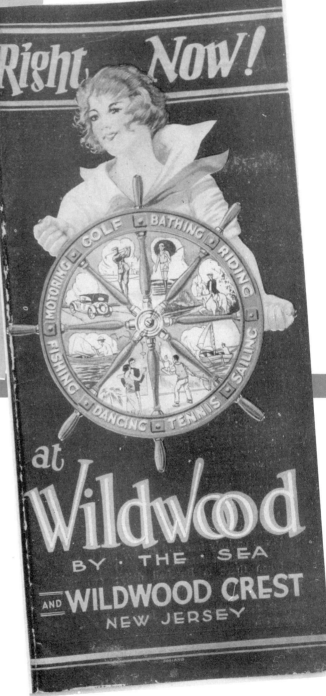

BY THE SEA

THE HISTORY OF AN AMERICAN RESORT

DAVID W. FRANCIS,
DIANE DEMALI FRANCIS,
AND ROBERT J. SCULLY, SR.

AMUSEMENT PARK BOOKS, INC.
FAIRVIEW PARK, OHIO

*Also by
David W. Francis
and Diane DeMali Francis*

Cedar Point: The Queen of American Watering Places
Luna Park: Cleveland's Fairyland of Pleasure
Summit Beach Park: Akron's Coney Island

OTHER TITLES BY

Amusement Park Books, Inc.

Cedar Point: The Queen of American Watering Places
Conneaut Lake Park: the First 100 Years of Fun
Euclid Beach Park is Closed for the Season
Euclid Beach Park – A Second Look
Harry G. Traver: Legends of Terror
Luna Park: Cleveland's Fairyland of Pleasure
The Incredible Scream Machine: A History of the Roller Coaster

DEDICATION

Dedicated to Lauren Alberto,
    with love.

    David W. Francis and
    Diane DeMali Francis

To my wife, Kathleen –
    our four children,
    Bob, Lee, Lori, Linda
    and our
    thirteen grandchildren.

    Robert J. Scully, Sr.

Published by

Amusement Park Books, Inc.
20925 Mastick Road
Fairview Park, Ohio 44126
(440) 331-6429

•

Copyright 1998 by
David W. Francis and Diane DeMali Francis
All rights reserved

•

03 02 01 00 99 98   6 5 4 3 2 1

ISBN 0-935408-06-1
Library of Congress Catalog Card Number 97-78258

Printed in the United States of America

Wildwood

Book designed by Edward Chukayne

Cover art by Ryan Hagler
Page composition by Bonita M. Albrecht

CONTENTS

FOREWORD

The scent of sunscreen, the spray of the ocean, the caw of seagulls, the thrill of amusement rides, the taste of salt water taffy, the chatter of children on the boardwalk...summer in the Wildwoods captures the Jersey Shore experience that has been treasured by millions of Americans. As this book's detailed history of the Wildwoods makes clear, the story of the Jersey Shore is filled with colorful characters, determined entrepreneurs, and investors seeking opportunities to capitalize on the enormous potential of our 127 miles of beaches. For so many New Jersey residents and visitors, the Jersey Shore story is also a very personal account – a family story. It is newlyweds taking their honeymoon at a seaside hotel. A mother teaching her son to ride the waves. A father taking his children to the same boardwalk amusements he enjoyed when he was young. Grandparents taking photos of their newest grandchild building her first sand castle. A youngster learning about clams and sand crabs while collecting seashells. Cousins getting reacquainted at their annual seaside reunion. A parent retrieving a child's fallen kite. Teenagers on their first date on the boardwalk. A college student holding down a summer job as a lifeguard. Generations reconnecting on a quiet stroll along the water's edge. Part of the magic of summer at the Jersey Shore is that every experience is different. Each family builds up different fond memories of places like the Iboardwalk or the Dayton Hotel or the Nut Hut. And even as the landscape changes, and as establishments come and go, those memories remain fresh in our minds and hearts. I know how much the Wildwoods – and, indeed, every part of the Jersey Shore – mean to our state. Our shore communities are a vital part of our state's identity. I want to help them thrive. In dedicating taxpayer dollars toward the shore protection, in making sure our ocean waters remain clean, and in investing state resources in tourism promotion, I hope to honor our coastal heritage by making it a lasting legacy for families to enjoy for centuries to come. More than a history of the Wildwoods, this book is a reminder of the remarkable potential in every Jersey Shore town. I hope that in offering a glimpse at the past, it also provides a window on a wonderful future.

Gov. Christine Todd Whitman
Trenton, New Jersey

ACKNOWLEDGEMENTS

This book was planned as a history of the summer resort industry in the seaside communities that comprise Greater Wildwood. Because of the focus of the study, many social, institutional, political, and economic aspects of the history of the Wildwoods have been omitted. For example, little attention is given to politics unless they related to the resort industry, and virtually no mention has been made of the churches, schools, and associations that have been so important in the development of the communities, but played a limited role in the resort activities. Similarly, many people who have been important citizens and were key personalities in the community's religious, social, economic, or political life do not appear in the following pages because they were not active along the Boardwalk or in related summer resort trades. It is left to others to write a comprehensive history of Five Mile Beach.

This book might never have become a reality had it not been for Jack Morey of The Morey Organization. Jack believed that the story of the Wildwoods needed to be preserved and told, and he spared no effort in convincing us to undertake the research and writing. Throughout the project, he has supported us in many ways, kept an interested eye on the progress of the book, and encouraged us to keep the writing moving toward completion. At the same time, he never attempted to dictate the content or the direction of the book. To Jack must go the credit for conceiving this volume and helping it materialize.

We also owe a great deal to another member of The Morey Organization, Rom Nardi. A distinguished teacher, former lieutenant of the Wildwood Beach Patrol, and current executive with The Morey Organization, Rom was in regular contact with us, providing photographs, arranging interviews, and handling uncounted details related to our research. Without his help, this project would have been a great deal more difficult.

Other members of The Morey Organization who provided information, photographs, and support, included Mr. and Mrs. Will Morey, Sr; Mr. and Mrs. Bill Morey, Sr; Mr. and Mrs. Will Morey, Jr; Mr. and Mrs. Bill Morey, Jr; and Mr. and Mrs. Barry Gehring.

We owe a special debt of gratitude to the Wildwood Historical Society and its fine museum. This organization open its files and microfilm collections to us and made available its excellent photographic collection. Among the officers and members that assisted us were Larry Lillo, President; Lena Adgie, Vice President; Patricia Nagel, Treasurer; Susan Mahoney, Secretary; Bob Bright, Sr., historian; Al Brannen; Rita Fulginiti; and Doris Mallek. We also wish to thank Bob Bright, Jr., who contributed many hours of research to this project.

Charles J. Jacques, Jr., the nation's premier amusement park historian, provided his usual support and expertise. Despite facing a tight deadline on his own book about Hersheypark, Charlie took the time to research the Wildwoods in his personal collections and to provide photographs in his possession. A long-time fan of the Wildwoods, Charlie's contributions were immeasurable.

We also greatly appreciate the assistance of the staff of the Wadsworth (Ohio) Public Library and especially Bobbie Richards, who arranged for the inter-library loan of microfilm that would not otherwise have been accessible.

Among the many people who provided assistance, information, or photographs were

BY THE SEA

Sueanne Agger; Jennifer Ambrose; Norman D. Anderson; Barbara Arenberg; Evelyn Bailie; Joseph Barnes, Jr; Pete Barnes; Debbie Bass; Richard Bonelli; June Douglass Bradley; Claude and Evelyn Bradshaw; Al Brannen; J. Carroll Bransfield; George D. Brightbill; James Byrne, Sr; James Cafiero, Sr; William J. Callahan; Madelyn Calloway; Domenic Capacchione; John Carlson, Sr; William Catanoso; Bill Cole; Asa Colson, II; Richard Curran; Michael D'Antuono; Robert Davenport; Richard Dietz; Victor DiSylvester; Bette Epstein; Amy Flemming; Loreen Flynn; Ron Franks; Dr. Ronald J. Gelzunas; John C. Gibson; Gregory J. Gill; Alan Gould; Reverend Tom Goslin; Laura Grauer; Earl A. Groff; John Harkins; Kirk Hastings; Gertrude Hubbard; Adel Hunter; David Ingersoll; Glenn Kay; William Kemp; John Kill; John W. Kille; Marge Koester; Jane Kohr; Randolph L. Kohr; Claire E. Lang; Barb Leveroni; Robert Lupp; H. Gerald MacDonald; Rita McAlarnen; Catherine McManus; George Meiser; Harry Mitchell; William Mitchell; Cozy Morley; C. Eugene Muson; Milton Nagel; B. J. Nickels; John Nickels; Steve Nickels; Gregory Neill; William Neill; Ed Nesbitt, Jr; Patty Nesbitt; Tom O'Leary; John Oliveri; James Osborn; Earl Ostrander; Marcia Palmer; Aldo Palombo; Jane Parson; the late Merrick Price of Seabreeze Park; Richard Ramagosa; Keith Rasmussen; H. V. Pat Reilly; Patricia Rhodes; Sue Rist; Stephen Ritchie; Lee Robinson; Joe Rozsa; Gary Rudy; Joseph Russo; Lillian Russo; Barbara St. Clair; Jim Salasin; James E. Salmon; Dr. Joseph Salvatore; George "Butch" Schmidt, Jr; Jim Schneeman; Sister Marcella Scully; Harold Sherwood; Edward Skipworth; Amie Smith; Richard Snyder; Elizabeth Terenik; Monica Trainor; Ernie Troiano, Sr; Irvin Unruh; Fred Wagar, Mayor of Wildwood; John Wallace; Patrick Ward; Palmer M. Way, Jr; Diane Wieland; Idna Williams; Ione Williams; John Williams; Peter Yecco; Ed Zaberer; and Jean Zajac.

Many organizations also contributed information or photographs. We very much appreciate the assistance of the Athenaeum of Philadelphia, Atlantic City Free Library, Atlantic County Historical Society, Aviation Hall of Fame of New Jersey, Camden Free Public Library, Cape May County Department of Tourism, Cape May County Historical and Genealogical Society, Cape May County Library, Cleveland (Ohio) Public Library, Delaware River and Bay Authority, Dinosaur Beach Adventure Theme Park, Douglass Candies, Free Library of Philadelphia, Heinz U.S.A., Historical of Society of Berks County (Pennsylvania), Historical Society of Pennsylvania, Kohr Bros., Curt Teich Postcard Archives, Lake County (Illinois) Museum, Laura's Fudge Shops, Library Company of Philadelphia, Library of Congress, National Archives, National Marbles Tournament, Newark Public Library, New Jersey Historical Society, New Jersey State Archives, New Jersey State Library, New York Public Library, Nickels Midway Pier, Philadelphia Toboggan Coasters, Inc., Princeton University, Reading (Pennsylvania) Public Library, Rutgers University, Urban Archives of Temple University, United States Marine Corps Band, Wildwood Crest Historical Society; and the City of Wildwood.

Finally, we are most grateful to Amusement Parks Books, Inc., who published our two earlier books about Cedar Point and Luna Park, and who have earned a reputation as the world leader in the publication of books about amusement parks, rides, and summer resorts. The dedication, faith, professionalism, and editorial contributions of Dick Hershey and Lee Bush represent a high standard in the publishing industry. Without Dick and Lee, this book might not have been published.

To everyone who helped make this book possible, we owe a sincere debt of gratitude.

Wadsworth, Ohio

July, 1997

**A segment of the Jersey Shore, where the sea,
the land, and the climate came together to
form the perfect summer resort atmosphere.**
– The Library Company of Philadelphia

New Jersey
Seashore
Resorts

Issued by
United States Railroad
Administration

1

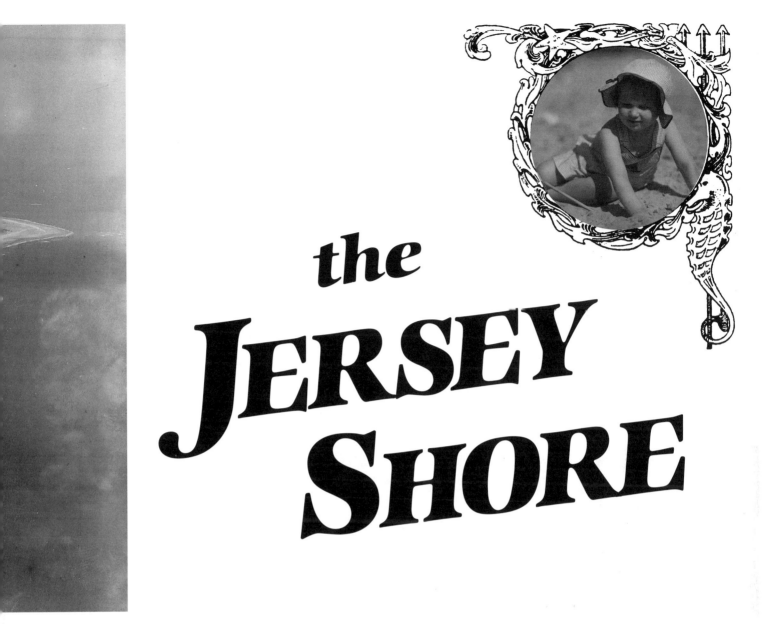

the JERSEY SHORE

*A*tlantic City ... Ocean City ... Seaside Heights ... the
Wildwoods ... Asbury Park ... Ocean Grove. The list of
summer resorts stretches almost as long as the Jersey Shore
itself — an impressive 127 miles of pale beige sand washed by
foaming ocean. For well over a century these seaside towns
have symbolized escape. Their very names conjure up inviting
images of salt air, sunshine, and sea breezes to blow away
every vestige of the grime, crime, and heat of the city. Just a
short drive from New York City, Philadelphia, Baltimore,
Washington, D. C., and thousands of points west lies the
Jersey Shore, legendary among the world's finest resort regions.

CHAPTER 1

More than a quarter of the New Jersey shoreline features spacious boardwalks that parallel the coast's justifiably famous beaches. The North Shore area and Cape May are located on New Jersey's mainland, but from Point Pleasant to the area southwest of Wildwood, most of the resort communities are situated on barrier islands tied to the mainland by bridges. Between Sandy Hook and Cape May are the summer resorts that have made the Jersey Shore famous: Asbury Park, Ocean Grove, Seaside Heights, Atlantic City, Ocean City, and the Wildwoods (North Wildwood, Wildwood, Wildwood Crest, and West Wildwood).

There is little doubt that the resorts of the Jersey Shore rival, and in many cases, surpass America's other luxury retreats. The Adirondack Mountains of New York, the beaches of Florida, and Michigan's Mackinac Island, despite their fame, cannot compare to the Jersey Shore as a summer playground. The statistics alone point to the significance of coastal New Jersey as a vacation destination. Publicity department claims that as many as fifty million people visited the shore during the 1950s are undoubtedly an exaggeration, but the fact remains that during those years, Atlantic City and Asbury Park alone could have entertained more than seven hundred thousand over a summer weekend. By about 1960, Stone Harbor's permanent population of eight hundred sometimes swelled to ten thousand on a pleasant weekend day. Wildwood, a far more popular summer resort than Stone Harbor, often saw its population of thirteen thousand expand to nearly one hundred fifty thousand on a busy summer weekend. This level of attendance at Wildwood resulted in a population density of thirty-four thousand people per square mile near the boardwalk.

The incredible popularity of the Jersey shore resorts can be attributed to a number of features shared by all: the incredible summer weather complete with fresh salty sea breezes; the mesmerizing sway of the Atlantic; broad sun-kissed beaches, well-maintained boardwalks, sprawling summer hotels; and quaint seaside cottages. In addition, Atlantic City, Wildwood, and Seaside Heights offered the boisterous energy of their amusement piers.

It's clear the Jersey Shore has much to offer visitors, but perhaps its most popular attraction is a nearly perfect summer climate. Directly influenced by the ocean the climate of the Jersey Shore differs markedly from the that of inland New Jersey. The warmth of the ocean and the nearby Gulf Stream cause a more gradual change of seasons while the heat of summer and the cold of winter are

less extreme than in other parts of the state. An Atlantic City press agent's claim that "it never snows on the boardwalk" is an exaggeration, but it is true that snowfall is generally light along the coast. History has recorded some temperature extremes, like the time in June and July of 1901 when the thermometer hovered at one hundred degrees in Wildwood, but usually Wildwood residents enjoy mean temperatures of 70°F. in June, and 75°F. in July and August.

Often during the summer season, the warming of the land and the comparative coolness of the ocean results in sea breezes that sweep in pollen-free air. During the 1920s the community of Beach Haven claimed to be the only New Jersey resort that could guarantee relief from hay fever. In fact, ocean breezes ensure that most visitors will see at least some relief from the ailments caused by pollen for much of the summer.

Yet despite its usual gentleness, the climate of the Jersey Shore sometimes shows a more dramatic side. Coastal storms and hurricanes can pound the shore at any time during the year, but they are most common during the non-tourist season; October to April. Over the years, countless coastal buildings have been flattened by winds that often approach hurricane velocity. Raging seas have flooded city streets and made beach erosion a common problem in Ocean City and other towns. From the 1820s to the 1920s such erosion claimed 5,521 acres of New Jersey beachfront property.

Interestingly, Wildwood has somehow evaded the problem of erosion. In fact, while the rest of New Jersey's shore was losing acreage, Wildwood's beach increased by 350 feet! This expansion of the Wildwood beach continues today, and has made it necessary for the boardwalk to be moved farther east a number of times to maintain its ocean proximity.

But, if the Jersey Shore can thank nature for its warm ocean, wonderful climate, and excellent beaches, several other man-made attractions are also indigenous to the area. Surely, the boardwalks, amusement piers, rolling chairs, and salt water taffy are as closely associated with the Jersey Shore as the fine weather and beautiful ocean.

ORIGINS OF THE BOARDWALK AND ROLLING CHAIR

Nineteenth century seaside resorts in England and France offered visitors promenades, but the boardwalk, lined on the land side with hotels and shops and on the ocean side with amusement piers, is truly a New Jersey innovation. The boardwalk (always

In spite of cold weather, hearty visitors strolled the Atlantic City Boardwalk or rode in rolling chairs equipped with blankets in March of 1936. Unlike Wildwood and many other resorts, Atlantic City's Boardwalk was busy throughout the year.
– David W. Francis Collection

In Atlantic City, rolling chairs were so numerous that they caused severe congestion on the Boardwalk and resulted in laws and special police details to control traffic.
– David W. Francis Collection

spelled with a capital "B" in Atlantic City thanks to a city ordinance passed in 1896), has been one of the enduring legacies of the Jersey Shore. Cape May had a primitive boardwalk called "Flirtation Walk" in 1868, but Atlantic City is generally credited for the invention of the first true boardwalk. In the spring of 1870, hotelman Jacob Keim and railroad conductor Alexander Boardman addressed the problem of beach sand on visitors' shoes being tracked into hotel lobbies and passenger cars. They called a meeting

Above left: The Boardwalk was an Atlantic City invention, and certainly its most valuable tourist attraction. – Library of Congress

In Atlantic City, great hotels emerged along the Boardwalk by the early 1900s.
The Chalfonte-Haddon Hall, center, was among the resort's best hotels in 1928.
– David W. Francis Collection

With the great success of Atlantic City's wooden promenade, other resorts built
their own boardwalks by the early 1900s. Ocean City, 1908. – Library of Congress

Ocean Grove's
Boardwalk in
1904.
– David W. Francis
Collection

Rolling chairs were made in one and two seat models, but were invariably constructed of wicker. – Library of Congress

The Sea Isle City Boardwalk, about 1930.
– David W. Francis Collection

of Atlantic City businessmen and suggested that a walkway constructed of boards along the beachfront would solve the problem. The idea met with approval and the first Boardwalk was opened on June 26, 1870, in Atlantic City. Gradually, the Boardwalk was lengthened and widened. By 1896, the Boardwalk, erected on steel girders, measured forty feet in width. In 1902, the city's fifth Boardwalk incarnation, was sixty feet wide and more than four miles long. The Boardwalk quickly became the symbol of Atlantic City and the center of all resort activity. By the 1890s, it was lined with hotels, shops, restaurants, shows, amusement rides, and bath houses.

Other seaside communities saw the value of a wooden promenade and followed Atlantic City's example. Ocean Grove's boardwalk started as just two boards in width laid directly on the sand. This primitive attempt was replaced in 1877 by a six-foot-wide elevated walkway illuminated by twenty-one street lamps. Ocean City, currently home of one of the world's great boardwalks, built its first promenade in 1883. Boardwalks were an outstanding attraction, but they were costly to maintain and subject to damage from several natural causes. Wood rotted and fires constantly ravaged sections of the walks. Storms were an even greater hazard, and in 1962 a severe northeaster swept away Cape May's boardwalk. Realizing how economically vital the boardwalks had become, seaside communities spent huge sums of money to maintain and repair the walks. When new boardwalks were warranted, they were designed with concrete and steel support structures to help resist the forces of nature.

Left:
The rolling chair was not invented on the Jersey Shore, but it became a symbol of the great seaside boardwalks.
– David W. Francis Collection

The famous boardwalk rolling chair, constructed of wicker and pushed by an attendant, is not exactly a Jersey Shore invention, but it was seaside businessmen who made it a boardwalk symbol. Evidently, the first rolling chairs were employed at the 1876 Centennial Exposition in Philadelphia. They made their appearance at Atlantic City in 1887 and have been there ever since. At one time, Atlantic City boasted three thousand rolling chairs, and traffic on the boardwalk became so congested that in 1905 a ten-man police force was assigned to control rolling chair traffic on Sundays. Rolling chairs were used throughout the year, and enterprising operators provided patrons with fur robes in winter and sun-shading umbrellas or canopies in summer. Other resorts again emulated Atlantic City, and by 1900, many were offering the pleasures of the rolling chair. In fact, by 1905, the rolling chair invasion had spread so far inland that Cedar Point, a large resort Lake Erie's shore in Ohio, operated rolling chairs on its own boardwalk.

SALT WATER TAFFY IS BORN

Unlike the rolling chair, which was invented elsewhere and later matured on the Jersey Shore, salt water taffy was born on New Jersey's Atlantic Coast. As early as 1880, the Richie brothers were selling taffy (but not "salt water taffy") in Atlantic City. Three years later, according to local legend, candy maker David Bradley arrived at his candy stand one morning to find that his stock of taffy had been doused with the ocean spray from a high tide. Unwilling to discard the candy, he sold it that day and called it "salt water taffy." The name appealed to the public as well as to other candy makers in Atlantic City. In 1889, Windle W. Hollis was selling salt water taffy and calling it the "original". That same year, Joseph Fralinger began a career that made him "The Taffy King." In 1905, Enoch James entered the market and introduced automatic taffy making and wrapping equipment. Soon, Atlantic City taffy makers were selling and shipping millions of pounds of salt water taffy around the world. Boxes adorned with colorful scenes of the Atlantic City boardwalk were as well-known in Japan and Europe as they were in the Midwestern United States. Although the Bradley name disappeared after the 1939 season, the Jersey Shore is still represented by a group of world-renowned taffy makers: Fralinger and James in Atlantic City; Shriver in Ocean City; and Douglass in Wildwood. Because Bradley neglected to trademark the name "salt water taffy," and because a 1923 court case failed to uphold the trademark claims of a Miami taffy maker who asserted that he first used the name in Atlantic City, the product's name remained in the public domain. As a result, salt water taffy signs appeared up and down every boardwalk and the treat seems forever bound with the Jersey Shore.

THE APPEARANCE OF AMUSEMENT PIERS

The idea for an amusement pier jutting out hundreds of feet into the ocean and anchored to land at the boardwalk was not conceived in New Jersey. It was, however, a group of New Jersey amusement entrepreneurs who developed the European concept to its fullest potential during the 1880s and 1890s.

The first piers evolved from stone jetties at English and Continental resorts. Visitors soon found a stroll on the jetty to be a pleasant, cooling experience, and by the late Victorian Period, ornate piers were a common feature of English seaside resorts.

Meanwhile, along the Jersey Shore, Long Branch offered at least an embryonic amusement pier in 1878. Built opposite the Ocean Hotel, the 600-foot pier was designed expressly for docking passenger steamships. However, it was not long before enterprising businessmen opened refreshment stands along the pier and provided benches to attract even those guests who were not waiting for a steamship. The Iron Pier, built at Cape May in 1884, stretched one thousand feet into the ocean and was dedicated more to pleasure than to vessel dockage. With more than half an acre of planking and an eight thousand square foot dance floor, the Iron Pier's pavilion played host to dances, band concerts, theatrical performances, and even the occasional light opera company. So spacious was the pier that it even allocated an area for fishermen.

It was Atlantic City, however, that made the amusement pier synonymous with the Jersey Shore. Colonel George Howard constructed the first pier in 1882. Destroyed in its first season by a violent storm, this pier was replaced with a new 850-foot structure that included a large ballroom which was suspended over the ocean. Howard's pier was joined by the Applegate Pier in 1884. In 1891, that pier was purchased by John Lake Young, a man who very soon would become Atlantic City's most renowned amusement entrepreneur and builder of ocean piers. The

Upper left: Of all the American amusement resorts, only New York's Coney Island could compete with Atlantic City, Asbury Park, and the Wildwoods. – David W. Francis Collection

Left: Heinz Pier was built along the Atlantic City shoreline to showcase the food products of the H. J. Heinz Company. Heinz considered building a similar pier in Wildwood.
– Courtesy of Heinz U.S.A.

ex-Applegate Pier was destroyed by fire in 1902, but in 1906 one of the city's best known piers, Young's Million Dollar Pier made its debut. The Iron Pier, built in 1886, became the Heinz Pier in 1898. The Heinz Pier was utilized as a promotional showcase for Heinz pickles and other food products until it was demolished due to hurricane damage in 1944. The world-famous Steel Pier opened in 1898, and in 1902 Coney Island park operator George C. Tilyou acquired the Auditorium Pier (1899), renamed it Steeplechase Pier and outfitted it with all of the amusements that had made his Coney Island park a household name throughout the world. A decade later, the Garden Pier and the Central Pier were added to the Atlantic City oceanscape. By 1910, Atlantic City post cards featuring views of the popular piers were being sent from coast-to-coast and the amusement pier was firmly entrenched as the resort's trademark.

THE JERSEY SHORE RESORT COMMUNITIES

While geographically, the New Jersey Shore is a single entity, each community is a microcosm exhibiting its own unique traits. Location, proximity to major cities, the arrival of the railroad and the attitudes and beliefs of the founding fathers meshed to give each community its distinctive appearance, traditions, and history.

Although New Jersey was one of the original Thirteen Colonies, much of the Jersey Coast was slow to populate. In fact, most of the barrier islands south of Atlantic City did not witness the development of towns until well after the Civil War. Yet communities on the two extreme ends of the coast—Long Branch on the north and Cape May on the South—were among America's earliest and most distinguished resorts. Some believe that Cape May, known then as Cape Island, may have hosted summer visitors a decade before the American Revolution. It is known that by 1800 there were taverns and inns at the Cape to accommodate visitors. Inevitably, other hotels appeared and soon steamship service from Philadelphia was made available. By the 1850s, Cape May was immensely popular with Southerners seeking to escape the heat and malaria, and neither New Jersey's Long Branch or New York's Saratoga could rival the South Jersey town. In 1851, the popular resort drew 120,000 visitors. But the Civil War promptly ended the annual influx of Southern vacationers and tragic fires in 1869 and again in 1878 eradi-

The idea of boardwalks and amusement piers spread from New Jersey to California by 1910. In many ways, the Long Beach amusement section was patterned after Atlantic City.
– David W. Francis Collection

cated much of the city, including many of the hotels. Cape May never fully recovered from the devastating events of the 1860s and 1870s, and it was soon overshadowed by the developing resorts at Atlantic City, Asbury Park, Ocean City, and the Wildwoods. However, the cloud of Cape May's decline held a silver lining. Because the community experienced little development from the 1880s until the 1970s, scores of its wonderful Victorian cottages were preserved for posterity. Today, many believe that Cape May exhibits the finest collection of Victorian architecture on the continent.

Long Branch, too, enjoyed early popularity but soon fell from grace. In 1788, Long Branch offered a boarding house that catered to shore visitors, and by 1850 the northern resort was challenging the popularity of Cape May. However, unlike Cape May, Long Branch's popularity as a resort was due to the availability of gambling, liquor and prostitution. Despite a reputation that rivaled Coney Island in infamy, Long Branch prospered until the New Jersey legislature made horse race betting illegal in 1894. Then in 1907, an anti-gambling bill closed the gambling houses, and progressive reform efforts made the operation of brothels difficult. Bombarded by reformers and progressive politicians, Long Branch declined in popularity and was soon overshadowed by its southern neighbors.

9

The wide beach that stretches from North Wildwood through Wildwood Crest is the finest of the Jersey Shore beaches and among the best in the world. – Wildwood Historical Society

While Cape May and Long Branch developed during the early stage of New Jersey's resort history, Atlantic City debuted during the middle period. Conceived by a group of entrepreneurs during the early 1850s, Atlantic City offered an excursion house, named the Surf House, in 1854 and benefited from railroad connections with Philadelphia that same summer. The year-round population of Atlantic City grew from 250 in 1855, to 13,037 in 1890 and to 27,838 ten years later. In 1880, the West Jersey Division of the Pennsylvania Railroad was extended to Atlantic City, and daily connections with both Philadelphia and New York City helped to expand the fast-growing resort. In 1888, the resort offered an amazing 506 hotels and boarding houses, and by 1902 the number had reached 739. Unlike Ocean Grove and Ocean City, which adhered to a strong Protestant moral code, Atlantic City's more liberal outlook tolerated gambling, prostitution, and the sale of liquor on Sundays — that is as long as violations did not prove too obvious or flagrant. The Boardwalk was quite racy by 1895, featuring nude portrait shows, living pictures, a bawdy phonograph parlor, and numerous exotic dancing shows from the Middle East.

In stark contrast to the liberal Atlantic City were the communities formed as religious camps with behavioral codes strictly enforced. Methodists were the most active along the Jersey Coast (Asbury Park was named for the great Methodist bishop, Francis Asbury), but other denominations were involved in camp developments as early as the 1870s. Among the seaside communities founded by men of determined religious principal were Ocean City, Ocean Grove, Asbury Park, Seaside Park, Cape May Point, Belmar, Atlantic Highlands, and Avon-By-The-Sea. Some of these resort villages had difficulty maintaining church-based regulations, but several have succeeded in holding onto their wholesome, family-centered traditions even into the 1990s.

Equally interesting in origin and history is Sea Girt, whose fame is based on military and political connections. In 1885, Sea Girt became a camp for the New Jersey National Guard, and frequently hosted summer visits by New Jersey governors. After the closing of the Louisiana Purchase Exposition in St. Louis, the state purchased the Louisiana building, moved it to Sea Girt and established the building as the "Little White House," summer residence of the governor. It was here that Governor Woodrow Wilson learned of his nomination to run for the presidency in 1912. Finally, in 1942, Governor Charles Edison closed the "Little White House" when the costs of maintaining and operating the attractive home became too high to tolerate.

It was in this rich, colorful, and diverse mosaic that the group of southern New Jersey resort communities known collectively as "The Wildwoods" began to develop during the 1880s. The Wildwoods did not have the religious foundation of an Ocean City, nor the political traditions of Sea Girt. City fathers did not permit the open debauchery of Long Branch, and The Wildwoods never attracted the society set as did Cape May. Although mayors and the police sometimes tolerated a very limited amount of gambling, illegal liquor sales, and prostitution, The Wildwoods never were as permissive or liberal as Atlantic City. Instead, the communities that made up Five Mile Beach developed their own special personalities and traditions. And, although it offered the same rolling chairs, amusement piers, and salt water taffy as most other New Jersey resorts, the Wildwood Boardwalk has always possessed a unique charm all its own.

RESORT

The island of Five Mile Beach looking north. Wildwood Inlet is at the bottom of the photo and Hereford Inlet near the top.
– The Library Company of Philadelphia

11

BEGINNINGS

Curiosities in Living Wood.

Ocean Pier.

Seaside Cape May County is comprised of the Cape May peninsula at the southernmost tip of coastal New Jersey and a series of barrier islands to the north of the peninsula. Moving north from Cape May, the five islands are comprised of Two Mile Beach (the site of Wildwood Crest after 1905), Five Mile Beach (Wildwood and North Wildwood), Seven Mile Beach (Avalon and Stone Harbor), Ludlam's Beach (Strathmere and Sea Isle City), and Peck's Beach (Ocean City).

CHAPTER 2

Although Cape May had permanent inhabitants by the 1680s, it would be 200 years before the barrier islands had any real settlement. Around 1723, Aaron Leaming, the new owner of Seven Mile Beach, moved cattle to the three southern islands to graze on beach grasses during the summer months. Eventually, the islands could boast of a few farmers, and by the mid-nineteenth century isolated life saving stations appeared on the barrier islands to deal with the tragically frequent shipwrecks along the coast. But, for the most part, the barrier islands remained a tangled mass of underbrush and salt marshes, inaccessible except by small boat, and shunned by land developers until fifteen years after the end of the Civil War. Then in 1879, dedicated Methodist clergymen and temperance movement leaders joined with a group of real estate developers to found Ocean City on Peck's Beach. Soon, interest in the barrier islands mushroomed. The development of the great South Jersey resorts had begun!

Charles K. Landis, among the greatest of the early South Jersey land developers and founder of Vineland, purchased land on Ludlam's Beach and began to carefully construct Sea Isle City in 1879. By 1884, the city had a tenuous railroad connection (until 1920, railway service was the single most important factor in resort development).

It was also in 1884 that the first of the settlements that would be known as "The Wildwoods" was founded at the northern end of Five Mile Beach. Anglesea, which became North Wildwood in 1910, was a sleepy fishing village with a few shacks and a small fleet of sail-powered fishing craft. Then, Humphrey Cresse sold Anglesea to the Five Mile Beach Improvement Company, a new firm headed by real estate and railroad man Frederick E. Swope of Philadelphia. By the early 1880s, Swope was selling land and building cottages for well-to-do Philadelphians looking to escape the city in summer. Swope soon built the Anglesea Railroad to connect with the growing West Jersey Railroad and operated a small steam locomotive named the "Mud Hen" by locals(so named beacuse the engine sometimes derailed in the mud after high tides washed out the road bed). By the mid-1880s, Anglesea was a small but growing seaside resort with the fifty room Hotel Anglesea, a narrow boardwalk laid directly on the sand, and about thirty summer cottages.

The next Wildwood community to be established was Holly Beach, named after the abundance of holly bushes native to the center section of Five Mile Beach. Holly Beach was conceived by John Burk, a trusted employee of Charles Landis, whom Landis accused of forgery and fraud. While Burk's guilt or innocence may be argued, it is a fact that he had an undeniable interest in developing Holly Beach without the assistance of his boss. In 1882, with the help of some investors, the recently-fired Burk founded the Holly Beach Improvement Company. The company acquired large tracts of land and pursued aggressively the development of Holly Beach. Although Wildwood would eclipse Holly Beach in the 1890s, during the 1880s, Holly Beach was the fastest growing community on Five Mile Beach.

The last of the original Five Mile Beach seaside communities to be established was Wildwood (Wildwood and Holly Beach merged and became the City of Wildwood in 1912; Wildwood Crest did not begin to emerge until 1905). The driving force behind the founding of Wildwood was Philip Pontius Baker (1846-1920), a merchant and hotel operator from Vineland who had been an original investor in both the Sea Isle City and the Holly Beach development projects.

ENTER THE BAKER BROTHERS

Baker enjoyed some fortunate political ties, having been elected to the state assembly in 1882 and to the state senate five years later. Because of his financial and political connections on the state level, Baker's development of the land situated south of Anglesea and north of Holly Beach was easily accomplished.

In 1883, Baker visited his brother, Latimer, and the two men walked north of Holly Beach and along an old Indian path into a beautiful but tangled forest. Maple, oak, poplar, magnolia, holly, and cherry trees were all bedecked with Spanish moss. The Bakers were impressed with the natural beauty of the undeveloped acreage and imagined a new summer resort and cottage colony set against the backdrop of this primitive fantasy forest. Joined by a third brother, J. Thompson, the Bakers purchased almost 100 acres for $9000 in 1885. The original name of their development, Florida City, just didn't seem to fit, so it was promptly changed to Wildwood in honor of the dense, twisted forest growth. The brothers formed the WildWood Beach Improvement Company, and began the tasks of clearing the land and surveying. In 1895, the Borough of Wildwood was incorporated. Three years later the Bakers bought 110 more acres that doubled the size of Wildwood and took their property to the Anglesea line in the north.

Early visitors to the island found dense undergrowth and many twisted trees and shrubs. Most famous was the "W" tree, which is now preserved at the Wildwood Historical Society. – Wildwood Historical Society

Dr. John Andrew was one of the founders of the Holly Beach Improvement Company and a pioneer developer of Holly Beach.
– Wildwood Historical Society

Early in the Bakers' development of Wildwood, there were rumors that the town would become a Baptist summer retreat complete with camp meetings but devoid of seaside amusements and diversions. It was also rumored that Wildwood would be built into an exclusive community of seashore homes for wealthy Philadelphians. But the coming of the railroad set Wildwood's future on a different course. Once trains began running from Philadelphia and other cities, Wildwood's popularity as a public summer resort and cottage colony was assured.

For five decades the Baker brothers were synonymous with Wildwood and its growth. They established a real estate office on the Boardwalk, aggressively promoted Wildwood through advertising and railroad excursions, produced brochures to help sell property and attract summer visitors, became deeply involved in local politics (Latimer Baker was elected Wildwood's first mayor in 1895), and were at the very center of Five Mile Beach society. In print and on signage, the phrase "Founders of Wildwood" was invariably linked to the name Baker Brothers. In fact, a brochure published about 1911 stated, "The history of Wildwood and of Baker Brothers, its founders, are synonymous. You cannot mention the one without thinking of the other."

An early real estate advertisement from the Baker Brothers attempted to list every attribute of the resort. The climate and geography of Wildwood was so pleasant that the Bakers had little need for exaggeration.
– Wildwood Historical Society

THE WILD WOODS OF THE WILDWOODS

In the mid-1880s, the three youthful communities of Five Mile Beach offered little tangible evidence that they would someday be sprawling resorts with boardwalks, amusement piers, hotels, and more than 200,000 visitors on a single day. Thomas Martindale, an early Wildwood booster, noted that "This island must have seemed uninhabitable and almost inaccessible to the early inhabitant." The first settlers came by boat. Later a ferry was operated and, before the railroad arrived, a rough corduroy wagon road crossed a crude plank bridge. Conditions on the island were described by Martindale as "...an impassable jungle." In fact, inhabitants of the 1880s referred to much of Wildwood as "The Jungle." Laboriously, a road was cut through not only tall stands of trees, but also blueberry and blackberry bushes, poison ivy, wild cactus, Virginia creepers, mistletoe, wild hope vines, and a myriad of flora. With the completion of the road, there was direct contact with both Holly Beach to the south and Anglesea to the north.

Described by Martindale as "Ocean Bound, Flower Gowned, Forest Crowned Wildwood," the small resort was a natural wonder. In addition to the scenic woodland and thousands of wild flowers, the island was home to numerous animal species. Most prolific were the birds, which included native birds, those that summered on the coast, and those passing through on north-south migrations. Among the birds observed by Martindale were woodcocks, egrets, gulls, Baltimore orioles, scarlet tanagers, bluebirds, yellowbirds, the yellow-throated woodpecker, king birds, osprey, robins, hummingbirds, kingfishers, bittern, marsh hen, king rail, blue heron, crane, yellow-legged snipe, gray snipe, curlew, willet, calico-back, bull head, and numerous types of wild ducks.

The birds were welcome visitors, but there were also some animals that brought early inhabitants their share of difficulties. Before the age of resort development, mainland farmers transported cattle in flat-bottomed boats to graze on Five Mile Island. Many were left on the island where they thrived on native grasses and grew in numbers. They also grew quite wild and aggressive. Many, it was said, were so dangerous that a man walking across the island was advised to carry a rifle and a good supply of cartridges. Eventually, as the towns developed, the cattle became bold, wandering the streets, harassing people and raiding fruit and vegetable stands. Finally, in the interests of the year-round residents and the summer visitors, hunters were hired to eliminate the wild cattle problem.

If the land of Five Mile Beach offered a bounty of natural beauty, the sea provided bounty for the table. Both sport and professional fishing industries were in full swing by the 1890s, and remain a major attraction of Five Mile Beach to this day. Clams and crabs made the Wildwoods famous, but fishermen of the 1890s also landed sea bass, bluefish, flounder, mackerel, weakfish, butterfish, kingfish, eel, sea robins, skate, Cape May goodies, ocean perch, porgies, tuna, sharks, oysters, and the occasional sea turtle. The abundant harvest of the sea ensured Wildwood's important role in the commercial fishing industry and as a destination for thousands of sport fishermen.

ANGLESEA

The three original Five Mile Beach resort communities grew slowly during the 1880s, hampered by the lack of major railroad connections to Philadelphia, Camden, Trenton,

The Inlet House, built during the 1880s, claimed to be Holly Beach's first hotel.
– Wildwood Historical Society

During the 1890s, visitors to the Wildwoods dressed somewhat formally for a stroll on the strand. – The Library Company of Philadelphia

and other population centers. Unlike Atlantic City, which developed rapidly because railroad service was immediately available, the Wildwoods came into being without a guarantee that they would ever have the benefit of passenger train connections.

Initially, Anglesea seemed to have the brightest future, and it was quickly and hopefully dubbed "...the youthful queen of seaside resorts." In early 1884, the community had but two houses, but before the season had ended, the Hotel Anglesea was open, several dozen cottages were either built or under construction, and a narrow boardwalk was laid directly on the sand to connect the few buildings and the beach. Hotel Anglesea was the center of all activity in those early days, and its proprietors were described as "jovial, kind and sociable." The sociability of the managers must have met with visitors' approval, for by late 1888 it was announced that Jonas Bowman, the current proprietor, was investing $4000 in improvements for the coming season. When the hotel opened in 1889, the rooms had been redecorated, the outside painted (it had probably been bare wood before 1889), a new kitchen was installed, and a barn was erected to stable guests' carriage teams. The hotel was often filled during the height of summer, and some of the cottage owners opened their cottages to guests. John Sturmer, an enterprising saloon operator, not only welcomed guests at his Rosewood Cottage, but hired a "first-class" French chef to assure that Rosewood guests enjoyed the finest cuisine in Anglesea.

Entertainment in early Anglesea was somewhat limited, and a favorite pastime was driving carriages over the large sand dunes and along the beach. However, it was not long before businessmen began catering to the visitors' desires. At the Germantown House, Anglesea's second major hotel, George Ent offered a barroom for gentlemen and a variety of musical entertainment. John Sturmer added a large pool room to his saloon, and Andrew Weeks built a combination billiard hall and news room where newspapers and cigars were available. These diversions were strictly for male visitors, as no proper lady would even consider entering saloons, billiard halls, or smoking rooms.

There were a few leisure activities that could be enjoyed by both sexes, however. Captain John Young ran sailing charters, and by 1888, spectators gathered for sailboat racing off Anglesea's shore. Of course, the wonderful sandy ribbon that ran along Five Mile Beach attracted both men and women. Charles Mace, an important figure in the real estate development of Anglesea, saw a great opportunity on the beach, and by 1888 he operated a pavilion that included a bathhouse and refreshment facilities. While propriety sometimes dictated when both men and women could be seen on the beach together, it was clear that the beachfront would be the focal point of the resort's future.

HOLLY BEACH

Further south, and mostly oblivious to Anglesea's growth, Holly Beach began its resort career. At a time when harvesting and shipping holly boughs to Philadelphia for the Christmas season was still a major business in Holly Beach, a newspaperman asked, "Why don't [sic] someone build a big hotel here. It would be a safe and money making investment." The question received a prompt answer with the opening of the Sea View House. It was followed in 1889 by the

Sunrise Hotel, erected by a group of investors from Millville, New Jersey. The Sea View House was immediately popular and was often booked to capacity from June to September. Once the railroad reached Holly Beach, the hotel sent carriages to meet guests at every train. Those who hadn't the forethought to make reservations often had to travel on to Cape May or even to Cape May Court House in search of accommodation at one of the larger hotels.

Holly Beach, during its early years, was still a gem in the rough. Despite its beautiful beach, sand dunes, and thick forested areas, wild cattle continued to assault the summer visitors. And, in the days before paved streets, it was necessary each spring for the street committee to arrange for the winter's accumulation of debris to be removed and the soggy streets made passable. Fortunately, sand was abundant, and both local officials and individuals used beach sand to fill holes in roads and lots. A breakwater, constructed in 1888-89, helped control high tides and storm waters, making the maintenance of streets and properties easier.

Not surprisingly, Holly Beach entrepreneurs were anxious to change the town's primitive conditions and fully serve the leisure-time needs of summer visitors. In 1888, Charles Bridges operated a small stand near the beach that sold candy, sarsaparilla, ginger beer and, on occasion, the most exotic of resort foods, bananas. At the same time, town boosters were busy trying to lure a photographer to the beach. A good photo studio, they believed, could make someone an excellent living producing souvenir tintypes. The same boosters were proud when noted stage actor Carl Haswin selected Holly Beach for his family's summer home. But their greatest accomplishment of the late 1880s, was the construction of the community's first "continuous boardwalk." The promenade was narrow, uneven, and laid directly on the sand so that it could be removed each winter and stored away from the ravages of the ocean. Many hoped that a larger boardwalk would be built for the following (1889) season, but others would have been satisfied just to have two or three oil-burning street lamps to prevent strollers from tripping on the uneven boards at night. Although the boardwalk was nothing like the twenty-foot wide, elevated walk that already existed at Atlantic City, by 1888 both Anglesea and Holly Beach had embryonic structures that would someday become the great boardwalks of the Wildwoods in the next century.

WILDWOOD

Wildwood, referred to as "A New and Attractive Seaside Resort" in 1889, initially grew more slowly than its neighbors to the north and south. Aside from the sea and the beach, Wildwood's featured attraction was a sixty-foot observation tower constructed of cedar and white oak and situated to provide spectacular views of the forest top, the beach, and a twenty mile stretch of sea. With carriage teams tied to hitching posts, visitors climbed the tower's shaky stairway for a breeze-swept survey of the natural wonders of Five Mile Beach. At this point in time, the beauties of nature were Wildwood's only assets. As late as 1890, Wildwood consisted of four muddy streets: Cedar, Oak, Pine, and Wildwood. The area north of Pine Street was nothing but vacant land entangled with undergrowth. However, just as with Anglesea and Holly Beach, early Wildwood businessmen wasted little time developing facilities that catered to the summer vacationer.

In 1888, the Excursion Pavilion was constructed on the sand at the end of Cedar Avenue. Although it was open on all sides to both soft breezes and storms alike, the pavilion was the initial centerpiece of the Wildwood resort. Refreshments were sold, rooms were provided for changing into bathing attire, and orchestras were imported from Philadelphia for dances or "hops." At one such festive event, the "dance deck" was festooned with holly branches and moss, intertwined with cedar boughs, and illuminated with Japanese lanterns. No doubt many lasting vows were sparked in such romantic surroundings! After the 1888 season, the pavilion was enlarged and street lamps were placed nearby to guide visitors on their way at night. In spite of these improvements, the pavilion's original proprietor elected not to operate the facility in 1889, and the owners leased it to J. W. Bond of Philadelphia. With Wildwood still lagging behind its neighbors in resort development, and with railroads only beginning to make an impact on the resorts, Bond apparently lost interest in a difficult business and failed to renew his lease for 1890. Fortunately for Wildwood, Bond's successor, Gilbert Blaker, would become one of Wildwood's most stalwart boosters.

The early resorts of Five Mile Beach were primitive, difficult to get to, fraught with a variety of hazards for the unwary vacationer. Visitors to the Jersey Shore of the 1880s were advised to bring opera glasses or spy glasses for amusement, medications for constipation and diarrhea, broad-brimmed

hats for protection from the sun, cotton to protect the ear drums from salt water, and a good length of strong rope with which to escape if the hotel should catch fire!

There is no question that the island offered one of the best, if not the best, beach on the continent, but those who ventured into the ocean were often warned of its dangers. In 1888, it was noted that "The sharks are getting unpleasantly numerous...and also growing increasingly bold...." But sharks were not the only challenge to be found in the ocean. The first beach fatality of 1889 was reported when a German baker who worked in a local bakery drowned in early July. Yet, nearly a decade would pass before any effort was made to provide the beach with lifeguards. During the coming years, the threat of sharks was mostly forgotten, lifeguards patrolled the beach, hotel conditions improved markedly, and getting to the Wildwoods became much easier.

Fire was the constant enemy of a summer resort constructed entirely of wood. To fight the common blazes, volunteer units like the Holly Beach Pioneer Hook & Ladder Company were formed. – Wildwood Historical Society

In 1890, the Public Drinking Pagoda was one of the first public conveniences at the resort. In the background are the famous Observation Tower and the first railroad station. – Wildwood Historical Society

The view from the southern end of the Hotel Dayton porch was dominated by the Wildwood Casino, with Blaker's Pier in the background. At this time, about 1900, the Casino did not yet have the long fishing pier that would soon stretch well into the surf.
– Wildwood Historical Society

RAILROADS CONNECT

The construction of a dependable railroad system was by far the most important watershed in early history of the Five Mile Beach resorts. The only major railroad in Southern New Jersey during the 1880s was the West Jersey Railroad, a line controlled by the mighty Pennsylvania Railroad. This line acquired the Cape May and Millville Railroad, played a major role in the resort industry at Cape May, and was also a primary artery into Atlantic City for the working-class visitors. Late in the spring of 1888, the West Jersey also acquired the now-defunct Anglesea Railroad, financed the construction of the Excursion Pavilion, promised a station at Holly Beach, replaced the tiny "Mud Hen" engine of the Anglesea line with a modern locomotive, and planned for a rail connection through Five Mile Beach to Cape May. Construction, however, was slow and delays were commonplace. Hopes that the line would be completed in 1888 vanished, and it was finally believed that track would be laid from Anglesea to Holly Beach by late May of 1889. But, by the time summer visitors started to trickle in during early May, trains ran only as far as Anglesea. Taking advantage of the situation, Harry Bright secured a contract to run a horse-drawn stage line from the Anglesea station to Wildwood and the Holly Beach hotels. After more delays, the track reached the Wildwood station in late June and although one dollar excursions began arriving on June 30, the Holly Beach hotels were still a half mile from track's end.

The railroad proved to be an instant success. It was precisely the catalyst needed to fully ignite resort development. Eight excursion trains rolled into Wildwood during August from Philadelphia, Vineland, and Frankford, while other trains ran twice weekly from Cape May. Rail-borne visitors came not only from New Jersey, but also from Pennsylvania, Connecticut, and New York to sample the joys of Five Mile Beach. On one Saturday night, when a train pulling five overloaded passenger cars stopped at Anglesea, the local hotels were strained to

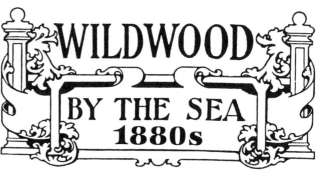

find accommodations for all the people. All around the railroad stations, businesses flourished. Near the Anglesea station, George Madara opened an ice cream parlor and soon expanded his business to serve fresh oysters to those stepping off the trains and waiting for return trips. The railroads brought thousands of people to the three resorts and they all came with spendable cash. It was now for the businessmen of Five Mile Beach to find the means to entertain and accommodate their summertime guests.

It behooved the railroad greatly to promote the Five Mile Beach resorts and it did so immediately. Meanwhile, the Baker Brothers purchased hundreds of inches of newspaper advertising in Philadelphia and Cape May. The resorts were hailed for their health-restoring climate. The Bakers claimed that mountain air might be exhilarating, but seashore air would lessen the severity of or even cure "...bronchitis, dyspepsia, insomnia, nervous debility and liver and kidney troubles...." The same sea air was touted as cure for poor appetites and as a tonic for the businessmen seeking relief from the pressures of daily urban life. Whether in search of better health or diversion from everyday care troubles and cares, trainloads of people began arriving at the three resorts.

The porch of Hotel Dayton provided an unobstructed view of the northern end of the Boardwalk and Wildwood's sparse commercial development. Arc lights illuminated both dusty Atlantic Avenue and the Boardwalk.
– Wildwood Historical Society

Below: Hotel Dayton, built in 1890 at Wildwood and Atlantic Avenues, was officially dedicated by President Benjamin Harrison.
– Wildwood Historical Society

Despite stiff competition from Atlantic City, Ocean City, Asbury Park, Cape May, Bellwood Park, Cranberry Lake, Nolan's Point on Lake Hopatcong, and Mauch Chunk, the "Switzerland of America," the youthful Five Mile Beach resorts thrived. A "fast and elegant train" left Philadelphia's Market Street Ferry on Memorial Day of 1890 with a full load of passengers enjoying the one dollar excursion rate. A typical Saturday train arriving in Wildwood carried four hundred visitors, and during the summer of 1890 more than forty special excursion trains steamed into Wildwood station. Over one four-day period in July, thirty-five hundred excursionists arrived. Another day two train sections of twenty-five coaches delivered twenty-five hundred passengers from a number of New Jersey towns! In addition to trains from the north and the west, the Baker Brothers arranged for several weekly rail excursions from Cape May. Surprisingly, Cape May busi-

nessmen failed to see Wildwood as serious competition and wholeheartedly supported the excursions. A few years later, relations between the older Cape May businesses and the upstart Wildwood businesses would be less cordial.

PROVIDING HOSPITALITY

The most immediate impact of the railroad was felt within the hotel and boardinghouse business. Like other coastal resorts, Five Mile Beach offered both types of accommodations. The distinction between them was based primarily on the number of rooms and the level of service offered. However, in most cases, the difference between a small hotel and a large boardinghouse was minimal. Whatever the distinctions, by the summer of 1890 there were not enough of either to accommodate the waves of visitors needing rooms.

The success of Hotel Wildwood in 1889 prompted construction of Hotel Dayton at Wildwood and Atlantic Avenues for the 1890 season. Officially dedicated by President Benjamin Harrison during his celebrated visit to Wildwood, the Dayton was the finest structure on the island. It offered a magnificent view of the beach and the ocean, and offered guests four floors of well-appointed rooms, a broad veranda, and a first-class dining room. So advanced was the Dayton that even in 1899, it was still the only hotel in the area to serve dining room guests on its own hand-painted china. For entertainment, the hotel engaged an excellent orchestra from Philadelphia. As one of its managers, William Crowell, noted, the Dayton never suggested that it offered lower rates. Instead, it offered the best location, the best food, and the "Best in everything...."

By 1897, the roster of local hotels included the Dayton, Marine Hall, Sea View, the Edgeton Inn, the Latimer, Ocean Villa, Tower Villa, Silver Dean, Brighton, Woodland, Selina, Stewart, Ivy, Wildwood, Trenton, Aetna, Ruric, Bartram, Pines, Oak Villa, Lower Villa, Seaside Cottage, and Homestead Cottage. Some offered only a few spartan rooms, while others, like the Marine Hall, provided sixty-five nicely decorated rooms. Each season new hotels opened, and, except at the depth of the depression of the mid-1890s, the demand for hotels usually exceeded the supply during July and August.

Even when business was at capacity level, the hotels vied with each other for the "best class" of customers. Every hostelry of merit dispatched its own carriage to the train station to meet trains, although soliciting potential customers at the station was considered unethical. Each of hotels strove to offer better services than its competitors. The Edgeton Inn was one of the first to boast of electric lighting and call bells in 1898. But it also touted its shuffleboard courts, fine dance floor, and private bathrooms. The Hotel Sheldon enticed guests with a new electric elevator "running to every floor," a barber shop, wide porches, a fine orchestra, unexcelled cuisine, and large, airy rooms with an ocean view from every window. At the older Hotel Germantown in Anglesea, George Ent was among the first to advertise a gentleman's barroom in the hotel, as well as a pool room, shuffleboard courts, and one of the best selections of fine cigars on the island. Mr. Ent, it appears, made his bid for business by appealing to the men and disregarding the women and children. Without doubt, the Dayton, the Sheldon, and the Marine Hall were all eminently more popular with the ladies. The older hotels were forced to upgrade and modernize as newer and better facilities opened. Many were improved, painted, redecorated, and expanded. At the Sea View House, the proprietor took delivery of an entire railroad car full of new furniture before the 1891 season.

Prior to the construction of the big boardwalks, the hotels were the centers of resort activity, and they continued to vie with each other to offer the finest in entertainment. During the week and on Saturdays, all of the major hotels provided orchestras, musical troupes, soloists, singers, and even vaudeville performers considered to be of the "better class." On Sundays, they opened their public spaces to church services, sacred concerts, and hymn singing sessions. At the height of the season, the hotels staged dances or hops and often the ballrooms were rented for special balls. In July of 1898, for example, the Hotel Latimer hosted a dance in honor of E. Palmer Goddard of Philadelphia's elite First Regiment. The hotels were also responsible for the first beauty pageant held in the Wildwoods, almost two decades before Atlantic City's renowned pageant began. The Five Mile Beach contest was held in August of 1903 and was staged at the Hotel

The fifty room Severn Hall hotel was built in 1900 by Mrs. M. B. Severn, one of the resort's first successful businesswomen.
– Library of Congress

Sheldon. The winner, Miss Anna Klienz, was an immediate local celebrity and other local hotels quickly picked-up on the idea of beauty contests.

Hotel rates during the 1890s ran the gamut from very inexpensive to pricey. The variation in price was based upon hotel location, social standing of the hotel, reputation, level of services, and the quality of the accommodations. A simple boardinghouse room in Holly Beach, complete with kitchen and utensils, could be rented for four dollars a week (sometimes less during the off season or if business was slow). The Silver Dean Cottage's rate schedule ran from seven to ten dollars a week, as did the modest, twenty-five room Oak Villa. The Oaklyn, a middle range house best known for Mrs. Wolfinger's excellent cuisine, had a top rate of twelve dollars a week. However, special rates were available for families and for extended stays. At the top end of the scale were hotels like the Dayton, where daily rates ran from $2.00 to $2.50, and special weekly rates were often not available.

During the 1890s, and continuing throughout the next one hundred years, the guests staying at hotels in the Wildwoods were predominately from the Philadelphia area. The next largest number came from Camden, followed by other New Jersey cities, Baltimore, Richmond, Washington, central Pennsylvania, Pittsburgh, and Cleveland. The hotel proprietors and local businessmen liked to believe that the Wildwoods were host to the cream of society. Indeed, it was not uncommon to see names in the hotel register followed by such descriptive phrases as "well-known Philadelphia businessman," or "prominent young merchant." However, the

fact that many of the hotels advertised "Terms Moderate" or "Terms Reasonable" belied the truth: middle and working-class patrons were really the core of the Wildwoods' summer hotel trade. Among this clientele, certain visitors attracted their share of attention. In 1898, it was noted that "Miss Nina S. Garsed, a handsome brunette, very prominent in social circles in Philadelphia..." was staying at the Latimer. If this news piqued the interest of young male guests, it was further noted that, "Every morning this popular maiden may be seen taking her daily spin on the beach."

By the end of the 1890s, the disastrous business depression that has begun in 1893 was over. Now there was even greater interest in hotel construction on the island. Between 1903 and 1904, the number of hotel rooms available in Wildwood alone increased by thirty percent. Among the new, first-class hotels constructed during the early years of the twentieth century was the Hotel Ottens in Anglesea. Opening on July 2, 1904, the Hotel Ottens was owned by the Five Mile Beach Hotel Company, of which Philip Baker was one of four prominent shareholders. Described as the finest hotel in South Jersey, the seventy-five room structure featured fourteen private baths, an electric elevator, modern fire escapes, a resident orchestra and dining rooms including the Roof Garden, the Grotto, and the Buffet. For the next decade, the Hotel Ottens was the showpiece of resort hotels and the obvious choice for important local social functions and dances. Although most resort hotels closed for the season by the end of September, the Ottens, like the Marine Hall and the Dayton, often remained open all year.

Most of the island's hotel owners and proprietors (those who rented the hotels from the actual owners, usually on a year-to-year basis) enjoyed excellent profits during the short seasons that ran from the first of July to mid-September. An example was Mrs. M. B. Severn, who skillfully managed the Marine Hall for seven years until she had enough money saved to build her own hotel. Her fifty-room Severn Hall opened in 1900. The same year she constructed an attractive cottage for her family in Holly Beach. In an era when women were denied most managerial positions, a number of ladies proved to be highly qualified and very capable hotel managers and owners at Five Mile Beach.

Mrs. Severn's new hotel was an immediate success, but other hotels were not as fortunate. Each year, a few of them were offered for sale. In 1900, Hotel Latimer was sold at auction at a Cape May County Sheriff's sale. Others succumbed to fire, an all-too-frequent fate of wooden hotel structures. Waters's Hotel and its attached pavilion burned to the ground after the close of the 1897 season, and in 1904, Hotel Ruric was consumed by fire. Rebuilt and renamed, it was again decimated by fire in 1928, was again rebuilt, and was destroyed by flames for the last time in 1960.

FOOD AND DRINK

While the natural beauty of the Wildwoods provided food for the soul, vacationers also required food of a more substantial sort. The hotels, of course, made every effort to satisfy the palate. On a typical summer evening the dining room of the Hotel Dayton served about three hundred people, approximately eighty of whom would have been hotel guests and the remainder, excursionists. As the resorts grew in popularity, restaurants and food stands offering lower-priced refreshments and faster service sprouted along the beach and along the streets. Harry Cills's Meadow Pavilion served a simple fare of cold soft drinks, cakes and candies; while William Cills's Arctic Refreshment Parlor, located on the lower level of the Marine Hall hotel, sold sparkling soda, ice cream sodas, dishes of ice cream, candies, fancy cakes, and even exotic fruits. Although ice cream cones would not be invented for another year or two, Mills & Company manufactured and sold more than 2000 quarts of ice cream on July 1 and 2, 1904. Dr. Tunis operated a little stand on the beach that offered paper bags brimming with fragrant, hot roasted peanuts. Salt water taffy, that perennial resort favorite, was not available at Wildwood until 1898. The famous candy maker, Lowe, first sold taffy at the railroad depot, but the stand was moved to the

beach when the large boardwalk was constructed. Naturally, seafood was always in good supply in the restaurants and at various stands along the beach. In 1892, an unnamed young lady was reportedly so fond of clams that she easily defeated all male competitors in clam-eating contests!

Naturally, a wide variety of liquid refreshments complemented all of these delicious foods. However, water was in short supply in the early resort days. There was virtually no fresh water available on the island and wells were often drilled in vain. In 1894, a well was sunk to a depth of 997 feet before it struck not water, but solid rock. Hotels collected rain water in cisterns, and quality drinking water was brought in by the railroad and sold to hotels and restaurants. One enterprising local, Jeanette Meech, bought bottled water in Vineland and sold the precious commodity for one cent a bottle at her store near the Sea View House.

Other beverages were in far greater supply. Numerous vendors offered flavored soda waters, the most popular flavors being root beer, birch beer, spruce beer, lemon, cherry, pepsin, ginger and, in a few places, claret. Stronger beverages were readily available in many of the hotels and in the bars of Anglesea, but even as late as 1898, there were still no saloons in Wildwood. Despite the deluge of prohibition literature that was circulated in Wildwood, the illegal sale of liquor was widespread and often connected to illegal gambling operations.

Obviously, ice was of primary importance to all of the resorts' beverage vendors, as well as restaurant and hotel managers. In the days before electrical refrigeration, ice was harvested on Magnolia Lake (at the present location of New York Avenue) during the winter and stored in an icehouse for summer use. In addition, freight cars loaded with ice arrived from the major Philadelphia ice companies. Finally, in 1891, Frank Smith of Holly Beach invested in the first ice making machine on the island, claiming that he could handle all of the resort's needs for the coming summer. By the end of the decade, new ice plants were processing and selling 30,000 pounds of ice per day and found it difficult to keep up with demand on humid August afternoons.

THE SAND AND SURF

In the evening, most social activity took place in the hotels, dining rooms, and saloons. But during the daytime, the wide, sandy beach of Five Mile Beach was the center of fun. In the early 1900s, the ocean reached a high water mark along the resort's coast.

Magnolia Lake was one of the early resort's most popular attractions. As the population grew, however, the lake was filled in to provide space for development. Today, the point where Magnolia and New York Avenues intersect is the site of the lake. – Wildwood Historical Society

During high tides in 1901 it was common for salt water to wash into the barbershop beneath the Hotel Seaside. Eventually, however, the beach began to expand and widen, partially because of pilings and breakwaters installed by the Baker Brothers. Incredibly, in some years the beach widened by as much as seventy feet! While Ocean City and Cape May struggled to maintain their beach line, the Wildwoods enjoyed an expanding beach and sometimes even had to find ways to dispose of excess sand.

During the resort's early years, the beach was lined with an assortment of bathhouses, stores, and pavilions. All were highly vulnerable during high tides, hurricanes, and nor'easters.

– Wildwood Historical Society

With an almost perfect summer climate, warm ocean water, and its wide expanse of sand, it's not surprising that beach activity accelerated throughout the 1890s. Perhaps part of the attraction lay in the fact that ladies' swim wear became more abbreviated and colorful during the decade. Some daring ladies eschewed stockings for bare legs, and hemlines on bathing skirts were shortened. Outraged moralists exaggerated that the new swimming suits would not fill the proverbial collar box! Another reason for the popularity of the beach was the increase in entertainment along the shore. For example, on Tuesday mornings, the United States Lifesaving Service's lifeboat crew held capsizing drills just off Wildwood's shoreline. Pretty exciting stuff in the days before television and "Baywatch."

All of this activity on the beach created a demand not only for bathhouses, but for bathing robes, towels, umbrellas, and chairs, all of which could be rented. In 1890, W. W. Thomas built new bathhouses in Holly Beach, added hot seawater baths, and opened a photo studio that specialized in capturing images of patrons in swim wear. A year later, Charles Mace opened bathhouses in Anglesea, and in Holly Beach, E. S. Hewitt built a structure that housed forty-eight changing rooms and a photo studio. Some, like Meech & Co., found their bathhouses operating to capacity. By 1895, many were doubling the

size of the their operations. While these bathhouses catered to the needs of the bathers, no one gave much consideration to their safety. Drownings were a commonly accepted risk that went along with the joys of swimming. As late as 1902, the only lifeguard on duty in Wildwood was a wrestling instructor from the University of Pennsylvania who was hired by the Casino's management to protect bathers in the area of Oak Avenue. At night, he doubled as a policeman in the Casino.

The amusement pier, like the beach and the Boardwalk, became symbolic of the summer resort industry on Five Mile Beach. The idea of the amusement pier was unquestionably borrowed from Atlantic City, but Wildwood's early piers grew from beachside pavilions. Gradually, as the beach area was enlarged, the pavilions spread eastward by a series of wooden decks and buildings constructed on pilings over the beach. Two of these pavilions, Blaker's and the Casino, evolved into piers, but it was not until the winter of 1904-05 that a true, Atlantic City-style amusement pier was constructed.

25

The Excursion Pavilion was acquired by Gilbert Blaker in 1890 and soon became Blaker's Pier. Located at the foot of Cedar Avenue, it was the resort's first amusement pier. – Wildwood Historical Society

G. H. BLAKER

The father of the Wildwood amusement pier was Gilbert H. Blaker (1853-1928). Gib Blaker was trained as wallpaper hanger during the 1870s and eventually opened his own paper hanging business in Frankford, Pennsylvania. In April of 1890, he visited Wildwood and secured a lease on the Excursion Pavilion near the foot of Cedar Avenue. Apparently, he didn't believe the amusement business would take all of his time, or perhaps he was just covering all bases, because he also opened a wallpaper and window shade store in Wildwood. Blaker expanded the pavilion by adding 100 new changing rooms stocked with new bathing robes. He then enclosed the pavilion with glass windows for protection from the elements. As the pavilion began to expand toward the sea, a pagoda was erected at the end of the new pier section. One of the big attractions at Blaker's in 1891 was a 2200 pound whale that had been stuffed by a Camden taxidermist and placed on display at the Pavilion. At the time, it was thought to be the only stuffed whale in the United States.

Gilbert H. Blaker (1853-1928) was the resort's first great amusement impresario. From 1890 into the 1920s, he dominated the Boardwalk scene. – John W. Kille Collection

One of Wildwood's first carousels was this small machine that offered both horses and chairs for riders. In the nearby pavilion are tables laden with picnic lunches (circa 1895).
– Wildwood Historical Society

Above: Blaker's Theatre, about 1904. On the extreme right are some of Blaker's bathhouses.
– The Historical Society of Pennsylvania

Above left: The Boardwalk entrance to Blaker's Pavilion and Theatre.
– The Historical Society of Pennsylvania

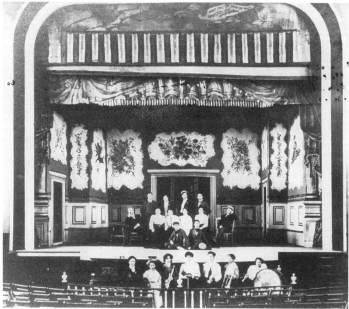

Left: The interior of Blaker's Theatre before the era of the moving picture. Vaudeville or stock company performers are on the stage, while an all-girl musical group is in the orchestra pit. –The Historical Society of Pennsylvania

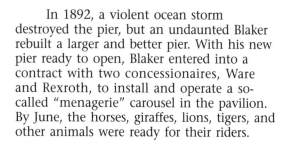

In 1892, a violent ocean storm destroyed the pier, but an undaunted Blaker rebuilt a larger and better pier. With his new pier ready to open, Blaker entered into a contract with two concessionaires, Ware and Rexroth, to install and operate a so-called "menagerie" carousel in the pavilion. By June, the horses, giraffes, lions, tigers, and other animals were ready for their riders.

The next few years brought a host of changes and improvements to the pavilion. By the time 1899 rolled around, Blaker's featured a lunch room, ice cream parlor, candy and soda water counters, a music stand, a 25 by 60 foot dance floor, bathhouses, and assorted other attractions. There was even an auditorium that later became known as Blaker's Theatre.

The resort's second amusement pier, the Wildwood Casino, was built in 1897 at a total cost of $18,000.
– Wildwood Historical Society

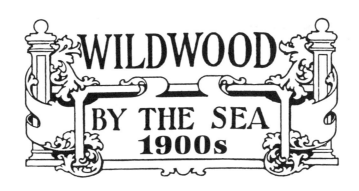

Blaker's Auditorium was originally designed to house vaudeville shows, but in 1904 it was completely remodeled, a new stage was built, and a large inventory of scenery and equipment was acquired. At that time, Blaker discontinued vaudeville (except during the winter months) and introduced stock companies. His manager, James Spencer, booked a number of small summer stock companies who performed a limited range of comedies. Black-face shows were also very popular around 1900, as was the occasional melodrama. Until the advent of moving pictures, Blaker's theatrical presentations were quite successful. All seats were reserved, the box office opened daily at ten in the morning, and frequently, evening performances were sold out.

Blaker also offered patrons a variety of musical entertainment. Dances and hops were held regularly, and he usually imported a well-known orchestra from Philadelphia to provide the music. Around this time, concert bands were enjoying the zenith of their popularity. Although Blaker could not afford bands like Sousa's or Brooke's, he did manage to engage William Payne's Millville City Band and Professor Lapatina's Orchestra. Crisply attired in white, Payne's eighteen-piece band offered the usual concert fare of standard marches, light classics, and favorite operatic selections. On Sundays, in keeping with New Jersey's Sabbatarian laws, the band restricted its repertoire to classical sacred music and hymns.

A lady who lived in Holly Beach during the 1880s and 1890s commented that Blaker's Pavilion was the best facility of its kind on the island and better by far than the small Holly Beach Pavilion. She recalled one memorable evening at Blaker's when it rained so heavily that employees scurried to find enough buckets to place under each leak in the roof. Undaunted, the good-natured dancers skillfully avoided the buckets as they whirled around the floor! It was not long, however, until Gib Blaker could easily afford a new roof.

THE CASINO

The success of Blaker's Pavilion during the early 1890s led to the construction of other pavilions and piers. In the spring of 1897, a new $18,000 pavilion, the Wildwood Casino (known as The Casino) was constructed immediately north of Blaker's. Unfortunately, The Casino was built during an unstable economic period and by the end of its first season was near bankruptcy.

In April of the following year, it was sold at sheriff's sale to a group headed by Dr. G. J. R. Miller. The Casino was personally managed by Dr. Miller in 1898, and he promoted a number of hops, as well as a midsummer carnival. The local newspaper reported that "The Casino and pier present a lively scene, especially at night, when the full moon makes a silver track across the shimmering sea." Alas, Dr. Miller was no

Although the streets were still dirt (or often mud), the Casino offered the modern convenience of hot salt water baths and a popular fishing pier with a pavilion at the end.
– Library of Congress

By 1903, the owners of the Casino had constructed a long fishing pier with a pavilion at the end. Without the amusements that would soon line the Boardwalk, a stroll on the promenade in the early 1900s was leisurely and quiet. – Wildwood Historical Society
– Cape May County Historical and Genealogical Society

more successful than the casino's original owners. When he was unable to make payments on $12,000 in mortgages, a Sheriff's sale awarded the property to James Butcher, Benjamin E. Harris, and James Davidson (The Wildwood Pavilion Company) for just one dollar!

Heading the group was former New Jersey State Senator James Butcher, a real estate investor, bank director, and Treasurer of Salem County. Under his supervision, The Casino developed into a facility that rivaled and sometimes even eclipsed Blaker's.

The Wildwood Pavilion Company enlarged The Casino and expanded its entertainment facilities. In the restaurant, two hundred diners could feast on oysters, clams, and fish "in every style" while a new piano provided musical entertainment. The Casino's dance floor, measuring 50 feet by 100 feet, was considered the finest in New Jersey and offered free dancing every afternoon, although there was an admission charge in the evenings.

For the convenience of ocean bathers, The Casino rented bathing suits and "first-class bathing robes." Three hundred and fifty changing rooms served thousands of bathers each day, as did the hot sea water baths. For just a nickel, one could enjoy ocean fishing from a five hundred foot pier without ever boarding a boat. Those who forgot to bring fishing tackle could rent what was needed from The Casino.

In addition to all of these attractions, there was a carousel, Sagel's candy shop, George Wonfor's photo studio, a shaded promenade, billiards, shuffleboard, ping pong, bowling alleys, a basketball court, a shop that sold sea shells, and another that sold red-flashed glassware custom-engraved while buyer waited. Vases, cups, goblets, plates and pitchers emerged from the shop sporting sentimental inscriptions such as "Mother// 1898" or "Mary//Wildwood Casino 1897." When electricity became available, the West Jersey Electric Company installed colored light bulbs throughout the pier, and by night The Casino shimmered with light and color.

Capitalizing on its major attraction, The Casino was quick to exhibit all natural wonders that came from the sea. In 1903, a turtle alleged to weigh 1100 pounds was displayed at the pier and drew huge crowds. The following season, a 1500 pound shark more than ten feet in length went on display. It, too, attracted much attention until the third day of its exhibition when the dead animal began to decompose. It was promptly dumped back into the sea, which must have distressed those people bathing in the area of The Casino and Blaker's Pavilion.

Like Blaker's, The Casino centered its entertainment around music. Starting in 1899, the dance floor came under the management of Professor Harry Roselle, a friendly, energetic man who became almost legendary

One of Wildwood's first large carousels (probably at the Casino Pier), was purchased from Philadelphia's celebrated carousel builder, Gustav A. Dentzel. Steam-powered, this machine featured not only nicely carved horses, but also other animals such as deer, camels, and giraffes. – Wildwood Historical Society

in his role as dancing master. Roselle, who taught dancing in Camden during the winter months, managed the dance hall, gave dancing lessons, arranged special events like masquerade balls, managed the Wildwood basketball team, and directed the Wildwood Scrap Iron Band. Many couples chose to dance at The Casino instead of Blaker's simply because of the gregarious and popular professor. Dance music was provided by the Wildwood Casino Orchestra, conducted by Samuel Corle, who spent the off-season as a railroad conductor in Philadelphia. While employment on Five Mile Beach was no doubt interesting and rewarding, it was limited to a three or four month season. In order to survive, one had to leave Wildwood at the close of the season and find employment in the larger cities.

In addition to dancing, the Casino offered an almost endless array of stage entertainers. Rosalie Washburn sang "coon songs," and the Real Georgia Minstrels was advertised as a traveling troupe made up

entirely of "Colored People." Such a group was a rarity in the early 1900s, as most minstrels were whites made up in "black face." In addition, there was Signor Nicoletta playing the harp, Madame Celeste imitating birds and animals, Ethel Ewan providing "darkey" songs and dances, a host of magicians, singers, and acrobats, and the Philadelphia Quartet, a seriously classical group composed of a soprano, a contralto, a tenor and a bass. As was the case at Blaker's, Sundays were devoted exclusively to sacred music. Most of the summer's entertainment at The Casino was decidedly adult in tone, but children's parties were a weekly event that included lighter entertainment and refreshments. Usually these events were held on a weekday afternoon when The Casino would not have been very busy.

As might be expected, a bitter competition grew between the Casino and Gib Blaker. Blaker called his facility the "Old

Once the fishing pier was built, visitors could enjoy ocean breezes and a view of the Casino from several hundred feet out at sea. – Ron Franks Collection

Reliable," while Butcher confidently advertised that The Casino was really the only facility of its kind in Wildwood. In Butcher's opinion, there was no comparison between the two piers. By the early 1900s, the small boardwalk that connected the two piers was torn down, and a fence was erected so that patrons had to make tramp over the sand to reach one pier from the other. When The Casino closed for the season, Blaker gleefully erected a sign that read, "This pier is open to the public," and suggested that The Casino's closing provided a disservice to those who still visited the shore in October. As the years went by and crowds increased, pier owners recognized that there was plenty of business for both operations and the bitter competitive struggle came to an end.

OTHER PIERS AND PAVILIONS

Although The Casino and Blaker's were major attractions, they were by no means the only pavilions in operation. The Holly Beach Pavilion was operated by C. A. J. Johnson and Levi Butts (an ocean pier was considered for Holly Beach in 1891 but never constructed). And, at the foot of Rio Grande Avenue, Y. S. Rogers operated a small pavilion. As early as 1889, Rogers had proposed that a two hundred-foot ocean pier be erected at the end of his pavilion, but nothing came of this plan, either. Other ideas were more successful.

For example, an old telegraph office was moved to the shores of Magnolia Lake in 1891. Verandas were added, refreshment services were installed, and penny arcade machines and a phonograph were purchased. The Severn House, as it was called, offered excursions on a twenty-two foot swan boat. Although this little pavilion enjoyed a modicum of success, it was quickly overwhelmed by the popularity of the beachside pavilions and piers. A tranquil lake held little interest for those who could easily bath in the roaring Atlantic. At about this same time, someone built a pagoda on a sand dune at Maple and Atlantic Avenues. Probably because it was not a commercial venture, the pagoda provided an excellent retreat for young couples strolling the beach in the evening. In fact, its popularity with young lovers earned it the nickname of "Sugar Bowl."

While interest and development dollars were being concentrated in Wildwood and Holly Beach, Anglesea continued aggressively courting the tourist trade. Charles Ludlam built a large bowling alley and shooting gallery in 1892. And, after Charles Mace's pier was destroyed by high tides in October of 1891, his pavilion was moved inland slightly. A new pier was constructed and new refreshment counters were added for the 1892 season.

There is evidence that Anglesea probably had the honor of exhibiting the first moving pictures on Five Mile Beach. In August of 1904, a small pavilion was erected next to Mace's Hotel Royal, and short films were shown there each evening. Within a few years, moving pictures would become a huge summertime attraction from Anglesea to Holly Beach.

THE FIRST RIDES AND ATTRACTIONS

Amusement rides also began to appear along the island's beach during the 1890s. Although there was a roller coaster in Atlantic City during the 1880s and another was built at Cape May in 1890, it was not until after 1910 that the Wildwood area got its first bona fide thrill ride. Meanwhile, riding the carousel was a favorite pastime in Wildwood and Holly Beach. A small carousel was operating in the area as early as 1890, and both Blaker's and the Casino featured the gaily painted circular rides. In 1904, a councilman placed a new merry-go-round on the beach, and several others were operating by the early 1900s. Most of the early carousels in the area were small and surprisingly portable. In fact, J. H. Ware, who owned the carousel at Blaker's, disassembled his machine each fall and moved it to larger cities where he could operate it at an indoor location during the colder months. In spring, he returned it to Blaker's.

In addition to the commercial entertainments offered by the big piers, the small pavilions, and the independent carousel and shooting gallery operators, simpler diversions were also available to summer guests. Lawn tennis and shuffleboard were played at many of the hotels, and by 1899 summer basketball was more popular than baseball in Wildwood. The Wildwood team originally made the Casino its home and built a respectable reputation playing teams like the Philadelphia All Scholastics. By 1904, the Wildwood team was drawing capacity crowds from July to September. That season, the team recorded six wins, one loss, and one tied game.

THE FIRST WILDWOOD BOARDWALK

In 1896, Atlantic City built its fifth Boardwalk, a forty-foot wide promenade that has served the city for more than a century. It was clear to Wildwood area businessmen and municipal leaders that if the communities of Five Mile Beach were to compete with Atlantic City, Asbury Park, and Cape May, they would need a boardwalk of their own. In fact, initial efforts to build a boardwalk had already been launched in both Wildwood

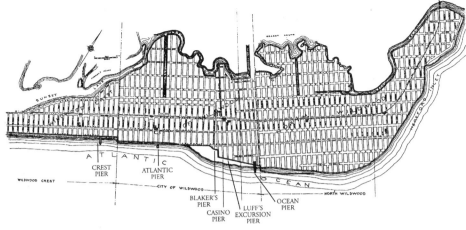

and Anglesea. In 1890, Messrs. Scott and Morts of Rio Grande were hired to lay a boardwalk directly on top of the sea wall built by the Baker Brothers in Wildwood. A year later it stretched the entire length of the sea wall, and in 1892 another two hundred-foot section was added. In another few years, Gib Blaker built a twelve-foot boardwalk on either side of his pavilion which sat on the south side of Cedar Avenue. Then he connected it with an existing walk on the north side of the street. Anglesea joined in the boardwalk rush in 1891 when the city council appropriated money for the construction of a five thousand-foot promenade along Central Avenue. By May of that year, a second walk was completed near the beach. Finally, in 1892, a narrow boardwalk was built to connect the Hotel Germantown with Beach Creek. All of these walks were narrow and portable, laid directly on the sand or the sea wall, and stored away from the shore in winter to prevent them from being washed out to sea.

Early in 1899 Wildwood leaders began campaigning for more impressive, permanent boardwalk. On March 14, 1899, Mayor Latimer Baker proposed a plan for a boardwalk 1,000 feet long, 12 feet wide, and elevated 3 or 4 feet above the sand. His plan also called for a few pagodas to be built along the walk to provide shady rest areas for strollers. Baker estimated the cost of constructing the boardwalk at about $1 per foot, plus about $75 each for the pagodas. Three bids were received for construction, but council members could not agree about the promenade's location, and it appeared that nothing would happen for the 1899 season. Not to be denied, Baker nevertheless moved ahead and constructed a small boardwalk along Atlantic Avenue. Like the earlier walk, it was laid directly on the sand and was removed for storage at the end of the season.

During the winter of 1899-1900, the council debate over a boardwalk was resumed without resolution. As spring neared, the subject again arose and this time approval was given to solicit bids. The winning bid was submitted by A. S. Miller and Sons of Camden for $2,400.66 (ranging from $1.15 to $1.18 a foot, depending on location). The 1900 Boardwalk (it was finally large enough and permanent enough to warrant a capital "B") was still not an elevated walk, but arc lights placed along it gave it a sense of permanency. The walk was constructed along Atlantic Avenue, and many argued that with the widening beach it should have been placed closer to the water's edge.

By 1903, it was clear that the Boardwalk had been located too far to the west, and council announced plans to build a larger, wider, elevated Boardwalk closer to the ocean. In March of 1904, council approved the issuance of $12,000 in bonds for the construction of a new Boardwalk, and a committee met with the influential Baker brothers to select a site. An ordinance was passed to allow the structure to be built 180 feet east of Atlantic Avenue, where it would connect with a new 32 foot-wide Anglesea boardwalk and the proposed Holly Beach Boardwalk. Voters approved the bond issue on May 10, 1904, and construction was rushed to completion. Proud of their new elevated Boardwalk, the council decreed that four street lights would burn all winter long to illuminate the wooden promenade.

Holly Beach was the last entrant in the boardwalk race. On October 5, 1904, the Holly Beach council voted to approve a new 32 foot-wide walk of red cedar to run from Cresse Avenue north to the Wildwood Boardwalk at Blaker's Pier. Built by George Burgeois of Ocean City, the Holly Beach Boardwalk ran 4925 feet and cost $19,641.75. Dedicated on August 17, 1905, the latest Boardwalk continued the series of wooden walks that now stretched for two and a half miles from Anglesea south through Holly Beach.

For many, the Boardwalk opened up new sources of income. Before long, buildings of all shapes and sizes sprang up along its length, especially on the west side of the promenade. Several enterprising individuals bought and operated Atlantic City-style rolling chairs. Grover Smith and a partner had chairs on the Wildwood Boardwalk in 1904, and both Smith and N. B. Long operated similar concessions on the Holly Beach Boardwalk a year later.

Not everyone, however, was pleased with the new Boardwalk. Commercial fishermen, who already viewed the summer visitors with some degree of contempt, complained that the new Boardwalk interfered with the landing of their boats on the beaches and the hauling of the catches to the loading docks. Their complaints fell on deaf ears, for it was already clear that the summer resort industry now ruled Five Mile Beach.

The advent of the great new Boardwalks gave the Wildwoods a chance to compete openly and fairly with Atlantic City and Asbury Park. Accordingly, the Wildwood Council approved ever increasing advertising budgets to place resort ads in newspapers in Philadelphia, Pittsburgh, Baltimore, Camden, Wilkes-Barre, New York, Washington, and other cities. The community's first public relations manager, Charles Shick, was appointed to place articles about Wildwood in the major newspapers. The communities also found that as the resorts grew, so did their municipal budgets. Boardwalk repairs were always needed, and adequate lighting, mosquito control, and additional police protection were all matters of concern. In 1902, for example, Wildwood hired an extra police officer for the months of July and August at a salary of ten dollars a week.

Joseph Roth's Candy Land was one of a number of salt water taffy stores to emerge along the Boardwalk and in the hotels of the Wildwoods during the early 1900s.
– Cape May County Historical and Genealogical Society

Holidays, of course, brought the largest numbers of visitors to the hotels and beaches. On Memorial Day of 1894, it was estimated that a thousand people strolled the beach. A decade later, on July 4, 1905, it was estimated that more than ten thousand enjoyed the new Boardwalks. Memorial Day was a particularly important day in Wildwood, as it signaled the start of the summer season. It was also the date of the annual naval memorial ceremony. In 1891, a local minister suggested that Wildwood hold a special ceremony to honor the nation's naval heroes, and on May 30, 1894, the first such event on the Atlantic Coast took place. Originally,

Like candy stores, photo studios thrived along the new Boardwalks. This photo, taken about 1900 at Matthews' Studio, featured a background of ocean waves and a prop made of twisted local wood.
– David W. Francis Collection

The new Wildwood Boardwalk of 1904 provided a better vantage point for watching bathers and enjoying the ocean.
– David W. Francis Collection

The new Wildwood Boardwalk from ground level. Note the signs atop the pavilion and the observation platform spelling "Success" and "Luck." Both were fashioned from the wildly twisted trees that grew on the island and gave Wildwood its name.
– Wildwood Historical Society

In 1900, Hotel Dayton was blessed by the construction of the Wildwood Boardwalk at its front door. Few hotels in the nation could boast of a better location.
– Wildwood Historical Society

flowers were cast upon the water, but Wildwood quickly invented the idea of launching a flower-decked boat into the sea during the ceremony. By the end of the decade, Memorial Day had become a huge event in Wildwood. On Memorial Day, 1899, an excursion train brought ten coaches full of people. The hotels and dining rooms were full, Professor C. E. Nash's New Jersey Training School Band played on the porch of the Hotel Dayton, and Miss Anna Smith of Philadelphia was presided over the festivities as May Queen.

BUT NEVER ON SUNDAY

Even though the summer holidays drew the largest crowds, the boardwalks were usually bustling with excursionists every weekend. Unfortunately for the boardwalk merchants, New Jersey laws made it impossible for most of them to operate legally on Sundays. In 1798, the state had passed a law forbidding travel, business, drinking, dancing, sports, or any other form of amusements on Sundays (this law was not officially repealed until 1978). In 1847, another law made it illegal to

sell any intoxicating beverages on Sundays. Atlantic City, which adopted a "liberal policy," mostly disregarded the laws, operating amusements and selling liquor on Sundays. Since these laws were meant to be enforced locally, city officials often turned a blind eye to such infractions. But, in 1901, the Vorhees Act forced local officials and police to enforce the Sunday laws or face a fine or jail sentence. This new law now sometimes forced a county to step in where local officials still refused to act (as sometimes happened in Wildwood). Finally, in 1906, the Bishop's Law threatened license revocation and stiff fines for any establishment found guilty of selling intoxicants on Sundays.

In fact, the Five Mile Beach communities were far more respectful of the Sabbath than was Atlantic City. Many of the early excursions to Wildwood were made by church schools from the large cities, and in 1891, Reverend W. W. Meech led the island's first worship service at Blaker's Pavilion. Illegal liquor sales and gambling did take place on the island, but most businessmen of the 1890s adhered to New Jersey's Sabbatarianism and remained closed on Sundays. Blaker's and the Casino were open on Sunday, but the facilities were dedicated to church services and sacred musical concerts. Nevertheless, Cape May citizenry viewed Atlantic City, Five Mile Beach, and some of the other resorts as dens of sin. "Cape May can boast of a moral, refined, and fashionable class of people; no Sunday desecration, no summer gardens line the boardwalk, no gambling dens, no drunken loafers found on every corner, but everything is respectable and of a high character." In a parting shot at Wildwood's spectacular beach, the spokesman stated that the Cape May beach was "...beyond dispute the finest in the world...." Apparently, Cape May's businessmen were finally recognizing that the upstart resorts of Five Mile Island had eclipsed the grand old resort of Cape May.

The resorts on Five Mile Beach were now so popular that visitors demanded souvenirs of their vacations at the shore.

When President Benjamin Harrison visited Wildwood on August 23, 1890, the only souvenirs available for the President were wooden crafts hand made by Joseph Jones. In the years following, Jones became the area's first notable souvenir dealer. During the fall he collected wood and then spent all winter fashioning souvenirs to be sold the following summer. By 1900, the souvenir industry was big business in Wildwood. R. W. Ryan offered ten different post card views in his Wildwood Bazaar, and in 1903, he opened a Japanese Bazaar to sell imported Japanese goods, sea shell art, and even more post cards of Wildwood. Not to be outdone by Ryan, Meech & Company offered nearly one hundred full color post card views of the island. By 1904, the Wildwood post office could attest to the increasing popularity of sending post cards.

GONE FISHIN'

While most people came to the island for a rest, to enjoy the beach and stroll the Boardwalk, it is important to remember that the island, and especially Anglesea, was the center of a thriving sport fishing industry. The railroad ran many "Fishermen's Specials," one dollar excursions that carried fishermen from Philadelphia to the island. Long fishing poles protruding from the coach windows prompted one observer to note that the trains looked like steam-drawn porcupines. During one week in August of 1898, Anglesea hosted more than a thousand fishermen chartering boats to catch sea bass, porgies, croakers, and flounder. Around this sport fishing industry grew a prosperous fleet of charter fishing boats. Typical was Captain Samuel Buck's boat that offered fishing excursions from Anglesea for only one dollar including bait and tackle! For those who did not fish, there were plenty of other diversions. Sailing parties were popular with hotel guests who often took picnic lunches on the yachts that sailed out to the fishing grounds on pleasant days.

"UNDER-STAYING" THEIR WELCOME

Obviously, summer was the choice season to visit the resorts of Five Mile Beach, but local politicians and businessmen never ceased their efforts to make the area a year-round vacation destination. The railroads, of course, supported their efforts. The Hotel Dayton, the Sea View House, and the Oak Villa stayed open all winter during the 1890s. Excursions to the resorts continued well into October and November, although never in the kinds of numbers that local businessmen had hoped. After a New Year's Day excursion in 1890 it was reported that holiday visitors strolled "...on the beach without winter wraps...and they were perfectly delighted..."

Ultimately, all efforts to make Wildwood a four-season resort were doomed to failure, mostly because of abrupt weather changes during hurricane season, not to mention the storms of winter. One of the first severe hurricanes of the resort era struck the island on September 8, 1889. Railroad tracks were washed out, Mace's Pavilion was destroyed, debris littered the streets, and damage was evident everywhere. A year later, a major storm destroyed twelve cottages in Holly Beach, and in 1896, parts of the Anglesea boardwalk were washed out to sea, Blaker's Pavilion was badly mangled, and numerous cottages were severely damaged by hurricanes. Then, in October of 1897, another storm wreaked havoc, totally destroying three Holly Beach pavilions at a cost of more than five thousand dollars. Businessmen like Gib Blaker learned to deal with the unpredictable weather of fall, winter, and spring, but vacationers could never be convinced that Five Mile Beach was anything but a summer resort.

The Baker Brothers and other land developers might have wished for a resort that knew no season, but they were practical men and were content to develop their land as a summer retreat. It was estimated in 1896 that there were 30,000 saleable building lots located between Atlantic City and Cape May. Of these, 5000 enjoyed prime locations overlooking the ocean. None were more desirable than the undeveloped properties along Five Mile Beach. The Bakers opened offices in Philadelphia and advertised heavily in newspapers from the Quaker City to Cape May. Land sold fast, and as many as one hundred new cottages were erected annually. Even during the dismal economic climate of 1893, Wildwood real estate developers sold more land than during the entire period from 1889 to 1892. Accordingly, the town's year-round population also grew. By 1900, Wildwood could claim 150 residents while Holly Beach had a more impressive permanent population of 560. Of course, in summer the numbers swelled into the thousands.

The Bakers were not content just to develop Wildwood, however. In 1905, Philip Baker bought a large tract of land south of Holly Beach and began the development of the last of the island's seaside resort communities, Wildwood Crest. By 1910, Wildwood Crest was large enough to be incorporated as a borough. The Crest, as it was known, never attempted to compete with its more established northern neighbors, but it did develop into a unique and prosperous segment of the Wildwoods.

MORE WAYS TO GET AROUND

The early success of the Five Mile Beach resorts owed much to the efforts of enterprising men like the Baker brothers, Gilbert Blaker, and James Butcher. However, it was the transportation network that made the resorts accessible to the major eastern cities and thus assured a prosperous future for the Wildwoods. As early as 1895, the steam yacht Wildwood made four trips daily, carrying passengers from Cape May to Wildwood. But steamships never played a major role in the resort's development. It was the railroad that brought most people to the resorts between the 1880s and the 1920s. The Pennsylvania Railroad (previously its West Jersey branch) aggressively promoted trips to the Wildwoods. Weekday excursions, which used to bring a few hundred people, were carrying several thousand by the early 1900s. On one weekend in August of 1904, sixty-nine passenger coaches carrying more than four thousand people arrived at the Wildwood station. At the end of that season, the railroad estimated that it had transported more than seventy-five thousand to Wildwood between June 1 and September 15. In addition, its baggage handlers had moved 6290 trunks destined for seaside hotels. In addition to regular line service, special seashore excursions ran from Philadelphia on weekends and holidays. Charging one dollar for the round trip, the trains left Philadelphia's Market Street Wharf at 7:30 A.M. and stopped at various New Jersey towns on the way to the Holly Beach platform. The return trip left at 4:40 P.M. and stopped in Wildwood and Anglesea before heading back to Philadelphia. It was not uncommon for these one dollar excursion trains to fill fifteen to twenty passenger coaches on a single day's run.

Meanwhile, city officials and businessmen turned their interests to transportation on a local level. On May 1, 1903, Italian laborers were nearly finished laying track for the island's streetcar line, the Five Mile Beach Electric Railroad. Five new electric cars arrived, and the line opened to the public in time for the 1903 season. The new streetcar line provided convenient transportation for those who did not enjoy making the long walk from one end of the resort to the other.

Gradually, county and local governments needed to direct their attention to the construction of access roads from the mainland. The first automobile, a French-built electric, arrived in Atlantic City in 1899, and

By the early 1900s, it was clear that Wildwood was growing. The clutter of roof-tops and a busy railroad freight station are evidence of a prosperous resort community. – Wildwood Historical Society

Soon after 1900, Atlantic Avenue featured the Boardwalk on the ocean side, a row of hotels, cottages, and boarding houses on the west side, and a new streetcar line in the center. – Wildwood Historical Society

In the 1890s and early 1900s, military units from Pennsylvania and New Jersey selected the resort for their summer camps. For most of the volunteer soldiers, camping at Wildwood provided a little drill and a great deal of entertainment. – John W. Kille Collection

Anglesea saw its first auto in 1902. Within a few years, autos would be a common enough sight at all of the resorts. No one at that time recognized the importance of the automobile, or the role it would play in the further development of the resorts. But everyone seemed to understand that Five Mile Beach would remain isolated until tied to the mainland by adequate roads. In July of 1901, the first road connecting Rio Grande to Pacific Avenue was opened. Primitive and often dotted with huge puddles of water, the road crossed creeks and waterways by way of crudely built timber bridges. In 1911, a higher grade was engineered to eliminate standing water on the road surface. A year later the Rio Grande swing bridge was completed. By this time, automobiles were on every street of the resort. The Borough of Wildwood, following the opening of the road to Rio Grande, took a more active role in street maintenance. By 1903, streets were scraped each spring and arc lights were placed along Atlantic Avenue. Eventually, the streets would be paved.

It was obvious by the early 1900s that the Five Mile Beach resorts had grown out of their infancy and were headed for adulthood. Outside investors viewed the resorts as golden opportunities for making great profits. Late in 1902, J. Willard Morgan and State Controller Frank B. Sweeten of Camden announced that they would spend $60,000 to build a new amusement pier at the foot of Poplar Avenue. Some of the lumber even arrived in town, but the enterprise never moved any farther. Nevertheless, it was clear that those with adequate funds were ready to invest in the resorts. By the end of 1904, Ocean Pier, the largest single amusement investment in the resorts to date, was being erected. Its construction symbolized the coming of age of the Five Mile Beach summer resorts.

Two of the Baker brothers, Philip (left) and Latimer, pose in one of the resort's popular rolling chairs. – Wildwood Historical Society

the COMING of AGE

OF A RESORT

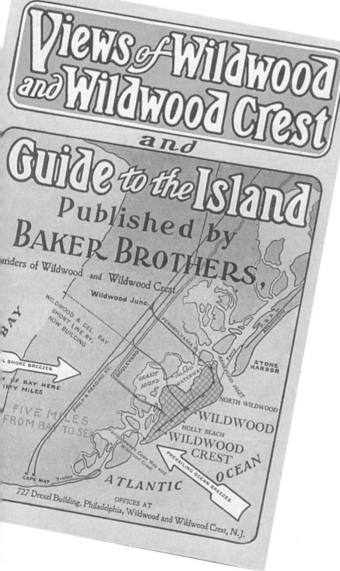

*I*n 1902, the Wildwoods were ranked fourth in resort popularity in Cape May County. Fifteen years later, they eclipsed all other county competition and were rivalling Asbury Park and even Atlantic City in some respects. In Wildwood alone, the population grew from 150 in 1900 to 898 in 1910. By 1920, Wildwood's population was 2,790. True, the 1912 merger of Wildwood and Holly Beach accounted for part of this growth, but much of the population explosion could be attributed directly to the city's economic development. In fact, despite a major national business depression and a serious county-wide recession, the resorts of Five Mile Beach were attaining regional prominence.

Lower left: With a design very much influenced by the Atlantic City piers, the Ocean Pier was the first modern amusement facility in the Wildwoods. – Wildwood Historical Society

CHAPTER 3

A number of indicators suggest that the Wildwoods had come of age by 1905. Bank deposits have always been the most obvious way to evaluate the success of a summer season, and by July of 1905, deposits exceeded those of 1904 by $100,000. More importantly, amusement investors from other cities and states were looking at the Wildwoods as a new frontier ripe for further development. Showmen from New York's Coney Island began visiting the Wildwoods to investigate local conditions. Pittsburgh's H. J. Heinz Company, which promoted its "57 Varieties" on Heinz Pier in Atlantic City, considered building another Heinz Pier in Wildwood. And John Lake Young, the premier amusement pier operator in Atlantic City, offered to purchase the Casino Pier for $70,000 in 1906. When James Butcher held out for $90,000, Young announced that he might build a new, Atlantic City-style pier elsewhere in Wildwood. Neither the Heinz Pier nor Young's pier materialized, but the trend of outside investors moving into the Wildwood area was well established. This trend reached its pinnacle with the construction of the $150,000 Ocean Pier during the winter of 1904-05.

Mostly due to the promotional efforts of the Baker brothers, Wildwood was an expanding community by the mid-1900s. – Cape May County Historical and Genealogical Society

Before benches lined the Boardwalk, chairs provided the only available seating when the rest pavilions were full.
– Wildwood Historical Society

OCEAN PIER

The construction of the Ocean Pier at the foot of Poplar and Juniper Avenues was an important bench mark in the history of the Wildwoods. It not only represented a sizeable investment by businessmen from outside the area, but it was also the first pier on Five Mile Beach modeled after Atlantic City's example. The pier was the financial dream of Herman Buckborn and Charles A. Reynolds, both officers of Camden's Keystone Leather Company. Apparently, they started planning for the pier in 1902, and, with the help of the Baker brothers, acquired the land with

180 foot frontage and riparian rights. By October, 1903, pilings had been delivered and the construction firm of Thomas Goslin and William Brannan had been hired, but actual construction was delayed until late in 1904. By mid-December of that year, pilings extended 400 feet out from the Boardwalk, installation of the decking had started, and it was expected that the buildings and another 200 feet of the pier would be finished by January of 1905. In the meantime, Frank W. Fowkes, manager of the Sea Isle City Ocean Pier, was hired to manage the new amusement venture.

Designed by Philadelphia architect Charles A. Brooke, the 1000-foot pier was painted bright white, trimmed in ivory, and sported roofs of peacock green. Nighttime illumination was provided by thousands of colored incandescent bulbs. The pier was designed to accommodate 10,000 visitors at any one time, and its main building was almost the size of a football field. On the main floor of the central pavilion were refreshment stands, Sagel's salt water taffy and ice cream stores, eight bowling alleys, billiard and pool tables, shuffleboard courts, boxball games, and a shooting gallery. Nearby, a grand carousel complete with band organ whirled delighted riders round and round.

The second floor housed a huge ballroom, basketball courts, and covered promenades with rocking chairs. The ballroom, quickly heralded as the best on the Atlantic Coast, featured a white maple floor, band stand, and elaborate decorations and lighting. Beyond the main pavilion was a theatre edifice built exclusively as a seaside home for first-class vaudeville. The theatre included a 35-foot proscenium arch and comfortable seating for 2,000 patrons.

Near the boardwalk end of the pier were the bathhouses, acclaimed the best on the beach. The Ocean Pier provided bathers with hot and cold sea baths, showers, bathing robes, and two large, clean towels for every customer. Tickets to the hot sea baths were forty cents each or three tickets for a dollar, and the baths were open until 10 P. M. every day except Sunday.

After a very successful 1905 season, the owners embarked on a policy of yearly improvements. During 1906 and 1907, a new

By 1906, the streets of Wildwood were being paved and carefully maintained. In the background is one of the resort's new carousel buildings. – Cape May County Historical and Genealogical Society

skating rink featuring a $10,000 band organ was built. Automatic pin setters were purchased for the bowling alleys, an art store was opened near the main entrance, the pier was extended, and a moving picture theatre was opened by Philadelphian H. P. Fox. Not interested in operating the pier on a day-to-day basis, Buckborn and Reynolds leased it to Manager Fowkes and James Powell starting in 1906. And under the direction of Fowkes and Powell, an outstanding entertainment bill was assembled.

Most popular, especially before 1910, was the roller skating rink. Afternoon and evening skating sessions and skating lessons were well patronized, and management tried new events like roller skate polo and high-speed races. In 1906, more than one thousand spectators bought tickets to watch brothers Ralph and Elmer Gifford compete in a three mile race. Ralph came out the winner by a full four inches! After the great race, both brothers offered to challenge all comers to one mile races. Much to their surprise, they were both promptly defeated by Howard Biggs. Another popular attraction was the African Scramble, a troupe of African-American skating comedians.

Fowkes, Powell, and the managers that succeeded them booked a wide variety of high quality musical entertainment and stage acts for every taste. Concert bands were the most popular attractions of the age, and, although the Ocean Pier could not afford organizations like Sousa's Band, they did engage Herbert's Marine Band, the band of the 3rd Regiment of the Pennsylvania National Guard, and the twenty-five piece Troilo's Royal Italian Band. Under the direction of the colorful Signor Cianfoni, the later group had scored a big hit at Atlantic City's Steel Pier. Energetic and volatile, Cianfoni was known for his "...hilarious gyrations with the baton." Admission to weekday concerts was just fifteen cents. On Sundays, when crowds neared two thousand, ticket prices were increased to twenty-five cents.

But bands were not the only entertainment offered. Throughout the 1905 season crowds were treated to Mrs. Doherty's Troupe of Snow White Poodles; Fred Poole's Chinese Festival Company; Uno the musical dog; magician Harry Morphet; the Dunbar Opera Company performing Gilbert & Sullivan; 14-year-old violinist Madeline McGuigan; and Lois Worden who sang her new composition, "Wildwood-By-The-Sea." While the women and children spent their time watching the shows and listening to the bands, gentlemen enjoyed the pleasures of a good cigar in the sumptuous Oriental smoking room of John Steigerwald's cigar store.

The younger visitors to Ocean Pier were not neglected either. A playground was erected on the beach, and every Thursday evening the pier hosted a children's party with music, singing, refreshments, and souvenirs. And there was the Funchase, an immense fun house with a barrel of fun, sliding floors, rocking staircases, a giant slide, a human roulette wheel, and a dozen other mechanical attractions.

The Ocean Pier was an instant success and quickly wooed both patrons and employees from the Casino and Blaker's. The Wildwood basketball team, which had made its home at the Casino, moved to the Ocean Pier in 1905, and promptly beat the Friends Central team, 36-28.

Most surprisingly, however, Professor Harry W. Roselle, the dean of the Casino dance floor, accepted a position as the Ocean Pier's dancing master in 1905. By now, Roselle was a respected figure in the Wildwoods. He was a common sight riding his horse, Two Step, around town or taking his dog, Beans, for a stroll along the pier. Beans, who became known as the "Ocean Pier Dog," was always surrounded by children for whom he happily performed a series of tricks and stunts. Roselle was apparently a competent manager, for in 1907, while still operating the pier's Floral Ballroom, he was appointed manager of the roller skating rink. Roselle was an excellent skater, as comfortable on skates as he was on the ballroom floor. He was reputed to have been the first man on Five Mile Beach to put on roller skates some years earlier.

The construction of the Ocean Pier was a boon to Wildwood, and a fine investment for Buckborn and Reynolds. However, the Casino's James Butcher and his old rival, Gib Blaker, were hardly enthusiastic about a new pier that lured away paying patrons, the basketball team, and Professor Roselle. Even before the Ocean Pier was completed, Butcher announced the renovation and enlargement of the Casino Pier. Meanwhile, Blaker expanded his theatre by several hundred seats, extended the stage, and purchased all new scenery.

CASINO PIER CHALLENGES THE COMPETITION

Early in 1907, rumors again surfaced that John Lake Young had purchased the Casino Pier. It was not so. Instead of selling the pier, Butcher spent $10,000 on a new 9,000 square foot roller skating rink. The entire island was described as "Roller Skating Mad" in 1907, and the new Casino rink had no trouble attracting skaters. Like the Ocean Pier, the Casino offered open skating sessions, lessons, races, marches, and other events. In 1908, African-American races proved to be the rage, with Snowball Jackson being one of the most successful and popular racers.

Right: The Casino Arcade (center) and the old Casino (right) as seen from the Boardwalk in about 1905. – Wildwood Historical Society

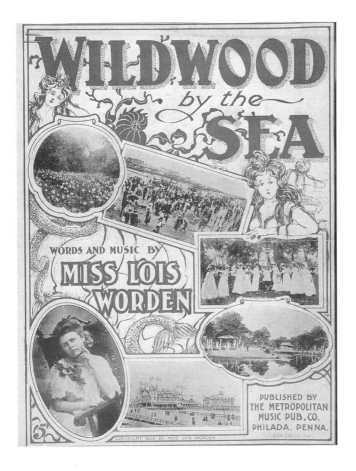

the crowd that descended on the Casino each summer. At one end of the entertainment spectrum was the Flying Lady, a mystical levitation act that had been a big hit at Coney Island; at the other was Johannes Sembach, a Wagnerian tenor from the Metropolitan Opera in New York. Not surprisingly, few came to Wildwood to hear Wagner, but a great many came to be entertained by acts like the Flying Lady.

A particularly active feature of the Casino Pier was the game room, managed by the promotion-minded H. A. Spencer. The game room was a predominantly male venue that featured pool tables, billiard tables, Manhattan tables, and shuffleboard courts. Gambling and cigar smoke abounded, and many of the ladies who dared to frequent the game room were there expressly to ply their trade. Spencer ran many promotions to entice men into the Casino game room from the Boardwalk. In 1907, he offered a box of cigars to the man with the highest score on the Manhattan tables. Ladies were offered a box of candy for the same achievement, but few respectable ladies of the early 1900s ever entered a game room. Two seasons later, Spencer hired J. F. Davis, an accomplished stilt walker, to walk up and down the Boardwalk with signs advertising the Casino game room. In many respects, the Casino game room mimicked the seamy underside of the Wildwoods that included off-Boardwalk brothels, gambling dens, and unlicensed liquor establishments. The game room may not have actually encouraged illicit activities, but it did offer men a more permissive environment than could be found in most of the other Boardwalk amusements. Such men-only entertainments were most obvious at large resorts like Atlantic City and Coney Island, but even strict religious resorts like Ocean City had their share of the usual vices.

Numerous other improvements were made at the Casino Pier. A new carousel and carousel building were installed in 1906, bowling alleys were constructed, new "shirt waist" dances were promoted in the ballroom, and David Dayan was convinced to move from New York City to open an oriental goods store on the pier. The Casino restaurant was leased to Ralph Carll and James Sams, "the peanut man," and was quickly transformed into the Casino Gardens. Carll and Sams renovated the decor, added new menu items, and hired an orchestra to provide music during dining hours. Entertainment was as varied and diverse as

Even though Ocean Pier proved to be a formidable competitor, the Casino Pier continued to prosper. In 1915, the Casino Pier Company announced that it would spend $30,000 for a convention hall seating 2,000 and a theatre that could seat 1,200. By the spring of 1916, the old carousel building was razed and both new facilities were nearing completion.

By the time Ocean Pier made an appearance in 1905, the Casino Pier was doing so well that James Butcher could afford to spend his winters soaking in the Florida sun. His competitor, Gilbert Blaker, finally had enough faith in his pier that he sold his wallpaper business in order to devote all of his attentions to the amusement industry. Indeed, pre-1910 business in the Wildwoods was booming. It was clear that there was, economically speaking, room enough for three, or even more, large amusement piers.

THE BLAKER PIER UPGRADE

After the 1905 season, Blaker spent more than $15,000 to revamp his pier. A Philadelphia decorating firm was hired, the stage was expanded yet again, 150 new bathhouses were constructed, and two new stores were built. One of these stores was rented to Lowe's salt water taffy confectionery, while the other went to R. W. Ryan for his Japanese Bazaar that merchandised a wide range of "fancy goods." Blaker also engaged B. F. Miller and C. F. Miller to open an ice cream parlor and to manage the amusement pavilion.

To keep up with the Casino and the Ocean Pier, Blaker unveiled unusual exhibits like a monster fish weighing an incredible 1,080 pounds. The exhibit was popular while it lasted, which, given the hot summer weather, wasn't long!

By 1905, Blaker had expanded his auditorium, enlarged the seating area, added a balcony, and formed his own theatrical group, the Blaker Stock Company. Managed by Maurice Stanford, the new stock company contracted with important vaudeville and stage stars for the summer season at Wildwood and engaged the Percival Ladies' Orchestra to provide music for each evening's performances.

Gilbert Blaker was well on his way to becoming the Wildwoods' premier amusement impresario. In addition to his other operations he obtained a permit to operate rolling chairs on the Boardwalk in 1906. By 1910, his land holdings along the Boardwalk were sizeable indeed. It could be said that before 1918, Blaker was the most important figure in the development of Wildwood's amusement enterprises.

Between the early 1900s and the First World War, the Wildwoods grew rapidly in terms of population, income, physical plant, and the number of annual visitors. Despite a county-wide business depression that began around 1910, the resort offered five major amusement piers and more than 300 hotels and boarding houses by 1916. A good indicator of resort growth was the number of souvenir post cards purchased and mailed from the resort each summer. In 1906, 15,082 post cards were mailed from the Wildwood Post Office between July 14 and July 21. John Reeve's Wildwood Post Card Company reported that heavy sales required them to print several hundred thousand cards in Germany each year to meet the seasonal

Left: Mr. and Mrs. Champ Clark (right) and Congressman and Mrs. J. Thompson Baker in front of the Casino Pier, 1913. A powerful Democratic politician and Speaker of the House of Representatives, Clark made a number of trips to the Jersey Shore during the summers of 1912-13. – Wildwood Historical Society

The Boardwalk entrance to Blaker's Pier, circa 1906. – John W. Kille Collection

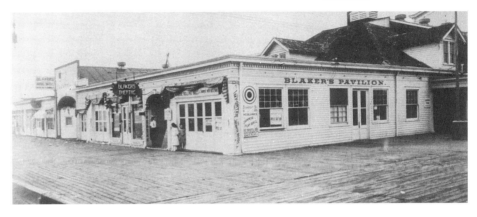

demand. In 1914, Postmaster George Smith announced that more than one million post cards had been mailed from Wildwood during that season.

CREST AND ATLANTIC PIERS

The phenomenal growth of the Wildwoods, and the success of the Casino Pier, Blaker's, and the new Ocean Pier enticed other investors to build piers and install various forms of amusements along the Boardwalk. After the Ocean Pier was built, the Crest Pier was constructed in the young community of Wildwood Crest. Not quite as glittery or bustling as its northern neighbors, the Crest Pier was opened during the middle of the 1906 season. The new facility included an 800 seat theatre, bowling alleys, roller skating rink, dancing pavilion, and a bathhouse. Original plans also called for a carousel, but it does not appear that it was ever installed. However, a few seasons later a Mirror Maze was added to the pier's attractions.

Throughout its early history, the Crest Pier seemed to be plagued by an unstable management structure. James Creamer was replaced by Harry D'Esta as manager in 1909. D'Esta had previously managed the Johnstown Flood Show in Atlantic City, and was quick to engage the Royal Italian Band, enhance the food services, promote fishing from the pier, and aggressively advertise nightly dancing. Under D'Esta's management, many predicted that the Crest Pier would rival Young's

Below left: The Crest Pier was never able to fully compete with the larger piers to the north, but it was a popular attraction offering band concerts, roller skating, dancing, bowling, refreshments, and a bathhouse.
– Wildwood Crest Historical Society

Below: Trying to emulate the success of the Ocean Pier, a group of investors constructed the Atlantic Pier during the winter of 1909-10.
– Wildwood Historical Society

46

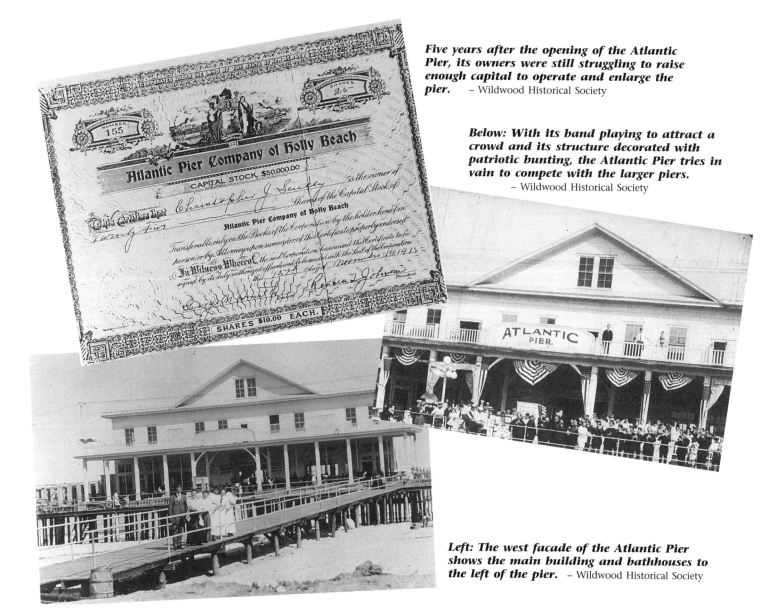

fabulous pier in Atlantic City. But attempts to compete with the well-established Wildwood piers proved difficult, and within a few years D'Esta was replaced by H. L. Strickler. The new manager replaced most of the food and game concessionaires, brought in a new concert band, and began directing more attention to the skating rink. Included in the special rink events was a walking race that was won by Joe Wilson, a "crack heel and toe walker," who covered ten miles in one hour and 29 minutes. Despite the fact that as many as thirty thousand people patronized the Crest Pier in a single week, it could not compete with the larger piers and soon stopped trying. Instead, it concentrated more on popular local events like sing-a-longs, dances, and children's parties. Once the Crest Pier ceased trying to emulate the bigger piers, it was quite successful until it was completely destroyed by fire 1917. Three years later it was rebuilt on the same site.

Less successful than the Crest Pier, was the Atlantic Pier located at Andrews Avenue in the Borough of Holly Beach. William Oaks, Eben Yenney, and Joseph F. Gorman obtained permission to construct the pier in 1909, and it was completed in time for the following season. The pier featured a salt water taffy stand, refreshment counters, a small concert area, and bathhouses. It was, however, far too small to compete with the Ocean Pier, the Casino, and Blaker's. By 1918, the Atlantic Pier was abandoned and decaying.

A GROWING RESORT

While the central communities of Five Mile Beach formed the heart of the amusement area, development continued in other areas of the island as well. In 1908, Henry Otten stocked his canal with various sea creatures and launched glass-bottom boats for cruises on the canal. The following year a small amusement pavilion opened at Ottens Harbor, but it was little more than a dance hall and failed to offer much competition to the big Boardwalk piers.

Numerous independent concessionaires began opening stores, counters, and amusement attractions all along the wide Boardwalk. Matthew's Photo Studio opened next to Blaker's, and the T. Sotto Company, one of a number of Japanese merchants who were attracted to Wildwood, unveiled a Japanese goods store and a ping pong parlor near the Ocean Pier. Typical of the Boardwalk merchants of this era were Max and Rose Mayer, who operated toy and jewelry stores on the Boardwalk during the summer, and another jewelry store on Pacific Avenue during the winter months. Less typical was Professor Lingerman's Palace of Amusements that came to Wildwood from Atlantic City in 1906. Sam Lingerman and his wife Lucy operated a variety stage show that included magic and ventriloquism. A giant, six-foot wooden face named Bobby ballyhooed the attraction to the passing crowds on the Boardwalk. The Lingermans remained in Wildwood for a few seasons before moving on to other resorts and amusement parks.

As the Wildwoods grew, the flowering resort business lured many new amusement, hotel, and restaurant operators to the island. Some, like the Lingermans, stayed only a few seasons, made some money, and moved on to other locations. Others came, liked what they saw, and became Boardwalk fixtures. Among the latter was a young Philadelphian, Sebastian B. Ramagosa, who opened a single game stand on the Boardwalk in June of 1914. A year later he owned five games. In 1916, he entered into a partnership with Ralph Carll, a Wildwood city commissioner. Ramagosa, who would eventually be known as the "King of the Boardwalk," parlayed his first boardwalk game stand into an amusement empire that included the Casino Arcade and Sportland.

THE FIRST COASTER – UP AND DOWN

Another newcomer to the area was the Amusement Construction Company of Scranton, Pennsylvania. An operator of amusement parks in Pennsylvania, New York, and Ontario, the company sent its president and chief engineer, M. J. Neary, to Wildwood in 1916 to design and build the resort's first roller coaster. The Yankee Dip, better known as the Ocean Pier roller coaster, was built between Poplar and Juniper Avenues. The

$12,000 ride operated six cars and reportedly entertained up to 60,000 customers between early July and late August. The popular ride was a great success in its first season. Then, in April of 1917, a heavy snow destroyed a portion of the Ocean Pier roller coaster. The owners were willing to invest the $2,000 necessary to rebuild the ride. Further, they agreed to the city's insistence that the collapsed section of the ride be rebuilt with strong reinforcement. But by June the ride had not yet been rebuilt, for the coaster's manager had been confronted with additional demands from the city commissioners. First, they demanded the coaster be painted to make it "more presentable." Then, they decreed that the ride must close promptly at 11:30 P. M. every night in order to eliminate complaints about the noise. Finally, they raised the annual license fee from $25 to $100. Manager Thomas Reddington refused to pay the new rate, and the company's attorney declared the rate excessive and discriminatory. By this time, the 1918 season was almost over, and the wartime lumber shortage made reconstruction of the coaster almost impossible. As a result, Wildwood's first roller coaster disappeared after just one season of operation.

TAKING A WALK ON THE BOARDWALK

What with the construction of the new piers and their countless amusements, it was clear that by 1905 the center of activity on the island had shifted from the hotels to the Boardwalk. In fact, by 1909 the Boardwalk so dominated the area that a popular five-cent cigar was called "Boardwalk of Wildwood." The elected officials of Wildwood, Holly Beach, and North Wildwood were quick to grasp the importance of the Boardwalk, and appropriations to maintain, improve and expand the promenade were increased annually. Normal daily maintenance of the wooden walks often escalated when storms washed out pilings or, as happened in 1910, marine worms infected and destroyed 150 pilings in the Holly Beach section. Maintenance of lighting was also undertaken by the local governments, although lights were never used during the off-season, except on Saturdays nights in April. As innovations in street lighting developed, the quality of Boardwalk illumination improved. About 1914 it was reported that, "The new inverted arc lighting system makes it at night bright as midday."

The local government officials and their Boardwalk Committee catered to the comfort of the spending visitor in other ways as well.

For example, during July and August, 1911, Wildwood paid 35 cents per 100 pounds of ice to keep the public drinking fountains along the Boardwalk cool and inviting. In 1907, Holly Beach approved $600 for the construction of three small pavilions to serve as shaded rest areas. Three years later Wildwood spent a similar amount to construct new restrooms in a pavilion along the walkway. Mr. and Mrs Edmond Brown were appointed restroom caretakers and the borough allocated them fifty cents per day provided that they also swept the bandstand each morning. It was assumed that the Browns would make up the rest of their income in tips. Boardwalk visitors proved none too generous, however, and a salary of three dollars a day was approved for the Browns. During this period the municipal officials began their first efforts to control how people dressed while walking on the Boardwalk or on the streets. In 1913, the City of Wildwood prohibited people from walking on the wooden way without suitable clothing over their swimming attire.

View of Boardwalk and Ocean Pier. Wildwood, N. J.

Above: When each new Boardwalk was built, it was positioned near the ocean so that waves swept under the walkway at high tide. The beach, however, was constantly expanding and soon the sea was far east of the Boardwalk. – David W. Francis Collection

Right: When the Boardwalk was moved east, it became necessary to move the entire Ocean Pier toward the sea. – Michael D'Antuono Collection

Right: After the construction of the new Boardwalk, the Casino (far right), was left land-locked. In order to connect the Casino with the new Boardwalk and give access to the beach, the Casino Arcade was constructed. – Wildwood Historical Society

Below: As the Boardwalk was moved eastward to keep pace with the expanding beach, Blaker's Pier was also moved east. – Historical Society of Pennsylvania

TAKING THE BOARDWALK FOR A WALK

This was also the era of continued Boardwalk construction and relocation due to the expanding beach. Late in 1909 the local newspaper editorialized: "Since the beach has made out so much between the Casino and the New Ocean Pier it seems necessary to

move the boardwalk out further near the water. Our summer visiting throngs demand that this be done...." Indeed, when the Boardwalk was first built, the ocean surged under it. By 1909, the nearest wave broke onto the shore several hundred feet east of the Boardwalk. The newspaper joined the Baker brothers in pressuring the borough (soon to be the City of Wildwood) for the construction of a new Boardwalk much nearer to the surf. The topic was taken up in December of 1910, and a bond issue for $20,000 was planned to pay for the removal of the old Boardwalk and construction of a new structure. The lowest bidder, Rufus Hays, received a contract for $13,552, and by October of 1911 the old Boardwalk was gone. The new promenade was 2,150 feet long, with 500-foot approaches, and three sets of access stairs. The relocation of the Boardwalk required that the Casino Pier be moved closer to the ocean, but no one seemed to object to this costly project. With the Wildwood Boardwalk once again nearer to the sea, the center of resort business gravitated eastward. Following suit in 1913, North Wildwood moved ten blocks of its Boardwalk east to allow for the construction of Surf Avenue. Twenty-six blocks long, the new street spanned a width of 100 feet.

The rolling chair continued as a fixture on the Boardwalk, and the Blaker Rolling Chair Company played a major industry role. Rates were 25 cents an hour for a single chair, or 75 cents for a double. Special day-long rates were available, and of course, the attendant anticipated a gratuity at the end of the tour. So busy did Blaker and the other rolling chair companies become that telephones were installed at the offices to handle reservations, and often those who failed to make reservations found themselves "strolling the Boardwalk." Inevitably, all those rolling chairs just added to the congestion of an already crowded Boardwalk. As a result, around 1914, special police officers were assigned to Boardwalk duty. Rolling chair operators were instructed to keep the chairs moving on the right-hand side of the walk, and bicycles were strictly prohibited.

At this time, the Boardwalk featured a rich and varied selection of games, amusements, food stands, theatres, and stores. In many cases, the operators of the Boardwalk stores were more colorful than the merchandise they sold. Miss Auburn, who ran a

Blaker Rolling Chair Co. 🌿 🌿

HARVEY & SOLOMON, MGRS.

Chairs by the Hour, Day or Week,
🌿 with or without attendant

Single Chairs, 25c per hour
Double " 75c " "

Attendant, 25c per hour Extra

By Day or Week Special Terms
🌿All Chairs New and Up-to-Date🌿
PHONE

popular shooting gallery, was known for her penchant for swimming in the ocean while snow was still on the Boardwalk and the air temperature was well below freezing. The hardy Miss Auburn was generally considered the first ocean bather of each new season.

MAKING CONCESSIONS

All up and down the Boardwalk were operations that sold refreshingly cold grape juice, fresh hot roasted peanuts, or just-pulled salt water taffy. And, to test one's skill, there was an almost unending array of games intended to "...attract your eyes and lighten your pocketbook." Indeed, as S. B. Ramagosa recalled many years later, the games of the 1914 era were almost always rigged to allow the operator to control if and when anyone left a winner.

For the unlucky game player, countless stores offered every type of domestic and imported merchandise. Carl Oldach's

Below left: In order to cater to every need of the resort visitor, the Boardwalk of 1914 featured men's clothing shops, women's apparel stores, toy shops, and jewelry stores.
– Wildwood Historical Society

Huge crowds brought prosperity to most Boardwalk merchants, even during the county-wide recession of the post-1910 years.
– Wildwood Historical Society

Charles Douglass, the king of the Wildwood candymakers, established the resort's most famous salt water taffy and fudge store.
– Douglass Candies

The Boardwalk at Cedar Avenue on a typical summer day in about 1910. The Japanese Tea room is on the left, while Sagel's candy store is on the right. – Wildwood Historical Society

Mexican store near the Ocean Pier sold beaded purses, jewelry, fancy knitted goods, and pyrographic gifts (wood and leather items with names and designs burned into them to take home as souvenirs). A reminiscent stroll along the Boardwalk of that era would take you past Wonfor's photo studio, Takamuri's Japanese goods, W. B. Craig's candy store, Gould's soda fountain, Murphy's pool room, Spencer's bowling alleys, the Casino novelty shop, Yamazaki's Japanese store, Mayer's novelty shop, Lowe's salt water taffy, Kawashima's Japanese novelties, Sweet's Baths, Marten's novelty shop, Saiber's photo studio, Schmeiz's novelty shop, Morse's art leather goods, and an orangeade stand built in the shape of, what else, an orange! There was also The Lemon, a lemonade stand in the form of a giant lemon constructed at Pine Avenue, where one could enjoy the cooling drink served by a "coy maiden." And, there was the Abbott Boardwalk Cow, an artfully constructed animal conceived by a local dairy to dispense cold whole milk and buttermilk from her bountiful udders. There

Left: By 1909, the Boardwalk's west side was lined with candy stores, novelty stores, ice cream parlors, restaurants, and businesses of all descriptions.
– Wildwood Historical Society

were, of course, scores of other shops, counters, and emporiums that dotted the west side of the Boardwalk and added to the growing color of the resort. All in all it must have been a memorable way to spend a summer's night or day, strolling the Boardwalk in Wildwood!

More than one million visitors were expected to visit the Boardwalk in 1914, and a major challenge was providing enough food and drink for these throngs of funseekers. At the time, the Boardwalk featured more than a dozen candy stores, the Royal Waffle Parlor in the Casino Arcade, the Ocean Pier Cafe, Whitcomb's Honey Chewing Candy counter, Joseph Douglass's cafeteria and ice cream parlor, Charlie's Ice Cream, The Hot Dog Kennel, the Louisiana Praline store, the I-Wan-A-Donut stand, and several fruit juice operations. There was Welch's Grape Juice Parlor, where the soon-to-be famous cold juice was sold in tall, clear glasses. And there was the Vineland Grape Juice Company pavilion, which included in its architecture a twelve-foot metal Vineland juice bottle.

Of course by this time, ice cream had become an absolute "must" for any summer resort, and Wildwood offered more than enough ice cream parlors to satisfy every patron. Joseph Douglass's ice cream parlor, which manufactured many flavors of ice cream on the premises, offered a big dish of ice cream for a dime. For twenty cents, hungry guests could buy the "High Hat," a single serving of more than a pint of ice cream! The Joseph brothers, operating in the Casino Arcade, not only made ice cream but also baked their own cones at the store. Lucky customers walked away with the still-warm cone melting the rich, cold ice cream inside.

Even more popular than ice cream, however, was salt water taffy. By the early 1900s, there were three major taffy makers and a number of smaller operators lining the Boardwalk. Lowe's sold taffy for twenty-five cents a pound and wrapped each piece in paper imprinted with their name to discourage imitators. One firm that didn't need to imitate Lowe belonged to Louis Sagel and his family of candy makers. Born in Russia in 1862, Sagel came to New Jersey in 1884, opened a candy factory in Bridgeton, and then moved to Wildwood in 1888. His first major Boardwalk store was in the Casino, where he sold salt water taffy and marzipan molded in the shape of fruits and vegetables. His son, Harry, opened a store at Lincoln Avenue in 1918, and another store soon followed. The newcomer to the salt water taffy market in Wildwood was Charles Douglass, whose candy stores outlasted all the competition and became a Boardwalk legend. Born in Philadelphia, Douglass operated a cabby business in the Rittenhouse Square district. It appears that by 1900 he was running his own candy factory in Philadelphia. Douglass showed up in Wildwood in 1917, and he soon opened a small taffy stand on Cedar Avenue. Following the First World War, Douglass bought an old barracks building from the naval base at Cape May, moved it to 3300 Boardwalk, and began selling his famous tartan-design boxes with their traditional black Scottish terrier logo. Although fudge would later replace salt water taffy as the favorite resort confection, in pre-1920 Wildwood, taffy was the true king of the Boardwalk.

Wheels of fortune were always popular on the Boardwalk, but another game that proved to be most profitable was Frank Henneway's Honolulu Dip in Sweet's Block at Schellenger Avenue. The attraction featured a garishly made-up individual described as an Irishman. He sat on a board above a tank of water and when patrons struck a target with a ball, he fell into the water with a huge splash. Balls were three for a nickel or seven for a dime, and Henneway, "...knew how to attract and hold an audience, and he also knew how to rake in the coins." A few curious customers asked Henneway why he

named his game the Honolulu Dip, as the name obviously had nothing to do with the Irishman perched above the water. Henneway explained that while a soldier during the Spanish-American War, his troop ship stopped in Hawaii on the way to the Philippine Islands. Ever since, he had loved Hawaii. A variation of the Honolulu Dip was the African Dip, which replaced the Irishman with an African-American.

Above: During the years before the First World War, Sagel's was the most famous salt water taffy at the resort. – John W. Kille Collection

Middle: At the height of the season, in July and August, the Boardwalk was literally a sea of people. – Ron Franks Collection

Bottom: Wildwood's famous beach on a wonderful summer day in about 1910. The Ocean Pier is in the background. – Library Company of Philadelphia

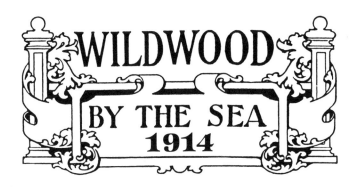

WILDWOOD
BY THE SEA
1914

Above: The lifeguards of the Wildwood Beach Patrol during the summer of 1918. – Wildwood Historical Society

Below: Three of the thousands of bathing beauties who, in 1915, enjoyed the less restrictive and more revealing bathing attire of the era.
– Cape May County Historical and Genealogical Society

ON THE BEACH

With the Boardwalk moved farther east, the beach was narrowed, but only temporarily. It would continue to widen at a rate of nearly 100 feet per year. The beach was heralded not only as a center of merriment, but also as a pathway to better health. Commented one brochure, "Children who play in the sand and splash in the surf lay up a stock of strength that will last them a lifetime." But, neither children nor adults needed the enticement of good health to flock to the beach. It was estimated in 1908 that one million bathers frolicked on the beach annually. By 1914, the number had increased to more than a million and a half. Fashions in swimwear were changing to keep up with the times. By 1907, bloomers had replaced skirts as the standard attire of lady bathers. Many were shocked to see store windows displaying mannequins dressed in these new bloomer bathing suits. Some were so repulsed by this daring fashion statement that they were sure that such suits had been "... purchased of foreign agents." Certainly, American agents would never sell such outrageous costumes! In any case, the modern bathing suits undoubtedly did their part to attract more than a few young males to the beach.

While the many attractions of the Boardwalk made for exciting evenings, the beach was the center of most activity during the day. As a result, many activities found an appreciative audience on the beach. In 1905, the Washburn and D'Alma Trained Animal Show pitched its tent on the beach and stabled its elephants, horses, monkeys, and dogs on the strand. At the same time, sand sculptors created elaborate masterpieces in the wet sand vied for tips from admiring onlookers. These sand sculptures were usually placed near the elevated Boardwalk where spectators could enjoy a full view the sand art. There was also the occasional beach parade, with prizes going to the best dressed participants. Many took part in the new fad of auto bathing in which bathers drove their vehicles to the edge of the water, swam, and re-entered their autos for the trip back to the city streets. Before long, animals and automobiles on the beach were outlawed by officials.

As the beach became more crowded, borough government recognized the need to provide protection for swimmers. Originally, only larger entertainment facilities like the Casino Pier provided lifeguards. But as the resorts grew, it was obvious that the Five Mile Beach communities would need to hire a beach patrol of qualified lifeguards. In 1905, Wildwood accepted a number of applications and on July 1, two guards, Daniel Briggs and John Wicks, went on duty. Twelve days later, Briggs died in a Camden hospital of injuries suffered in a dive from the Casino Pier into shallow water. A year later, Holly Beach hired a Mr. Schada as lifeguard, partially it seems, because he already owned his own "outfit." Although Schada did not return after the 1906 season, Holly Beach's lifeguard force grew to three by 1909. Wildwood, too, expanded its lifeguard patrol. In 1912, there were six guards on duty, and for the first time, all were uniformed in regulation swimsuits and hats (purchased by the city at a total cost of $39.50). Four years later, the season opened with "...seven husky young men who are ever ready to risk their lives...." Captain Thomas Needham, in command of the beach patrol, increased the Wildwood force to eighteen guards. In addition to uniforms, the lifeguards were equipped with surf boats for rescues, a motor ambulance, and an Indian motorcycle for use on the beach. In 1916, they also received their first pulmotor, a device used in attempts to resuscitate drowning victims. The pulmotor was centrally located on a platform near Sweet's Baths on the Wildwood beach.

The increased beach activity also created a demand for more bathhouses. In 1907, Joseph M. Sweet built a large facility at Schellenger Avenue that boasted 300 rooms for changing into swimming attire. He included additional locker rooms with showers for men and even a drying room that could handle a thousand wet swimsuits per hour. Sweet's Baths, it was said, compared favorably with anything that Atlantic City had to offer. Many felt that Wildwood bathhouses charged exorbitant fees and, as a result, their business suffered. D. F. Hallahan, discouraged when the city asked him to pay a $70 license fee for the establishment of a new bathhouse, stated that Wildwood's locker fees were four times the rates charged in Atlantic City. On one day in August, he claimed, a bathhouse in Atlantic City had handled five thousand bathers, while a similar establishment in Wildwood had only five paying customers. The city's license fees, Hallahan charged, necessitated high rental rates which, in turn, discouraged customers from using the facilities. Nevertheless, it seems that most bathhouse operators were quite satisfied with the level of business and realized that city license fees were necessary to help finance the lifeguard force.

Above: A typical crowd on the Wildwood beach on a sunny summer morning in 1912.
– Cape May County Historical and Genealogical Society

In a time when dogs were still permitted on the beach, ponies and pony carts were rented to children on the Wildwood beach.
– Wildwood Historical Society

Blaker's Theatre, during the vaudeville and stock company era, with the bathhouses on the right. – John W. Kille Collection

The streetcar tracks curve from Atlantic Avenue onto Schellenger Avenue, passing Blaker's Theatre, Blaker's Baths, and a "cottage" owned by Gib Blaker. At this time, about 1906, these streets were still unpaved.
– John W. Kille Collection

The performers of the Blaker Theatre Company are transported from the railroad station to their hotels at the start of the theatrical season in June of 1907.
– John W. Kille Collection

STAGING EVENTS

After a day in the sun on the beach, resort visitors were ready for a different kind of entertainment at night. Theatres made up a major portion of the entertainment fare, at first presenting vaudeville acts and stock companies, then later, silent moving pictures. Most aggressive of the theatre operators was Gilbert Blaker, whose entertainment bill often included groups such as the Stanford Players, who performed each evening at the Blaker Theatre or the Manhattan Player. Blaker was so encouraged by the success of these live performances that in 1910 he constructed the 3,000 seat Hippodrome. It featured a large stage and a circus ring for acts provided by the Philadelphia Hippodrome Company. At the same time, Blaker was canny enough to realize that the future success of theatres lay in moving pictures. Accordingly, his Wonderland Motion Picture Exhibition opened in 1907.

Between 1906 and the beginning of the First World War, a number of other theatre operators offered motion picture programs in Wildwood. In 1906, the Comique was opened on the Boardwalk charging ten cents for adults and five cents for children. There was also Frank Worden's Bijou Theatre in the Blaker Block that advertised both foreign and domestic movies, plus illustrated songs by Lois Worden. Within a few years these pioneering theatres were joined by moving picture exhibitions at the Casino Pier, the Ocean Pier, and the Crest Pier, as well as at the Fern, Regent, and Star theatres. The latter establishment claimed that it showed only imported movies interspersed with vaudevillians such as black-face comedian Al Wilson, and Zeda, the fiery dragon.

WILLIAM C. HUNT

The burgeoning moving picture industry caught the attention of one William C. Hunt, and his decision to move to Wildwood gave the resort its leading entertainment entrepreneur. Born in Port Jefferson, New York, in 1872, Bill Hunt opened a nickelodeon in Camden in 1906. When it was instantly successful, he and a partner each invested $150 and opened the eighty-seat Bijou Dream Theatre in the same city. At about this same time, Hunt bought a one dollar excursion ticket to Wildwood and was immediately struck by the potential of the growing resort. He promptly opened a theatre at Garfield and Atlantic Avenues and secured a job with the West Jersey Electric Company in order to survive during the winter months when his theatre was closed. His reputation as a promoter and businessman assured his future. Blaker hired him to manage his theater, and the young showman went on to operate the Comique, Bijou, Casino, New Avenue, and Crest Pier theatres. For a time while under Hunt's direction, the Casino Theatre operated as the Airdrome, and featured vaudeville acts. It was soon reconverted to the Casino Theatre, however, and it became Bill Hunt's flagship motion picture facility. In 1913, Hunt leased the Blaker Theatre, but a disagreement over rent caused Blaker to forcibly evict Hunt from the theatre's office. A decade later, Hunt owned the Blaker Theatre.

Bill Hunt was a first-rate showman and a dedicated promoter. He advertised heavily and eventually purchased the resort's primary newspaper. Each Christmas, he gave free movie admission to local children. When Atlantic City theatres raised admission to twenty cents in 1915, Hunt maintained a ten cent ticket price prompting one local to note, "They improve the pictures, but they don't increase the price." Although he was a man of high moral standing, Hunt did not object to occasionally enticing customers into his theatres with allegedly risque movies (which, in fact, were quite innocent productions). In 1916, he booked a film that portrayed the terrible consequences of "...vice and physical ruin that follows abuse of the moral law." Admission for this special show was raised to twenty-five cents, and no children were admitted unless accompanied by their parents.

For more than sixty years, Bill Hunt would be at the very center of the resort's growth, in many ways replacing the Baker brothers, Gib Blaker, and James Butcher as the area's premier entertainment entrepreneur. Although he sometimes found himself the subject of controversy, Hunt led the way in civic development, resort promotion, and politics. As his theatre chain grew in Wildwood, as well as elsewhere in New Jersey and Pennsylvania, he attained wealth, respect, and power. His accomplishments include positions as a newspaper publisher, state senator, bank president, founder of the Wildwood Golf Club, hospital benefactor, active member of the Board of Trade, and one of the first advocates of a passenger ferry from Cape May to Lewes, Delaware.

CONCERT BANDS AND DANCE ORCHESTRAS

Rivaling the theatres in popularity, at least until the time of the First World War, were concert bands and musical programs of all types. Dance orchestras remained a most popular attraction and, in fact, dancing continued to increase in popularity with the introduction of new dances, many pioneered by Vernon and Irene Castle. Among the new dances popular along the Boardwalk in 1914 were the Tango, the Castle Walk, and other "high falutin' dances." In the Wildwoods,

indeed, throughout the country, controversy erupted over the propriety of the new dances. When Blaker's new Danceland opened on his pier in 1913, it was made abundantly clear that only "Refined Dancing" would be permitted there. To insure that no "new" dances were performed at Danceland, Blaker hired Professor Walter G. Wroe to manage and oversee the ballroom. Those who dared to try out any of the new dance steps risked ejection by Professor Wroe and his employees.

Concert bands were also favored at the time, and scores of professional bands toured the country before 1920, often settling into summer resorts and amusement parks for the entire summer. Bands such as John Philip Sousa's played only at the most prestigious locations like Manhattan Beach on Coney Island, Willow Grove Park in Philadelphia, and Atlantic City. Resorts such as Wildwood, Ocean City, and Cape May could not afford the country's leading concert bands, but they saw to it that visitors were entertained by high-quality bands each summer.

Both Holly Beach and Wildwood chose to underwrite the cost of engaging these summer concert bands. As usual, bands were invited to bid for the annual contract, and in most cases, the lowest bidder received the contract. However, in 1911, Holly Beach could not decide between J. W. Harrison's Band from Philadelphia and Briton's Third Regiment Band. Both bands were invited to play one concert in late May. Following this contest, Briton's eighteen-piece band was hired to give forty-eight concerts over an eight-week period at a rate of $360 per week. In Wildwood, slightly more expensive bands were engaged. In 1912, Cianfoni's Band played a ten-week season for $4570. Cianfoni was followed by Passeri's Band in 1913 and Weaver's American Band in 1914. Cianfoni wanted to return in 1915 and even offered a low bid of $3600. However, the hot-tempered bandmaster had been arrested for assault during his previous engagement in Wildwood. Consequently, the city rejected his bid and instead hired Frank Donado's Band for $3960. By 1916, the traditional concert band had been replaced by Walter Pfeiffer's Orchestra which included members of the Philadelphia Orchestra and..."several of the world's most celebrated singers...." Although bands would return in a few years, Pfeiffer's Orchestra was considered a step up the resort's cultural ladder.

Not every merchant, however, was pleased with the community's commitment to providing concert music. The Boardwalk Mens' Association asked Wildwood officials to stop the music, alleging that business along the Boardwalk suffered during concerts. Their complaints fell on deaf ears, however, and Wildwood continued to pay for bands into the 1920s.

Where to stage the band concerts was an issue from the very beginning. In fact, in 1905 there was really no suitable place for band concerts on the Boardwalk. That season, the Baker brothers and the Board of Trade jointly financed the construction of a bandstand near the Casino and Blaker's, and it was arranged for the Millville Band to sleep in the borough hall during its engagement. A new bandstand was erected in 1908, but it was not much of a structure. One member of the Board of Trade referred to this bandstand as a "sausage shed" and began campaigning for the construction of a municipal pier to house concert bands. Some merchants, hoping to profit from the concerts, offered to donate land if the city agreed to construct a new bandstand near their Boardwalk operations. In any case, the city did not have the funds to construct a major municipal pier or auditorium at the time. Then in 1916, the Casino Pier Company offered to provide a facility for the band complete with electricity, a ticket seller, and a janitor in return for fifteen per cent of the ticket sales. This plan was quickly endorsed by the Board of Trade.

Professional musicians were visiting the Wildwoods in increasing numbers, and many of them wrote pieces of music dedicated to the resort. In 1905, Mrs. F. A. Breck wrote the lyrics to "Wildwood, Beauteous Wildwood," and Lois Worden composed "Wildwood-By-The-Sea." A year later, the musical director at the Ocean Pier, William Rushton, premiered his new "Wildwood Ocean Pier March." In the years to come, additional songs and marches would be inspired by the beauty of the Wildwood resorts.

GROWING PAIN AND PUBLIC BEHAVIOR

With annual summer attendance at Wildwood now exceeding one million visitors, and with every Five Mile Beach community expanding, it was inevitable that issues of public morals and clashes with state and local laws would arise. The police received complaints that ranged from a fourteen-year-old girl being employed for arduous work on a carousel to loud music and singing emanating from hotels and boarding houses until well after midnight. There were also those who complained that some of the motion pictures shown in Wildwood were vulgar and offensive. In response, F. Ogden Carll, manager of Blaker's Theatre in 1915, assured customers that Blaker's offered only photoplays that were "absolutely clean."

But even more distressing than these complaints was the fact that professional criminals had begun to haunt the resorts. In 1914, a robbery at Lowe's candy shop was foiled by the owner and an employee, while another robbery at Kline's Restaurant resulted in a police officer firing shots at the fleeing robber. On Labor Day of that season, the local police force was bolstered by Philadelphia detectives and three pickpockets were arrested and fined.

A constant bone of contention was the old Sunday closing law. In general, city officials and the police sympathized with Boardwalk merchants and did not enforce the law unless the issue was forced. Understandably, amusement operators lamented that Sunday was the busiest day of the week and without Sunday income many businesses could not be profitable. A case in point was the carousel operated by R. Arthur Long and Son. Long was part of a distinguished family of carousel builders and operators. In 1907, he brought a large, ornate carousel to Wildwood that had been built by his family in 1895 for Rochester's Ontario Beach Park. This beautiful machine included not only horses, but also a lion, seahorse, giraffes, camels, goats, zebras, donkeys, and four chariots. Long refused to close down his carousel on Sundays. It became a matter of course each Sunday for the local police to issue

During the annual Tall Cedars of Lebanon conventions, bands from the fraternal organization offered free concerts for the members and their families. – Cape May County Historical and Genealogical Society

Cianfoni's Band was hired in 1912 to play ten weeks of concerts for $4570. – Wildwood Historical Society

Long a citation for which he paid the borough a token fine. Then in 1909, the local officials were pressured by the county prosecutor to enforce the Sunday laws or face possible imprisonment. The borough issued orders for absolute Sunday closing, but Long, Jaquett's shooting gallery, and a number of other merchants challenged the law and were arrested. Unable to tolerate Sunday closings, Long moved his carousel to Eldridge Park in Elmira, New York, in time for the 1910 season.

The 1909 enforcement of the Sunday law, however, was not the end of the issue. Gradually, as the county took less interest in enforcing the law, merchants began to reopen on the Sabbath. By 1916, most of the Boardwalk operated freely each Sunday and one local politician ran on a platform that favored a liberal Sunday policy and open defiance of the state law. But once again, in 1917, a petition signed by fifty citizens requested that the county prosecutor close all unnecessary entertainments on Sundays. According to the petitioners, such unnecessary amusements included all Boardwalk games, vaudeville and motion picture theatres, bowling alleys, pool rooms, and similar operations. The problem of Sunday closings continued for some time, but by the 1920s it had taken a back seat to the much larger one of illegal beer and liquor sales during Prohibition.

Alcohol consumption had always been a controversial issue at the resorts, and officials were torn between catering to thirsty visitors with full wallets or pleasing indignant teetotalers. The communities, in fact, did not allow liquor to flow without restriction. In 1907, Holly Beach wanted all liquor-serving establishments to be at least two hundred feet from the Boardwalk. And in 1913, the well-respected Casino Pier was denied a license to sell liquor on its second floor. So much profit was derived from liquor sales, however, that a license was often merely an unnecessary formality. In 1910, an illegal tavern was operated by a Mr. Hand on the Holly Beach Boardwalk, and "speakeasy bathhouses" seem to have been common. Accommodating bathhouse attendants would slip bottles of liquor or beer into the dressing rooms and would quietly receive payment from the customer. Although some raids took place, the restriction of liquor sales in a large resort dedicated to leisure time amusements was difficult.

Cottage renters and hotel guests began to complain that local bars were noisy, rowdy, and a bad influence on their families. One Philadelphia businessman who had rented a cottage in Wildwood for years, protested the city's liquor situation and moved his family to Ocean City for the 1914 season. Others were concerned about hotels serving liquor on Sundays, a practice that had been tolerated well into the 1913 season. At that time, county prosecutor Matthew Jefferson announced that hotel bars would close on Sundays or the proprietors would face prosecution and jail sentences. Grudgingly, hotel bars officially closed on Sundays, but, as with Atlantic City, it was always possible to find a cold beer or a glass of whiskey on the Sabbath.

In the pre-world war era of reform, even dancing came under attack by local ministers. According to one clergyman, federal regulations stated that dancers must always be separated by at least five inches. Worse yet, he said he had actually witnessed dancers on the beach attired only in bathing suits! Reverend A. Q. Bailey of St. Simeon's Church asked city officials if they would like to see their daughters dancing in swimsuits while their partners were similarly attired. Reverend Keiter demanded an end to immoral dancing, especially on the beach. The mayor, who had greater concerns, patiently assured the ministers that dancing on the beach would be prohibited and that police officers would be instructed to supervise all dancing. By the end of the 1915 season, the dancing issue apparently had been resolved to everyone's satisfaction.

At the rate that the Five Mile Beach resorts were growing, it was inevitable that public morals would be compromised. Any crowd that exceeded one million people naturally contained both the best and the worst of society. And even those at the top of the moral ladder might enjoy a beer on a hot Sunday afternoon. Nor was it always the lowest class of visitor that sought the gambling den or the brothel. Indeed, the lowest class visitor could afford neither. The merchants and the elected borough officials faced a common dilemma. Large crowds meant large profits, but they also meant rowdyism, drunkenness, and the certainty that gambling, drinking, and prostitution would vie with the traditional Boardwalk merchants for visitors' dollars.

ATTRACTING PEOPLE WITH MORE ATTRACTIONS

As happened at almost all summer resorts throughout the United States, even highly ethical men overlooked the immoral aspects of the resort crowds and solicited even larger numbers of visitors. As a result, the Board of Trade, the Boroughs of Wildwood and Holly Beach, and, after 1911, the City of Wildwood, spent increasingly large sums of money to attract America's families to the Jersey seashore. In 1905, Holly Beach appropriated a mere ninety-nine dollars for advertising in Philadelphia newspapers. This budget was tripled a year later, and by 1911 the borough had hired an Atlantic City advertising agency and set aside $1000 for resort promotion.

After the merger of Holly Beach and Wildwood, the Casino Pier installed a Bureau of Information to help promote the area, and advertising budgets for the resorts increased annually. Five thousand dollars was earmarked for advertising in 1915, and 30,000 resort brochures were distributed. A year later, the Pathe Motion Picture Company was hired to produce a promotional film about Wildwood, and distribution to theatres in the east and the midwest was arranged. Finally, in 1918, with the munitions and war materials plants operating around the clock, the Board of Trade bought thirty billboards to entice workers and their families to the Boardwalk during their limited leisure time.

These advertising efforts, combined with Wildwood's growing reputation as a great seaside resort, brought vacationers in great numbers. They also attracted groups looking for a resort for conventions and meetings. Despite the fact that retreats like Ocean City offered an alcohol-free environment, the Wildwoods continued to host church groups and Sunday schools from Philadelphia and throughout New Jersey. In addition, large fraternal organizations thought the Wildwoods were ideal for their conventions. For many years the annual New Jersey Red Men's convention was held in Wildwood, and 1914's event was especially memorable. That season, a blockhouse and forest were constructed on the beach, and a mock battle between colonists and Indians was staged. To add authenticity, Chief Two Moons, allegedly the last surviving Indian leader to have been present at the slaughter of Custer and his command in 1876, travelled to Wildwood from his reservation home in Montana. Chief Two Moons was a sensation along the Boardwalk, spending each day shaking hands with young boys and being interviewed by newspaper reporters.

More and more organizations were finding Wildwood to be every bit as hospitable as Atlantic City and Asbury Park. In 1917, the New Jersey Fraternal Order of Eagles held a three-day event that brought more than twenty-five thousand people to the resort. And, when the National Advertising Club held their annual convention in Philadelphia, hundreds of conventioneers boarded a train to investigate the charms of Wildwood. They were not disappointed.

Among the many groups visiting the Wildwoods before 1920 were military schools and independent military companies that found the resort ideal for encampment, drill, and a few non-military activities. While the New Jersey National Guard units encamped at Sea Girt, other units came to the Wildwoods. In 1909, Philadelphia's Cooper Battalion visited the resort. Formed in 1898 for the Spanish-American War, the battalion never saw service but remained in existence and planned annual summer camps. While

at Wildwood, the unit engaged in infantry drills, artillery demonstrations, rifle and revolver competitions, and battle drills using blank cartridges in outdated Krag rifles. The week was climaxed with a grand military ball at the Ocean Pier, and both officers and enlisted men returned to Philadelphia with a high level of pride in their military proficiency. By 1913, military units from as far away as Pittsburgh held their summer camps at Wildwood, and even the Wenonah Military Academy set up camp on the Wildwood beach. Summer camp in Wildwood was an extraordinarily happy event that included strolls on the Boardwalk, glittering military balls, and drills in full-dress uniform. No one realized that within a few years many of these units, especially those with National Guard affiliations, would be fighting in France as part of the American Expeditionary Force.

GETTING THERE BY RAIL, SAIL, AND TRAIL

Most groups arrived in the Wildwoods on passenger trains, at least until 1920. Despite increasing automobile sales, the railroad was still favored for trips to the seaside. It was not uncommon to see eighteen or more trains arriving at Wildwood on a Sunday. Around 1905, a Philadelphia newspaper announced that of all the shore resorts, only Atlantic City welcomed more railway passengers than did the Wildwoods. On one single day during that season an estimated twenty thousand people detrained at the Wildwood station. Soon after, the West Jersey and Seashore Railroad was acquiring land for a new station. Two years later, the line added two more daily trains from Philadelphia, making a total of six scheduled trains a day.

Until 1912, the Pennsylvania Railroad (originally through its West Jersey and Seashore division) had total control of the railroad transportation to the Wildwoods. However, in 1909, many local merchants began complaining that the Pennsylvania system was no longer adequate to serve the needs of the growing resort. Early in 1910, stock was issued to help finance the construction of the Delaware Bay Short Line. The new line would connect Wildwood with the Reading Railroad's tracks to the west, thereby doubling railway access to the resort. Operation of the new line began in December of 1912. The Reading line was pleased with its new access to Wildwood and, at the end of the 1913 season, reported that Reading trains had carried three times as many passengers to Wildwood as had it to Cape May. The Reading line had also transported twice as much freight to Wildwood as it had to Cape May and 120,000 pounds more than it hauled to Ocean City. Initially, there was adequate business for both railroads, although, during the 1920s, automobiles and buses began to cut deeply into passenger ticket sales. Soon, both lines found themselves struggling to sell enough tickets to survive.

The relationship between the railroads and the local communities was a bittersweet affair. Both railroads claimed that they turned an excellent profit during the summer months, but lost money during the winter. Both railroads asked the boroughs to subsidize their winter operations, but they were never successful in obtaining this financial commitment. At the same time, city officials and Boardwalk merchants constantly complained that service was never adequate during the season, excursion rates were too high, and the equipment the railroads placed on their seashore lines was not their best rolling stock. As long as the railroads remained profitable, the cities were usually successful in forcing the railroads to lower or maintain excursion rates and to continue expanding service.

Electric railways also thrived during this period, although a coal shortage in 1916 (precipitated by the war in Europe) caused a temporary reduction of service by the Five Mile Beach Electric Railway. A year earlier, an electric bus began running from Cape May to Wildwood at a fare of 25 cents.

Passenger boats and ships also flourished from about 1905 to 1918, but they never seriously challenged the railroads for supremacy. Just after the turn of the century, the Anglesea Transportation Company's steamer Wildwood sailed four times a day between Anglesea and Stone Harbor, giving the resorts a connection with Avalon, Sea Isle City, Ocean City, and Atlantic City. In 1913, the Coast Transportation Company and the Pennsylvania Railroad consolidated their four boats to provide service every half-hour between Anglesea and Stone Harbor. These boats were responsible for carrying 90,000 passengers in 1914, while another line handled 70,500 people on the route between Cape May and Wildwood Crest. Finally, in 1916, the 251 foot steamer Cape May provided service to Cape May, Wildwood, and Philadelphia, with additional trips from Lewes, Delaware, to the Cape May County resorts. These passenger vessels seem to have been very successful, but, like the railroads, they were about to lose ground to the automobile.

The horseless carriage was still a novelty along the Jersey Shore in the early years of the century, but local magazines and newspapers were quick to predict that the automobile would prove to be very important to the seaside resorts. It was reported that early in the 1905 season, a group of Philadelphians motored to the shore in a huge Panhard vehicle, and, in April, a man drove the distance from Philadelphia to Atlantic City in

The Oak Avenue passenger station of the Wildwood & Delaware Bay Short Line, which connected Wildwood with the Reading Railroad and provided fast service to Philadelphia. – H. Gerald MacDonald Collection

Right: By 1910, railroad facilities in the resort communities were becoming fairly large, despite the fact that most railroad business was confined to the summer months. – Wildwood Historical Society

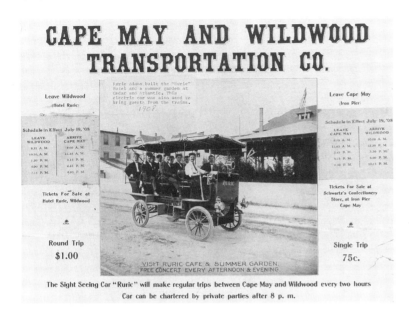

In 1908, the Hotel Ruric's electric bus, which met hotel guests at the railroad stations, was also used on regular trips between Wildwood and Cape May. – Wildwood Historical Society

just two hours and fifteen minutes. Soon, adventurous motorists were driving from New York City to Atlantic City! It was just a matter of time before the automobile made its presence known in the Wildwoods.

Bowing to the needs of motorists, Ocean Boulevard was extended to Five Mile Beach just before the start of the 1910 season. It wasn't long before other streets were paved and hotels were offering parking places for automobiles. The sale of gasoline became a necessary business at the resort.

As usual, with change came controversy. The State of New Jersey failed to agree on an auto licensing plan of reciprocity with Delaware and Pennsylvania in 1911. In retaliation, New Jersey forced automobile tourists from these two states to buy a New Jersey license for fifteen dollars. Since Pennsylvania and Delaware contributed heavily to the

An automobile parade on the Boardwalk passes the Wildwood Manor Hotel at 24th Street in 1907. – Wildwood Historical Society

annual influx of summer guests, businessmen from Wildwood and other resorts protested by sending a delegation to Trenton to meet with Governor Woodrow Wilson. Wilson promised a solution to the problem, and soon relations with the other states were normalized. In the future, the automobile would cause further problems at the resorts, but at least the issue of out-of-state licensing was solved. The Hotel Dayton gave proof positive that the automobile was here to stay when, in 1916, it retired its horses and carriages and purchased a seven-passenger car to meet guests at the train station.

MAKING ROOM FOR MORE ROOMS

The need for more and more hotel accommodations grew with each new season. In fall of 1906, it was announced that at least five new hotels were planned for the following season, including the Wildwood Manor between 24th and 25th Streets. The Manor was as close as the Wildwoods ever came to the huge, rambling hotels of Atlantic City. With 200 rooms, 50 baths, a dining room, cafe, and two electric elevators, the sprawling Wildwood Manor cost an eye-popping $200,000 to construct. Built in 1914 by Harry Witte at Pine and Atlantic Avenues, The Adelphi-Witte became another legendary Wildwood hotel. For decades to come, these two hotels were among the best known at the resort.

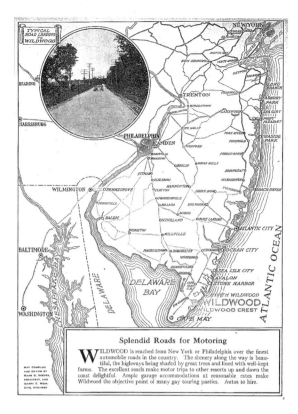

Splendid Roads for Motoring

WILDWOOD is reached from New York or Philadelphia over the finest automobile roads in the country. The scenery along the way is beautiful, the highways being shaded by great trees and lined with well-kept farms. The excellent roads make motor trips to other resorts up and down the coast delightful. Ample garage accommodations at reasonable rates make Wildwood the objective point of many gay touring parties. Autos to hire.

Both the Manor and the Adelphi-Witte were successful operations, but due to poor management, bad location, or simply hard luck, other hotels were not so fortunate. The Ocean Crest Hotel opened in 1906 as Wildwood Crest's first major resort property. A first-rate hotel, the Ocean Crest offered a grotto, a bar and fifty rooms, each with a phone. Within four years, however, the Ocean Crest was clearly in financial trouble and was offered at a public sale. The top bid of $17,500 was deemed unacceptable, but the hotel was later sold privately.

The Wildwood Manor, the island's largest hotel, was an elegant structure that represented the new seaside hotel architecture of the early 1900s. For decades, the Manor was the most stylish resort hostelry.
– Wildwood Historical Society

63

Hotel Dayton, the favorite hotel of the 1890s, was still among the resort's best hotels in 1912. – Wildwood Historical Society

Left: The Ocean Crest Hotel, Wildwood Crest's first large hotel, nears completion in 1906.– Wildwood Crest Historical Society

The Adelphi-Witte Hotel, from a 1915 brochure. – Wildwood Historical Society

The well-maintained Hotel Sheldon in an era when the streets were still mud and arc lights illuminated the night. – Library of Congress

Wildwood

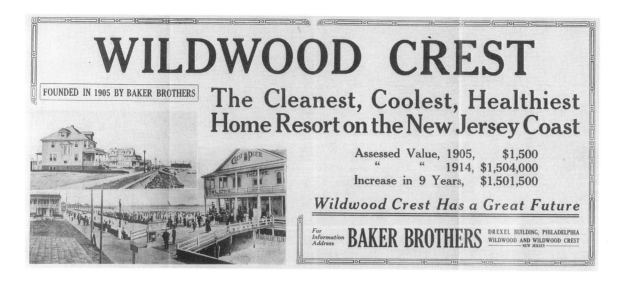

The construction of new, modern hotels forced many of the older hotels and boarding houses to appropriate money for improvements and remodelling. The Aetna Hotel, for example, added 27 rooms (making a total of 47), renovated the lobby in weathered oak, added a grand stairway, and a mahogany-paneled dining room.

To attract customers, the hotels kept room rates moderate and offered a variety of entertainment. In 1914, rates ranged from two to ten dollars a day, with the better hotels charging slightly more during July and August. The Hotel Ottens, which fell into that category, also provided some unique attractions. In the lobby was a canary who sang "Yankee Doodle," while the hotel's rathskeller featured an electric fountain. New dances like the Tango were all the rage, and local stores advertised special petticoats and dresses suitable for dancing the Tango at the Ottens ballroom.

HOLIDAYS AND SPECIAL EVENTS

Hoping to attract even more people to the Wildwoods, city officials worked together with hotelmen, Boardwalk merchants, real estate agents, and amusement pier operators to stage a number of special events. Some were highly successful and became annual events, while others quickly fell by the wayside. Some were also attempts to extend the season beyond the usual Labor Day end of summer. As a rule, they met with limited success.

The unofficial opening of the season was held during Easter weekend and was often accompanied by cold weather and sometimes snow. Some of the hotels opened for this weekend, as did many of the Boardwalk stores and amusements. The event usually brought out several thousand people

to stroll the Boardwalk in their Easter finery before attending Oglesby's Famous Concert Band, a basketball game, foot races, or an Easter cantata at Blaker's. Easter Sunday was reserved for church services, concerts on the piers, and more strolling of the Boardwalk. A good turn out over Easter weekend could herald a great season, and merchants kept a close eye on how well this preseason promotion fared. One year when a heavy Easter weekend blizzard blanketed the Boardwalk, delayed trains, and brought down trees and wires, the merchants worried little. Obviously, bad weather had kept the Easter crowd away. But, when the weather was sunny and warm and the crowds still did not come, the outlook for the coming season was bleak.

After Easter, merchants could look forward to the big three seasonal holidays: Memorial Day, July 4th, and Labor Day, all of which were well promoted. Of course, Memorial Day was the most restrained of the three with its traditional memorial service for America's sailors, patriotic band concerts, and a May Pole ceremony on the beach. At the other end of the holiday spectrum, July 4th was colorful, noisy, and packed with special events. There could be a yacht race from Ocean Pier, a motorboat race off Anglesea, motorcycle races on the beach, an auto parade on the Boardwalk, an automobile race at the speedway, or an auto run from Philadelphia to the Casino Pier. And, of course, there were the obligatory band concerts and fireworks. Despite its heralding the end of the season, Labor Day was no less colorful than July 4th. Labor Day festivities in 1909 included a Japanese Feast of the Lanterns with music by Pullo's Marine Band. There was also a parade of decorated rolling chairs occupied by Troilo's Royal Italian Band. Four seasons later, Labor Day was so popular that every hotel was filled to capacity,

The Brighton Cafe, a popular restaurant and night spot, in 1914.
– Wildwood Historical Society

Left: John A. Ackley, one of the resort's premier realtors and the founder of the Baby Parade in 1909 (he served as Grand Marshal of the 1929 Baby Parade).
– Wildwood Historical Society

and many private homes rented rooms to stranded visitors who had arrived on fifteen special trains.

With the exception of Easter weekend, holidays usually meant capacity crowds and big spending. There were, however, only four major holidays during the season, and only two fell during the height of the summer season. Therefore, it was necessary to invent other special events to stimulate business between holidays. The most enduring of these events was the annual baby parade that debuted in 1909. Real estate executive John A. Ackley came up with the promotion, but the idea wasn't a new one. Asbury Park introduced the first such event in 1890, and by 1910, the annual parade was attracting 100,000 spectators. Ocean City also presented an annual baby parade beginning in 1909.

Wildwood's first baby parade, held on August 28, 1909, attracted more than one hundred fifty entrants who dressed in fancy costumes or rode in gaily decorated baby car-

riages. Led by Pullo's Marine Band, the baby parade moved down the Boardwalk and past the judges who awarded cash prizes for the prettiest, cutest, fattest, best dressed, and smallest baby, as well as the best decorated carriages. The best costume award went to S. Edwin Corle, Jr., who rode a big hobby horse. The smallest baby weighed just eight pounds and was three weeks old. Pronounced a great success, the event grew each year, and within a few years there were more than four hundred children taking part in the parade dressed as birds, Indians, cowboys, Japanese ladies, Uncle Sam, Charlie Chaplin, and farmers, among others. Entrants were all given small gifts such as toys, boxes of Lowe's candies, and tickets to Hunt's Theatre and the Ocean Pier. A new twist was added to the parade in 1914 when Tillie Woods was crowned as the first Queen Oceania.

One somber note in the baby parade tradition came in 1916 when the threat of infantile paralysis caused the Board of Trade to cancel the event for that year. Even though the merchants lost revenues due to the cancellation, one good thing did come from the scare: believing that the disease might be caused by unhealthy conditions, a campaign to clean up garbage, vacant lots, and city streets was undertaken in September of 1916. The baby parade resumed in 1917 and was as popular as ever.

Hoping that dogs might be as popular as babies, the Board of Trade initiated a dog parade in 1915. That first canine stroll included 387 furry entrants and moved from the Atlantic Pier to the Ocean Pier. One hundred blue ribbons were awarded, and a motion picture company was on hand to record the event for movie theatre audiences. Despite the success of the first dog parade, the number of entrants dropped to 118 for the second event. And in spite of such impressive prizes as silver loving cups, Italian marble dog statues, and silver dog collars, interest seems to have waned. Although Wildwood continued to have pet contests annually, dog parades were discontinued after the 1916 event.

Motorcycle and automobile races were still something of a curiosity in the early 1900s, and consistently drew large crowds of spectators from about 1908 to 1913. Motorcycle races were sometimes held on the beach, but in 1909 they took place on Central Avenue in North Wildwood, with grandstands constructed along the curbs of the street. An automobile race in 1908 drew twenty thousand spectators which prompted much conversation about constructing a race course and scheduling races regularly at the resort. In 1910, Charles Warren drove his Stoddard-Dayton racer at 59 miles per hour, won two races, and left the resort with two sterling silver loving cups. Other events used Wildwood as the terminal of a longer race. For example, in 1913, 67 cars participated in an auto run from the Camden ferry docks to Wildwood. Although these auto runs did not attain the peak speeds of the track races, they were exciting events in an age when most families did not have automobiles.

But, even more thrilling than motorcycles and speeding race cars were airplanes. Only a decade after the Wright brothers made their famous flight, amusement parks and summer resorts were using flying exhibitions to draw crowds. Actually, Wildwood was a little slow in picking up on this trend. Most large amusement parks had tried dirigible flights by about 1905, and many had engaged airplanes by 1909 or 1910. The summer of 1913 brought two pilots to Wildwood, Marshall Reid in a flying boat and George Gray in a land-based craft. Each gave daily flight exhibitions over the beach and the ocean, and in late July, Gray pitted his Wright flyer against a motorcycle in an unusual race over a course of two-and-a-half miles. Cyclist Charles Glenn won by a fraction of a second, but this in no way diminished interest in flying and eager resort visitors lined-up for rides in Gray's fragile-looking plane. Reid, too, received his share of

publicity. It seems that the officers of the Aero Club of Pennsylvania agreed that Reid's plane was up to crossing the Atlantic. But just to make sure, a series of tests were conducted off the shore of Wildwood. Whatever the tests may have shown, Reid ultimately decided that flying exhibitions were a great deal safer than trying to cross an ocean.

George Gray returned to Wildwood in 1914, but was plagued by mishaps. A string of minor accidents on the beach caused damage to his plane. In August, a broken drive chain was responsible for a crash into the ocean. Just two weeks later, Gray landed near the water's edge, running over a seven-year old girl who was bathing. Fortunately, the girl suffered only minor cuts and bruises. Despite these and other misfortunes that season, Gray managed to execute sixty successful daytime flight exhibitions and five unique night flights.

In order to stretch the summer season as long as possible, the Board of Trade was constantly scheduling special events well into September and even October. After all, they argued, the golden month of September offered the seashores most pleasant weather, the crowds were greatly diminished, and hotel rates were usually lower. At the end of the 1913 season, the board tried a Japanese lantern festival. A year later, it was a "Night of Fun" beach party and masked ball. Five hundred free watermelons, ten thousand free clams and more than one hundred other prizes were offered as added inducements. But, try as they might, Wildwood would remain a summer-only resort. Labor Day was clearly and definitely the end of the season, and no amount of promotion managed to get crowds to return after the season ended.

THE ECONOMY OF THE 1910s

A more serious concern than extending the season was dealing with fluctuations in the economy. The Wildwoods seem to have been little affected by the major national recession of 1907, but a few years later, all of Cape May County entered a multi-year business decline that caused a great deal of concern. After vigorous and almost uncontrolled growth during the first decade of the century, the Wildwoods entered a period of economic decline that lasted until about 1920. The causes of this recession, which did not seem to affect either Atlantic City or Asbury Park, are not clear. Some blamed shark scares that kept visitors away from the beaches and diverted them to the northern resorts. Others felt that the threat of infantile paralysis, which was very real, dissuaded families from coming to the island. Whatever the causes,

By comparison to the wide Wildwood Boardwalk, the first Wildwood Crest Boardwalk was narrow and uncluttered. A severe storm demolished this Boardwalk in 1908. – Wildwood Historical Society

Left: Although Wildwood's promoters liked to claim that the resort's mild climate made it a resort for all seasons, the mound of ice in front of the Atlantic Pier during the winter of 1917-18 reveals the extremes of the coastal climate. – Wildwood Historical Society

the effects were swift and dramatic. Many hotels, including the great Hotel Ottens, were placed on the selling block. The famous Sagel Candy Company declared bankruptcy after the 1913 season, and the Boardwalk store at Poplar Avenue was offered for sale. In 1914, it was reported that, "The better cottages at Wildwood this year are renting slowly...." Boarding houses, which always offered the lowest rates, were doing better than the more expensive hotels. After a fair 1915 season, the Gennesee Cream Fudge Company considered building a second Boardwalk store, but many others who rented stores made the decision not to return to the Boardwalk in 1916. In order to make up for the poor summer trade, the owners of Lowe's taffy store decided to remain open all winter. The most stable and well established operations, like the Ocean Pier, survived the worst of these years and, in some cases, prospered. Crowds were still large, but because the Wildwoods had expanded so rapidly between 1900 and 1910, there were simply too many taffy stands, games, hotels, and restaurants to survive a recession. In many ways, the years between 1910 and 1920 were simply a period of adjustment for a resort that had evolved at too rapid a rate.

Adding to the economic woes of the resort were disasters such as fire and violent weather. While hurricanes were not a serious concern between 1905 and 1918, severe northeastern storms, especially in 1908 and 1914, did considerable damage. The earlier of these storms demolished the Wildwood Crest Boardwalk and inspired the Wildwood Crest Company to build a sea wall west of Atlantic Avenue. The storm of December, 1914, sheared the end of the Ocean Pier, and part of the Crest Pier fell into the ocean, taking with it pool tables and bowling alleys. The information bureau was destroyed, and portions of the Wildwood Boardwalk were swept into the surf.

The resort was fond of touting its salubrious climate, and a 1914 brochure proclaimed, "The latitude of Wildwood also helps to insure a mild climate in winter. It is on the same parallel as Washington, D.C., which is practically a southern city." But the fact that Wildwood was thirty miles south of the Mason-Dixon Line did not ensure the much publicized mild winters. In 1915, Easter visitors were greeted by eight inches of snow, and heavy snow falling from the roof of the Ocean Pier crushed the roof of a

building below in 1918. That same winter, a water pipe froze and burst in Louis Sagel's candy store. Upon returning from a Florida vacation, Mr. Sagel found that his water bill reflected the fact that 93,000 gallons of water had flowed through the damaged pipe.

Fire also caused major damage on January 21, 1915, when an entire block of Boardwalk buildings between Oak and Wildwood Avenues was razed by flames. The blaze was started in Philip Gould's restaurant, allegedly by an oven in which a turkey was being roasted. Spreading fast through the wooden buildings, most of which were closed for the winter, the flames destroyed Gould's restaurant, the Welch's Grape Juice store, an orange juice stand, Frank Snyder's photo studio, three novelty shops, and a lace store. Loss was estimated at $10,000, very little of which was covered by insurance.

Despite the difficult economy of the 1910-1920 period, the Wildwood real estate and land development business flourished, possibly presaging the ruinous land boom of the 1920s. In 1906, the Baker brothers sold in excess of seven hundred lots in Wildwood Crest. Eighty new homes and hotels, as well as the Crest Pier were built at a cost of more than a half million dollars. Four years later, the Bakers bought all of the land from Cedar Avenue to the North Wildwood border and from Atlantic Avenue to the beach. It was expected that development of the area would cost more than one-and-a-half million dollars. That same year, the Wildwood Crest Improvement Company purchased (from the Bakers) the land between Rambler Road and Turtle Gut Inlet and began the development of fourteen streets. At Ottens Harbor, $100 to $400 lots could be purchased for as little as five dollars per month. The cottage community continued to grow and, in fact, there was often a shortage of available cottages for summer rental. Portable cottages were offered for sale at $300, while in 1907, a large, twelve-room cottage could be purchased for $2,800. Annual land auctions set new records for sales each year, and Cape May County's poor economy seems to have had no impact on land investments.

OVER THERE

The beginning of the war in Europe in 1914 had no immediate effect on the Wildwoods, except for the occasional coal shortage during winter. With the United States declaring neutrality, many of the area's German-Americans donated to a German-Austrian relief fund, an act that focused much suspicion on these people when America finally joined in the war. When America's entering the war seemed imminent, a patriotic martial spirit swept over the resort. The Wildwood Coast Artillery was formed. It soon became a trench mortar battalion and was sent to Fort DuPont for training. A few days before the declaration of war, the Wildwood Battalion held a preparedness rally at Hunt's Avenue Theatre and former congressman J. Thompson Baker was a key speaker.

The resort immediately felt the impact of a nation at war — most notably in the presence of airplanes and airships in the sky and thousands of servicemen in uniform on the Boardwalk. Within a few days of the country's entry into the war, officers from the U.S.S. Wisconsin were in Wildwood on recruiting duties. In nearby Cape May, Wissahickon Naval Training Barracks, an officers' training camp, and a naval air station were established. The military also took possession of the failed amusement pavilion at Sewell's Point. Before long, fifteen thousand men were stationed at bases around Cape May, and several Wildwood area businesses were among those selected to provide them with food and supplies.

The people of the Wildwoods reacted with patriotic enthusiasm to the war. In fact, one overzealous patriot was arrested in June of 1917 for distributing free liquor to marines strolling the Boardwalk. Pfeiffer's Orchestra, which played at the Casino Pier in both 1917 and 1918, was issued a new contract specifying that all of the unit's musicians must be American citizens. War gardens appeared in every vacant lot and behind many homes, with the largest field set aside for growing only potatoes. A local branch of the American Red Cross was organized at the

Hotel Dayton, and a benefit dance for an ambulance fund was held at the Ocean Pier. At the Casino Pier, patriotic speeches were promoted and community sings were added to the performances of Pfeiffer's Orchestra. At the Crest Pier, Passeri's Band offered decidedly patriotic concerts. Throughout the summer of 1918, Wiener's Ice Cream Parlor, located near the Casino Pier, donated a portion of its sales to the Red Cross, and at the cafe of the new Colonial Hotel, nationality nights featured the foods of the allied nations. During the week, the cuisine of England, Italy, France, and Belgium was featured, while Saturday night was reserved for strictly American cuisine.

For the most part, the day-to-day Boardwalk routine was not affected by the war, but some merchants catered to servicemen with special offerings. Blaker's Theatre engaged a new show called Don't Tell My Wife, "A Smashing, Dashing Girlie Show" that could be viewed from the balcony for only fifteen cents. Another show advertised twelve "Pretty Big Darlings." The beach was as crowded as ever, and on one day when twenty thousand people covered the sand the lifeguards handled some thirty rescues.

The government had assured the resorts that nighttime black-outs would not be required, so the 1917 season proceeded as usual. By 1918, however, the real impact of the war was beginning to be felt. The opening of the season was met with severe shortages of coal, gasoline, lumber, meat, bread, and sugar. Construction in the Wildwoods came to a standstill, and at least one lumber company was forced to close. The candy and ice cream operations were always low on sugar, and restaurants were constantly having to change their menus. At the Severn Hall dining room, broiled mackerel and stewed chicken replaced beef and pork on the Sunday menu. The coal shortage was not felt much during the season, but the winter of 1918 was the coldest at the shore since 1880.

Shore birds froze on the beaches and schools closed when there was not enough coal to provide heat.

The most significant shortage, however, was that of railroad locomotives and rolling stock. The summer of 1917 passed without major interruption in railway service, but in February of 1918, all excursion trains to the resorts were cancelled and prospects for the coming season appeared gloomy. New Jersey senators fought for their seashore resorts, and by March the government had agreed to permit both the Pennsylvania and Reading railroads to run Sunday excursions starting on Easter weekend. However, excursion rates were raised from $1 to $1.35, a rate hike that the Board of Trade feared would discourage patronage, especially with a war tax added to the ticket price.

Depressing predictions for the 1918 season proved all too true. Although a substantial business increase during August of 1917 provided some hope, the decreased rail service and continuing local recession ensured disaster for 1918. Few hotels were filled to capacity, even in July and August. And, in fact, the Hotel Royal was sold at a Sheriff's sale for the bargain price of $11,300. As attendance at the concerts of Pfeiffer's Orchestra declined, afternoon concert tickets were reduced in price from a dime to a nickel, and advance sale tickets were offered at a twenty per cent discount. Up and down the Boardwalk, the recession that had plagued the resort since 1910 was aggravated by railway service cutbacks, food shortages, and, finally, the horrific influenza epidemic of 1918-19.

Yet, the end of the war seemed to coincide with an end to the Cape May County business recession. Except for the national depression of 1920-21 and the collapse of the Wildwood land boom near the end of the 1920s, the decade following the war brought new prosperity to the beleaguered resort.

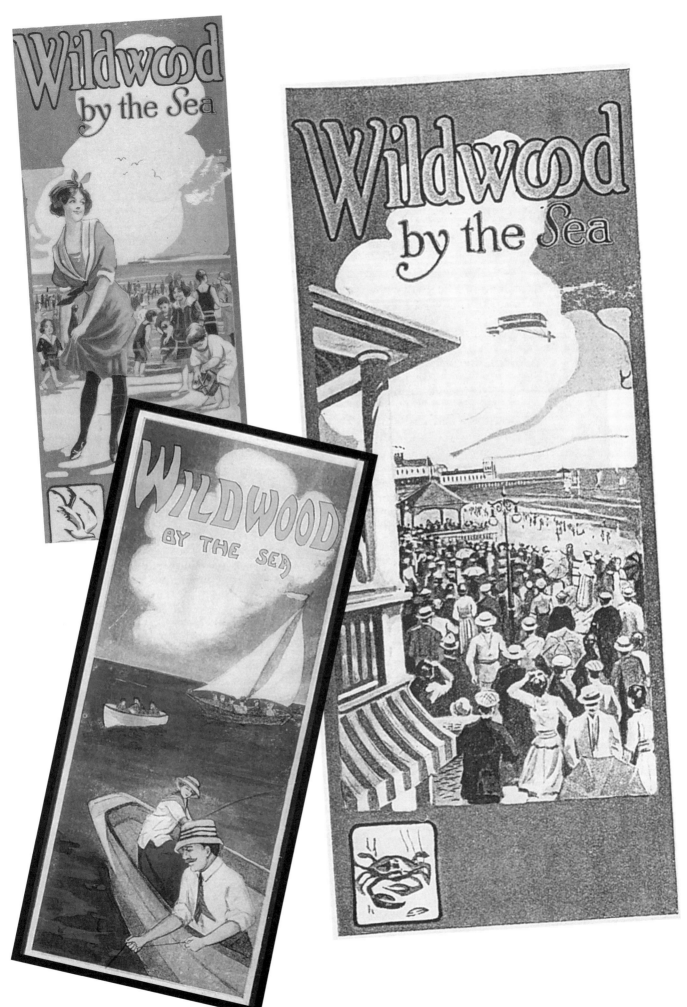

the 1920s
BLENDING
the OLD
WITH THE
NEW

*T*he decade of the 1920s has been stereotyped as the age of
gangsters, speakeasies, flappers, jazz, and loose sexual mores.
True, the '20s encompassed all of this and more, but the average
American family lived a quiet, sober life. Most Americans never
saw a gangster, never tasted bathtub gin, did not wear flapper
dresses, never learned to dance the Charleston, and may not
have appreciated jazz. Yet, while the average person enjoyed a
continuity of life carried over from the pre-war years, change
was in the wind.

CHAPTER 4

While the real wealth was concentrated within the upper class, the middle class also enjoyed a relatively prosperous decade. Most men made enough to afford homes, automobiles, electrical appliances, and even the occasional extended vacation. Despite the unstable economy of the 1920s and the agricultural depression of that decade, people flocked to amusement parks and summer resorts in increasingly large numbers.

In Greater Wildwood, the decade embodied an interesting mix of the new and the familiar. In some ways the Boardwalk never changed. On the other hand, such factors as Prohibition, rising prices after the end of the war, the post-war depression of 1920-21, and the ascendancy of the automobile over the railroad made change unavoidable. Perhaps the most obvious change was the passing of the old guard resort developers. Two of the famous Baker Brothers who founded Wildwood, passed away during this era; Thompson in 1919, and Philip a year later (Latimer Baker lived on until 1932). Joseph M. Sweet, the premier bathhouse operator who had arrived in Wildwood in 1900, died in 1919 at age fifty-five, and Gilbert H. Blaker succumbed to throat cancer in 1928. By the end of the 1920s, most of the resort's pioneers were gone, and a new generation of entrepreneurs had come on the

Atlantic Avenue looking north, about 1921. Hotel Sheldon is the large building on the left. – Wildwood Historical Society

scene. This group included Bill Hunt, S. B. Ramagosa, Charles and Joseph Douglass, and a number of recent arrivals.

The postwar depression had a major economic effect on the resort during the 1920 and 1921 seasons. In fact, the 1920 season was so bad that advertising budgets were cut drastically, the July 4th firework display was cancelled, and tickets to band concerts at the Casino Pier were raised from ten to fifteen cents in an attempt to reduce losses. But, despite the dismal season, businessmen were optimistic. Late in 1920, building permits representing $100,000 in new construction were issued during a two-month period. The Sagel family, now operating three candy stores, added a new facade on their Casino Arcade store and installed new glass showcases at all locations. The other candymakers — Lowe, Bergman, and Douglass — also made improvements. Their optimism was rewarded with a slightly healthier business climate in 1921. Although unusually wet, the summer of 1922 was even more successful, and for the next five years business skyrocketed.

A construction boom increased the cost of building projects from $146,000 in 1919 to $1,000,000 in 1922. Wildwood's population also increased, from 2,790 in 1920 to 5,330 in 1930. The 1920s, despite uneven levels of prosperity, a true depression for farmers, and a shaky economy, brought relatively good times to the resorts of Five Mile Beach.

PROHIBITION

Among the many changes seen after the First World War, Prohibition was probably the most noticeable. Even before the Volstead Act could take effect, the War Prohibition Act made the sale of intoxicating beverages illegal after June 30, 1919. Indeed, during the winter of 1918-19, saloons in the Wildwood area were included in an order to close all bars within a five-mile radius of the Cape May Naval Base. Saloon owners, city officials and the Board of Trade battled with the navy to rescind the order. However, by the time they began to make any progress, the War Prohibition Act was in effect.

With the legitimate saloons closed, illegal operations began to spring up, and the smuggling of beer and liquor became commonplace. Coast Guard vessels stationed at Cape May waged a constant battle with rum

runners and many of the chases could be seen from the Wildwood beach. Occasionally, lawlessness turned violent, and in one episode Wildwood Chief of Police Oakford M. Cobb was wounded during a gun battle.

The most flagrant violators of the Volstead Act were the area hotels that depended heavily on bar revenues. Before the end of the 1920 season, federal agents raided a series of hotels in Wildwood and North Wildwood. Liquor was confiscated at four hotels, but Hotel Ruric, allegedly a major offender, received early warning of the raid and no liquor was found. During the coming years, certain hotels, especially the Pacific, Brighton and Penn-Wood, were raided on an almost regular basis. In 1927, a raid at the Pacific Hotel netted twenty-four pints of whiskey and three gallons of alcohol. Often, hotels were padlocked after a raid that yielded liquor, as were the Brighton and the Elmira in 1925. In the meantime, shipments of alcohol, sometimes as large as a thousand cases, were landed at places like Ottens Harbor.

Citizens of Wildwood held differing views regarding Prohibition. The police, for the most part, made little attempt to help the federal agents, and, in some cases, actually opposed raids. In July of 1925, during a raid on the Hotel Bradley, police officer Michael Sheehan was allegedly beaten by federal officers when he and one other policeman tried to interfere with the raid. Although accounts of the incident were rather confused, it is clear that many locals had little sympathy for federal agents.

On the other hand, the Wildwood Hotel Association and local clergymen, took an opposite stance. In 1927, they claimed that the liquor situation in Wildwood was out of control. Teenage girls, they stated, were regularly seen staggering out of cabarets at three or four in the morning. Despite the federal raids, the sale of liquor along the Boardwalk, in cabarets, and even in ballrooms on Sunday evenings, was all but unrestricted. Many local businessmen were anxious to squelch such efforts at reform, and one editorial in a local newspaper stated, "There are no chronic social reformers here who are seeking to make our life miserable." In fact, there were reformers present, but their outcries were generally silenced by those who realized that a summer resort needed an atmosphere that "...breathes freedom of the soul and body...."

Meanwhile, there were other ethical issues that sometimes divided the community. During the 1920s, the Ku Klux Klan was a powerful organization that held rallies at various locations throughout the state,

Left: Taken in 1926, this aerial photo reveals the tremendous growth of the resorts since 1900.– Library Company of Philadelphia

including at Wildwood's Atlantic Pier. However, in 1924, when the Klan burned a cross in Wildwood, a scuffle ensued and a fisherman who tried to tear-down the cross was beaten.

Gambling, illegal, but widespread nonetheless, also had its proponents and opponents. The local police and city officials showed little interest in curtailing illegal gambling operations, but a crusading county prosecutor launched raids on gambling dens, as well as speakeasies and stills. In the meantime, the City of Wildwood outlawed games of chance on the Boardwalk. Unfortunately, city officials were ambiguous about what type of game constituted an illegal operation. As a result, licenses were granted to virtually all operators and only during future inspections was the legality of a game determined. During mid-July of 1922, the city launched raids that closed dart games, cane racks, and various ball games, while leaving Japanese Roll Ball games free to operate. Game owners threatened to test the law in the courts, but most simply awaited the results of similar cases in Atlantic City. Far from being settled, the issue of games of chance versus games of skill (and how to differentiate them) remained a heated topic well into the 1950s and beyond.

BOARDWALK EXPANSIONS

At the conclusion of the First World War, the Boardwalk was badly in need of maintenance. It was rotting and, by some accounts, unsafe. However, due to the constantly expanding beach, the Boardwalk was once again far removed from the water's edge. Just after the close of the 1919 season, the city attempted to appropriate $100,000 for a new Boardwalk, but there was considerable opposition to spending this much money, and the ordinance failed to pass. The mayor then regrouped his supporters and asked instead for $50,000. This time the ordinance was passed. In December of 1919, the city authorized the construction of a 2,300-foot walk from Cedar Avenue to Montgomery Avenue, with a 628-foot section connecting this new walk with the older structure to the south.

The passing of the ordinance prompted immediate legal action by Gilbert Blaker, who claimed that the city had breached a promise with him not to move the Boardwalk for another two or three years. In addition, Blaker questioned the legality of bonds issued by the city to pay for the construction of the new promenade. The city moved ahead with demolition of the old walk north of Montgomery Avenue despite a court-ordered injunction to halt the removal of portions of

Left above: The old Boardwalk was demolished in preparation for the construction of the new promenade. To the right is the original Regent Theatre. – Wildwood Historical Society

Left middle: Demolition of the old Boardwalk, 1919-20. Note that the new Jack Rabbit roller coaster is east of the old Boardwalk. The new Boardwalk would soon position the coaster west of the walkway. – Wildwood Historical Society

the walk. Both E. S. Culver and demolition crew foreman, John James, were charged with contempt of court, fined ten dollars each, and sternly rebuked by the judge.

The complicated legal actions brought the construction of a new Boardwalk to a stand-still. As of February, 1921, no further action had been taken; merchants and railroad officials worried that the 1921 season would open with huge gaps in Wildwood's Boardwalk. During one of the most interesting episodes in the 1920-21 Boardwalk controversy, city commissioners allowed a crew to tear out a large section of Boardwalk decking during the night, thereby forcing action on a new structure for the coming season. The extra-legal action aroused a flood of angry protests and the demand for a recall election. In the ensuing election, the two men most responsible for the action were removed from office and replaced. In the meantime, Blaker dropped the last of his legal actions and the city was free to begin construction.

In March, 1921, the city accepted the $44,425.12 bid of Cecil E. Ober and Israel T. Woolson, who were also the low bidders on a project to construct a 1,000-foot fishing pier at Ottens Harbor, and on March 22, the first pilings were driven. A few weeks later, the city won a legal action against Albert Mowitz, who had claimed that the Boardwalk denied access to his property. With this decision, all legal roadblocks had been hurdled by the city. Crews worked feverishly to complete the new walkway and to construct the right angle section that would join the newer section to the more westward older section at Montgomery Avenue. Even so, the new Boardwalk section was not completed until late August.

Late in 1924, the city again addressed the Boardwalk problem and proposed construction of a new section from Oak Avenue north to the border of North Wildwood. Most merchants favored moving the walk from Atlantic Avenue to a new location closer to the beach, so action on this proposal proceeded much more smoothly than it had in 1920-21. While buildings on the east side of the old walkway were demolished, a con-

Captain Samuel A. Buck's fishing steamer, which offered daily deep water fishing trips for $2.00 per person, including lines, bait, and accommodations for ladies. Most of Captain Buck's customers arrived on the Fisherman's Special Train from Philadelphia. – David W. Francis Collection

– David W. Francis Collection

Opposite: Ottens Harbor in August of 1926. Many boats from the island's great fishing fleet (one of the largest on the Atlantic Coast) are seen docked at the wharf.
– Newark Public Library

A portion of the North Wildwood Boardwalk, with the small Surfside Hotel behind the Beecher-Kay Realty offices.
– Cape May County Historical and Genealogical Society

The Wildwood Crest beach, Boardwalk, and fishing pier, circa 1920.
– Wildwood Crest Historical Society

tract in the amount of $123,167.88 was issued to J. W. Schwier of New York City for the construction of 2,160 feet of Boardwalk. Spruce decking would be used for the new section that included a concrete roadway for rolling chair operations. The Boardwalk was rushed to completion, and on Memorial Day of 1925, Mayor E. S. Culver and Commissioner Ralph Carll drove the last nails and viewed a gala parade celebrating the opening of the new section.

Two years later, J. W. Schwier won another city contract with a bid of $190,942.71 to construct the southern-most section of the Wildwood Boardwalk from Montgomery Avenue to the border of Wildwood Crest. This section was completed by July, 1927.

In the meantime, officials in North Wildwood and Wildwood Crest were kept busy with their own Boardwalk improve-

ments. In the early 1920s, Wildwood Crest replaced the wooden walk with a paved street; and, in 1929, council approved a cement walkway from Heather to Cresse Avenues connecting with the wooden Wildwood Boardwalk to the north. Unlike the northern promenades, the new Wildwood Crest walkway was constructed at ground level and departed from the traditional broad, elevated, wooden Boardwalks.

North Wildwood, on the other hand, maintained its large, wooden Boardwalk that offered amusements and stores to the west and a view of the beach to the east. In June of 1927, a contract for $237,486 was awarded jointly to the Craythorn-Nickerson Company and Versaggi Brothers Construction Company

for a new North Wildwood Boardwalk. The construction firms attempted to start building in July, but merchants protested that razing sections of the old walk would destroy business during the busy months of July and August. Careful not to interfere with summer business, construction began in July and the old Boardwalk was razed after Labor Day. Completed during the winter of 1927-28, the new concrete and wood walk ran from 26th Street north to 16th Street and was dedicated on July 4, 1928, by Mayor George Redding. With the completion of the North Wildwood Boardwalk, the famous wooden way stretched 9,771 feet from 16th Street in North Wildwood, south through Wildwood to the border of Wildwood Crest. Fifty feet wide at most locations, the new Boardwalk of Greater Wildwood emerged as one of the world's premiere structures of its kind, imperiling the supremacy of the magnificent Atlantic City Boardwalk.

The grandeur of the new walk inspired many Wildwood businessmen to invest in renovations of their own buildings and even attracted new merchants from out-of-town. Throughout the 1920s, the business community along the west side of the Boardwalk thrived and expanded. In 1928, a newspaper reporter strolling along the planks from 26th Avenue to Cedar Avenue counted eight restaurants, twelve food stands, two theatres, eight candy stores, and numerous toy stores, games, and camera shops. Although the 1919 season set a new record for the month of June, 1929 was considered a banner season overall. For decades to come, the 1929 season was the benchmark against which all seasons would be judged.

Inevitably, the construction of the new Boardwalk resulted in number of changes among the merchants. New enterprises appeared and some old standbys disappeared. One of the most popular new sensations was the Pig Slide that opened in 1921. Customers threw baseballs at a target that, when hit, released a pig to slide down one of four slides. Those who successively released three pigs won a doll or a box of candy. Ten pigs were on duty at any one time, and customers developed a fondness for pigs with names like Bacon, Dubb, Babe, and Jersey. Dubb made big news in 1928 when the 300 pounder gave birth to six piglets.

Another new attraction was silhouette artist Otto Greenberg, a New Yorker who billed himself as a "...traveler, artist, student, physiologist, inventor, and doctor of medicine." Greenberg had travelled through Europe, Mexico, and South America making a living with scissors and black paper. Among his clients, Greenberg boasted, were Teddy Roosevelt, the crown heads of Europe, and dozens of other notables.

Games of chance were still the source of controversy. Nevertheless, they retained their popularity with visitors and introduced many new game operators during the 1920s. The most successful newcomers were Ralph and Charlie Franks, who had operated games at county fairs in Delaware. The brothers visited Wildwood in 1929 and befriended candy-maker Harry Sagel. Sagel rented them a Boardwalk store and provided 100 boxes of taffy as prizes for their new dart game. Despite their Wildwood debut at the decline of a prosperous era, the Franks family built a seaside empire that included arcades, rides, shooting galleries, a monkey speedway, and games such as the Kentucky Derby and Pokereno. They also operated a number of food stands including Texas Lunch and Walkaway Malties. Still going strong in 1970, the Franks family established Wildwood's popular Nut Hut.

Not every Boardwalk merchant, however, owned a building or rented a store. Provided that they first procured a city license, performers were permitted to present acts on the Boardwalk in return for voluntary donations from appreciative spectators. Typical of these were the Reckless Recklaws, a husband and wife team that offered comedy bicycle stunts and fancy roller skating along the Boardwalk in 1920.

TASTE BUD EXPANSIONS

The construction of the new Boardwalk and the return of prosperity to Cape May County after the war enticed many new restaurant and food stand operators to the shore. The renewed economy also provided established operators the opportunity to expand and grow. Innovations in resort food items during the 1920s included the now-standard cotton candy. In 1922, H. W. Grambow, a food concessionaire at the short-lived Rendezvous

Park in Atlantic City, opened the Kotton Kandy Kitchen in the Casino Arcade. A season later, a big hit with visitors was Frozen Snow, finely chopped ice covered with chocolate, pineapple, or cherry syrup. These new treats were immensely popular, but they never ousted old favorites like the hot dog. Indeed, there was room enough and hungry patrons enough to support scores of food operators. In 1922, more than forty stands vied for Boardwalk strollers' patronage with hot dogs (known locally as "Burk's Roosters"). Most famous was Pop Schaeffer's stand, which owed much of its success to the fresh and often still-warm hot dog rolls delivered daily from Seiber's Bakery.

Unique among Wildwood's food concessionaires was Henry F. Merkel. Merkel's Root Beer stand was famous for its creamy Liberty Root Beer, fruit juices, and Wildwood Cocktails (a concoction of grape juice and orangeade), all served in big glass schooners. But what really set Merkel apart from the other cold drink stands were the two young alligators that he brought from Florida to display in the stand. Many of Merkel's customers bought cold root beer, postcards, and Florida sponges while marveling at the two reptiles.

Taffy, fudge, and other confections were still among the most popular concessions along the walk. During the 1923 season, Clayton Lowe's candy store shipped 2,500 pounds of taffy each week to addresses in the United States, Alaska, Japan, and even Fiji. Charles Douglass was doing so well with his candy store that in 1922 he built a courtesy pavilion opposite his candy store and fitted it with seats for tired strollers. The Douglass Pavilion made good business sense, for while people escaped both sun and rain under its roof, they saw hundreds of shoppers leave the Douglass store with boxes full of fresh taffy, fudge, and caramels. One imagines that it wasn't long before these spectators became Douglass shoppers themselves!

Nineteen twenty-six brought another new merchant to Wildwood. One who would put a smile on the faces of candy lovers for decades to come. That summer, Joe Laura was out of work, but his wife, Kate, opened a wheel of fortune game and gave away her own homemade fudge to the lucky winners. In 1928, she lost her game concession in a fire, but remembering the popularity of her fudge, opened a candy store at Pacific and Pine Avenues. The store prospered, and a few years later she moved Laura's Fudge to new quarters in the Dayton Hotel. Each morning a line would form outside of Laura's shop, for those who loved Kate's fudge knew that

daily quantities were limited. The doors opened at eleven in the morning. By two in the afternoon, the stock was sold and Kate closed up shop until the following day.

While candy shops and hot dog stands prospered, so did restaurants and cafeterias. A Chinese restaurant, dubbed the Oriental Tea Room, was established on the Boardwalk, and Joseph Douglass founded his Douglass Cafeteria at Oak and Atlantic Avenues. Joseph Douglass (Charles' brother) had operated a candy and ice cream business in Philadelphia's Fairmount Park before coming to Wildwood in 1919. He opened a small hotel, a restaurant and, finally, his popular cafeteria, which became famous for serving Douglass's own brand of ice cream.

One of the resort's most enduring restaurant operations began in 1918 when Earl M. Groff came to Wildwood from Pennsylvania. The lumber mill worker first opened some ball games on the Boardwalk, but, tiring of the struggle between game operators and the county government, he eventually opened a hot dog stand in 1925. The Groff family lived behind the hot dog stand which they used for cooking their meals. Soon, the wonderful aromas from those home-cooked meals brought requests from customers for something a little more substantial than hot dogs, and in 1928 Groff's opened a full-service restaurant. Groff's business grew rapidly, and by 1935 the brick-front restaurant occupied three store fronts along the Boardwalk at Magnolia Avenue. Then the Groffs purchased the property behind their restaurant for a second dining room. A new, modern kitchen was also built and here they created their famous specialties and home-made desserts, including peach glaze, strawberry glaze, and black bottom pies.

THE SILVER SCREEN

Nationally, the motion picture industry experienced amazing growth during the 1920s. In 1922, American theatres sold 40,000,000 admission tickets per week; by 1928, this number reached 65,000,000. Even while enjoying summer vacations, Americans took time to see the latest movies. Entertainment in the Wildwoods kept pace with national trends, and at the center of the resort's theatre business stood Bill Hunt, known as "Vacationland's Impresario." Capitalized at $1,000,000 in 1922, Hunt's Theatres, Inc. owned 17 theatres with a total seating capacity of 15,000 people. These movie houses included the Avenue, Casino, Regent, Comique, Blaker's, and the Strand in Wildwood; the Crest Pier Theatre in

Uniformed in white and lead by a drum major dressed as a clown, a band marches past Nixon's Vaudeville Theatre (probably during a Baby Parade of the early 1920s).
– Wildwood Historical Society

Wildwood Crest; three more theatres in Cape May. The other seven were scattered throughout New Jersey and Pennsylvania. As early as 1921, Hunt's theatres in the Wildwoods alone were showing at least twenty-two different movies per week.

Bill Hunt purchased the Regent Theatre in 1921 and moved it from Atlantic and Lincoln Avenues to the Boardwalk. The Casino Theatre was destroyed by fire in 1922 and was promptly rebuilt for the next season. The new Casino was a showplace designed for year-round use. It boasted 1,500 French grey seats, a huge Robert Morton pipe organ, bevelled glass mirrors, miniature candelabra, a brilliantly illuminated entrance canopy, and a large electric sign. That same year, Hunt built the new Plaza Theatre, also with seating for 1,500, and featuring a row of Boardwalk stores at the front of the building. Hunt had leased Blaker's Theatre for a number of years, and in 1925 he bought the theatre, along with the bathhouses and adjoining cottage. The old Blaker was totally renovated for the 1927 season with new seats, plush carpets, and the latest in projection equipment.

Although vaudeville was losing popularity, Hunt's movie houses continued to present live entertainment acts between movies throughout most of the 1920s. The first motion picture featuring sound was shown in the Wildwoods in February, 1929, at Hunt's Casino Theatre. Within a month, the Casino was showing "talkies" almost exclusively.

Many of the films of the 1920s were considered racy for that time, but Hunt's theatres presented primarily family-oriented movies. One rather naive theatre manager even went so far as to claim that the movies at Hunt's were so entertaining that "spooning" in the theatres was a thing of the past. There were, however, a few controversial presentations. One was The Unwanted Child, a stage play given at the Casino Theatre in 1923. The play, which dealt with sensitive subject matter, was represented as an educational tool, and mothers were encouraged to bring their daughters.

EXPANDING ATTRACTIONS

While Bill Hunt aggressively promoted his movie theatres, he also ventured outside of the motion picture industry in 1925 when he bought a reconditioned carousel from the Philadelphia Toboggan Company and installed it on the Boardwalk. Originally built for a park in McKeesport, Pennsylvania, the carousel operated at Wildwood until 1930. It was then moved to Lawnside, New Jersey, and dismantled fifteen years later.

Hunt was also active in Wildwood's Board of Trade and was one of the resort's most ardent promoters. In fact, Wildwood's self promotion reached new heights during the 1920s. In December of 1922, members of the Wildwood Hotel Association attended the National Hotel Exposition in New York City. Armed with 5,000 Wildwood brochures, 200 pounds of Douglass candies, and hundreds of Wildwood souvenirs, the hotelmen enter-

A prize winning float in one of the well-attended Baby Parades of the late 1920s.
– Wildwood Historical Society

tained more than 10,000 visitors in their booth and gave away free Wildwood vacations. The resort cities and the Board of Trade also appropriated large sums of money for advertising and in 1928, the City of Wildwood hired an advertising agency to handle $17,000 in newspaper and radio advertising.

The Baby Parade continued to be the resort's largest annual promotion, and in 1921 the committee added a pony competition, although only three ponies were entered. By the end of the decade, the Baby Parade drew as many as 150,000 spectators, including Governor Morgan Larson of New Jersey and Mayor Harry Mackey of Philadelphia. In 1929, Governor Larson presented the Governor's Cup to the winning baby. The popularity of the Baby Parade in August, 1925, tempted the Board of Trade once again to try to prolong the season with a September minstrel show on the beach. Although hailed as a success, the minstrel show suffered from the same mediocre attendance as previous post-season events. Once again, the merchants would learn that the Wildwoods were, and would remain, strictly a summertime resort.

In the 1920s there was still a great deal of interest in airplane exhibitions. Thanks to a surplus of war aircraft and large numbers of former military fliers, the resort industry could choose from an abundance of flying

exhibitions. In 1920, Lieutenant Arthur L. Cox and his plane, the Jazz Baby, arrived in Wildwood to provide daily exhibitions and on July 4th he parachuted 1,500 feet into the surf. Cox was quickly followed by other fliers, including Captain Victor Dallin of the Aero Service Corporation; Cleon Krause, the son of the mayor of Stone Harbor; and Captain D. K. Steele, a flying instructor from Princeton University. Public interest in aviation was high throughout the entire decade and flying exhibitions did much to attract visitors to the shore. (In later years, other pilots flying from the beach included Bill James, Harold Sherwood, Curt Young, Andre Tomalino, Ed Kotz, and Pat Ward).

NOTEWORTHY PEOPLE

Like flying exhibitions, musical entertainment retained its popularity. Band concerts were still attended, but the era of the great concert bands, like Sousa's, was all but over. Throughout the 1920s, the band concerts continued to lose audiences to the modern entertainments of the jazz age. Nevertheless, Wildwood maintained a contract with a concert band throughout the decade. In late 1920, the Casino Auditorium was rented to out-of-town interests, prompting fears that without a concert hall the Board of Trade might not hire a band for 1921. As a result, the city took responsibility for booking a musical organization and replaced Pfeiffer's

Queen Oceana and her court reign over the Baby Parade events of 1929.
– Wildwood Historical Society

Orchestra with Roselli's Band. Throughout the summer, the twenty-piece group gave free concerts on the somewhat dilapidated Atlantic Pier.

The city considered band concerts so important to the season's success that it increased the budget for bands from $5,000 in 1921 to $22,000 in 1928 (a year in which ten bands bid for the contract). In 1927 and 1928, the city booked one of the country's best bands, that of Patrick Conway. In fact, had Conway lived, his contract with the resort would have been renewed in 1929. Instead, the city contracted with three bands for shorter engagements. First came Roy Smith and his Kiltie Band in full Scottish regalia, followed by Everett Moses and his band from

St.Petersburg, Florida, and lastly, the Royal Venetian Band. Concerts were moved to the new Convention Hall in 1928, and amplifiers were installed so the music could be heard by people relaxing on the beach.

While the older timers reminisced to the music of the band concert, the ballrooms and modern dance orchestras attracted the younger set. In 1921, Byrne and Dillard, part owners of Atlantic City's Rendezvous Park, leased the Casino Auditorium where they laid a new maple dance floor that could accommodate 400 couples, surrounded the floor with a railing for spectators, and entirely redecorated the auditorium. The first bands to appear in the revamped facility were the Novelty Five String Orchestra, composed of students from Columbia and Indiana Universities, and the Royal Marimba Band, a popular group with records on both the Columbia and Victor labels. Jazz was king at the new Casino Danceland, and soon residents who lived near the Boardwalk were complaining about the loud music from the "jazziest of the jazz bands." Danceland was again redecorated in a rainbow of colors in 1928. That summer, Haffer's Orchestra played while Helen and Norman Smith gave an exhibition of the daring Adagio on the hall's dance floor.

An army surplus "Jenny" gave airplane rides from the beach during the early 1920s.
– Wildwood Historical Society

The Casino Danceland was an immediate hit, but it was not the only place to dance in the Wildwoods. On the Wildwood Crest Municipal Pier a number of bands appeared, including the very popular Holmes-Baker Orchestra, lead by Ralph Holmes. Bill Hunt also entered the ballroom business, opening Hunt's Plaza Pier Dance Hall. The featured band at Hunt's was the Roy Seagraves Orchestra, which played every evening and on rainy afternoons. Dancing had been popular in the Wildwoods since the 1890s, but it reached new heights during the 1920s.

Wildwood enjoyed a promotional windfall in 1922 when a Philadelphia company published the song, "I'm Wild About Wildwood" by Harry Keating, David Morrison, and Ed Ward. The song was a moderate success, quickly selling 2,000 copies in 100 cities. It was played on the band organ at Rhoads's carousel, and featured by performer Ed Morton in his act on the Keith vaudeville circuit. But the song had more ties to Wildwood than just its name and the beach scene depicted on sheet music. Composer Keating had lived in Wildwood since 1900, and he opened a music store at the resort in 1922. Singer Ed Morton was also a Wildwood resident, and, when vaudeville began to decline, he built three stores on the Boardwalk at 26th Street.

PIER EXPANSIONS

By the time the First World War ended the resort's piers and amusements had endured several years of shortages of both construction and maintenance materials. With the war over, materials again became available, piers were revamped and modernized and new facilities were constructed. Once again, amusement entrepreneurs and investors from up and down the East Coast were turning an eye toward Wildwood. In 1924, for example, Coney Island music hall and restaurant operators Louis Stauch and James Hildreth visited Wildwood and considered the resort for an expansion of their operations.

In 1922, the Atlantic Pier, which had suffered from a lack of maintenance in recent years, was leased to J. A. Miller, an experienced concessionaire from Cleveland who had operated midway attractions at Chicago's 1893 World's Fair. Miller began plans to recondition and expand the pier

and established year-round boxing matches in 1923. Allison's Pier also initiated boxing matches and attempted to compete with the larger Ocean Pier during the early 1920s. Allison's Pier, however, suffered a major publicity blow in 1924 when two people were seriously injured when a portion of the floor collapsed onto the sand below. After this incident, this pier seems to have faded away into obscurity.

Built during the winter of 1919-20 at Wildwood Avenue, the Wildwood Excursion Pier was generally known as Luff's Pier. The structure was owned by Edward Luff, F. H. Luff, and F. H. Luff, Jr., all from Palisades Park across the river from Manhattan. Luff's Pier was small by amusement pier standards, with a total length of just 400 feet. Decorated in white and green, the pier had a fishing area, some concessions, and one amusement

The Atlantic Pier during the 1920s. The streets near the pier are lined with small hotels and boardinghouses.
– Wildwood Historical Society

Luff's Pier (center) had too few amusements to seriously compete with Ocean Pier or Casino Pier. – Wildwood Historical Society

Luff's Excursion Pier (foreground) was one of the first amusement enterprises built after the war. – Wildwood Historical Society

ride, the Whip. This ride was something of an innovation in 1920 having been invented only a few years before by Coney Island ride builder, William Mangels. The Luffs also obtained a permit to operate a Shetland pony track next to the pier in a rope-enclosed corral. The track featured six bareback ponies and another six ponies to pull small chariots.

Probably because of its limited offerings Luff's Pier was not able to compete with the much larger Ocean Pier. In 1922, the Luffs lost their lease on the property when the land owner, Asa Colson, sold his Boardwalk properties. Luff's pier stood idle and decaying until late in the 1923 season when it was taken over by Frank D. Allison and renamed Allison's Pier. Allison, who had been an operator of concessions on the Boardwalk, hired a Philadelphia decorating firm to revamp the neglected pier. Exposed pilings were covered, new planking was laid, and the weakened structure was buttressed with fifty new pilings. New electric lights were installed, buildings were painted, a new dance floor was constructed, and flags of all nations were placed on the building roofs. Although he wasn't much more successful than the Luffs had been, Allison did manage to keep his pier open for a number of seasons.

Farther to the south, the Crest Pier in Wildwood Crest was destroyed by fire in 1919. Out of the ruins came a new Crest Pier that opened in late May of 1921. This pier featured a billiards hall, Hunt's Crest Theatre (complete with a fire-proof projection booth), a confectionery that served Breyer's ice cream, and a combination auditorium and dance hall that was initiated with the music of Julia Baker's Ladies Orchestra.

The Crest Pier was always more sedate than the raucous piers to the north. Children's parties were held every Monday afternoon, and on Sunday nights, Ted Nash led customers in traditional "song-fests." The Crest Pier never attracted huge crowds, consequently, it was difficult to keep concessionaires. In 1929, when bids went out for the 1930 season, only one bid each was submitted for the operation of the gift shop, bowling alleys, and billiards hall. No one even bothered to submit bids for the novelty stand, post cards, cameras, tobaccos, ice cream, candy, or light lunch operations. By then, however, Wildwood Crest Council had already determined that the Crest Pier, although less than a decade old, was a worn out disgrace. Council voted unanimously to begin plans for a new pier.

The Ocean Pier continued to reign as queen of the Wildwood piers, and because of its popularity, the owners were constantly able to upgrade and improve it. The original

The southern end of Wildwood Crest was still largely undeveloped during the mid-1920s. In the distance is the Crest Pier and the fishing pier. – Library Company of Philadelphia

The second Crest Pier, constructed after the original pier was levelled by fire.
– Wildwood Crest Historical Society

owners, Buckborn and Reynolds, decided to cash in on their success, and in the winter of 1921-22, sold the Ocean Pier to the Wildwood Pier and Realty Company for just over $350,000. A key shareholder in this newly formed company was William Lipkin, a Philadelphia real estate agent who would play a prominent role in the development of Wildwood amusement facilities during the 1920s. The new owners invested more than

The Ocean Pier after it underwent a major renovation and the addition of a new facade during the early 1920s. Note the huge electric sign on top of the Funchase structure and the giant slide enclosure protruding from the roof to the right of the sign.
– Newark Public Library

$50,000 in the pier. They constructed a facade along the Boardwalk, installed a balcony, enlarged the ballroom, re-equipped the bath-houses, and added a 100-foot pavilion for weary customers. Another $25,000 was spent to install a massive, Atlantic City-style electric sign on the pier that measured 37 feet high by 80 feet long. A year later, the company purchased a new Ferris wheel and several other rides. Other innovations of the 1922-23 period included a pogo stick race course and a radiophone designed to receive radio transmissions from far out at sea.

The pier's great roller skating rink was leased to Joe Barnes, Sr., an experienced rink manager who operated the Rollerdrome at Philadelphia's Woodside Park, Skateland at Willow Grove Park, and another rink in the Adelphia Building in Wildwood. Under his direction, the Ocean Pier rink soon became the leading skating palace in Wildwood, offering afternoon and evening skating sessions, numerous skating contests, and classes in roller skating.

The new ballroom, now expanded in size to 90 feet by 150 feet, was acclaimed one of the largest and most beautiful in New Jersey. The walls were accented in shades of green, and orange shades were installed over the lights to impart a soft, romantic atmosphere. Harry Roselle, who had already been at Wildwood for twenty-four years in 1922, was appointed Director of Dancing and was assisted by his daughter, Laura. Roselle

engaged the most popular East Coast bands of the early 1920s, including Bud's Orchestra, Sam Lilley's University of Pennsylvania Sextette, and Mike Fish's Varsity Six, also from Penn. Roselle initiated an unending array of contests and special events, one of the most successful of which was the 1922 Flapper Contest. Contestants were entered in one of four categories: red hair, blond hair, brunette hair, and best dressed flapper. Predictably, Roselle's Flapper Contest drew in hundreds of young men willing to pay for a ticket to see several dozen attractive, well-dressed young ladies in flapper attire.

SPORTLAND

The Ocean Pier enjoyed phenomenal business during the 1920s and William Lipkin, as one of the major shareholders, made enough money to allow him to invest in other major properties including the large Wildwood Manor Hotel. Then, prior to the 1928 season, Lipkin sold the hotel for $175,000 in order to help finance his most ambitious project, Sportland. Built along the North Wildwood Boardwalk between 23rd and 24th Avenues, Sportland was conceived as a complete sports facility for the entire family. With construc-

The magnificent swimming pool at Sportland.
– David W. Francis Collection

The solid, brick facade of Sportland (right) was in marked contrast to the flammable, wooden construction of the Ocean Pier (left).
– Historical Society of Pennsylvania

Much of the North Wildwood Boardwalk property was still undeveloped when Sportland (right) opened in 1928.
– Wildwood Historical Society

which was equipped with a music platform where orchestras provided "music to swim by." Lipkin's ultimate sports facility also incorporated hand ball courts, a boxing ring, running tracks, golf practice nets, quoits, broad jump pits, basketball courts, volley ball and tennis courts, a children's play area and wading pool, and even a physician to advise customers regarding exercise and health. For those who motored to Wildwood, Lipkin provided a parking lot that could accommodate 1,000 cars.

Sportland opened on June 30, 1928, to great fanfare and a full bill of athletic events. There was an eight-mile marathon race featuring a Penn State cross country champion and the man who had recently taken third place in the Coney Island Marathon. There were also swimming competitions and professional boxing matches in the arena that became famous as the "Punch Bowl."

tion costs variously estimated between $300,000 and $750,000, Sportland featured a solid brick front housing eight Boardwalk stores. Behind this brick facade was a massive swimming pool with a depth of almost 10 feet and a 2,500,000 gallon water system that pumped, filtered, and, when needed, heated seawater for the pool. Sixteen hundred pagoda-style bathhouses surrounded the pool

Rhoads's carousel featured four rows of exquisitely carved horses and two large chariots for those who did not wish to sit astride a horse. – Philadelphia Toboggan Coasters, Inc.

This elegant carousel, built by the Philadelphia Toboggan Company in 1917, became the centerpiece of Rhoads's new Amusement Center. – Philadelphia Toboggan Coasters, Inc.

The Jack Rabbit coaster and the Amusement Center are clearly visible in this mid-1920s photograph. To the right of the Amusement Center is the Casino Pier, and further north is the Ocean Pier. – Library Company of Philadelphia

Lipkin, who apparently preferred to be a developer rather than an operator, enjoyed a successful first season and then promptly sold Sportland to the First National Mortgage Corporation of New York City for $1,500,000. Considering that the local economy was already faltering early in 1929 and the national economy was soon to collapse, Lipkin's uncanny timing allowed him to walk away with more than $1,000,000 in profits and distanced him from the terrible financial crisis that Sportland faced during the 1930s.

THE AMUSEMENT CENTER

Others also saw the post-war years as an excellent time to install new amusement facilities in the Wildwoods. Gilbert Blaker, who had been active in the development of the resort for three decades, had become one of the area's largest landholders. Over the years, and especially between 1912 and 1913, Blaker had acquired all of the land between Cedar and Schellenger Avenues. This area, known as the Blaker Block where it fronted the Boardwalk, was ideal for further development. However, Blaker, by now sixty-five, appears to have had no personal interest in any grandiose plans for developing the Blaker Block. In 1918, Blaker was approached by Edward E. Rhoads, who owned Carsonia Park in Reading, Pennsylvania, and also operated amusement rides at Old Orchard Beach, Maine. Rhoads proposed to convert the Blaker Block into an amusement park. In return for stocks and bonds in the Carsonia Park Company and in other Rhoads enter-

prises, Blaker would contribute the use of the land and Rhoads would build the park and acquire the rides.

The first step in the construction of what came to be called the Amusement Center was the installation of a carousel for the 1918 season. Rhoads contacted the Philadelphia Toboggan Company, one of the leading builders of carousels and roller coasters, and purchased a one-year-old carousel for $15,000. Installed at the corner of Cedar Avenue and the Boardwalk, Rhoads's carousel was a wonderfully ornate three-abreast machine, with elegant horses, heavily carved chariots, oil paintings on the frame, and 1,564 electric light bulbs. These lamps were originally to have been multi-colored, but wartime shortages forced Rhoads to settle on clear bulbs for the 1918 season. Nevertheless, the new carousel was a glorious sight and the most attractive carousel ever installed in the Wildwoods.

After the 1918 season, Rhoads returned to Wildwood and announced that he would install a roller coaster, Old Mill, Ferris wheel, Whip, a Frolic, and other rides for 1919, "...if the proper encouragement is extended to him." In mid-October Rhoads and Blaker appeared before the city commissioners and outlined plans for the $100,000 amusement park. However, in order to construct the park, Rhoads needed fifty feet of vacated city land on Ocean Avenue. In exchange for other land, the city deeded this property to Rhoads and Blaker. Later, Rhoads complained about the electric rates that he was to be charged and noted that he paid far lower rates at his parks in Pennsylvania and Maine. Obligingly, the West Jersey Electric Company reduced its rates for the Rhoads enterprise. Much later, Rhoads again appeared before the commissioners and requested special tax considerations. Clearly, the "proper encouragement" had been extended to Rhoads.

With all of the obstructions cleared and wartime shortages abating, Rhoads was ready to proceed with construction. In December of 1918, he hired John A. Miller, a prolific roller coaster engineer from Homewood, Illinois, to design the Jack Rabbit roller coaster and the Old Mill ride. By early 1919, Ed Lauterbach was supervising the construction of both rides. While Rhoads raced back and forth between Wildwood and his Philadelphia home in his six-cylinder Packard, he advertised for carpenters and laborers to begin work in February. Carpenters were offered sixty cents an hour and ninety cents for overtime; laborers were given from $3.50 to $4.00 for a ten-hour workday. By spring, rides, shooting galleries, games, and food concessions were in place and the new Amusement Center opened for the 1919 season.

The Amusement Center seems to have been a profitable venture, but by 1925, Blaker's health was failing (he died in 1928), and Rhoads found that he needed more time to devote to his other holdings. As a result,

When the new Boardwalk was completed, the carousel and Jack Rabbit roller coaster at Ed Rhoads's new Amusement Center faced the new walk. – David W. Francis Collection

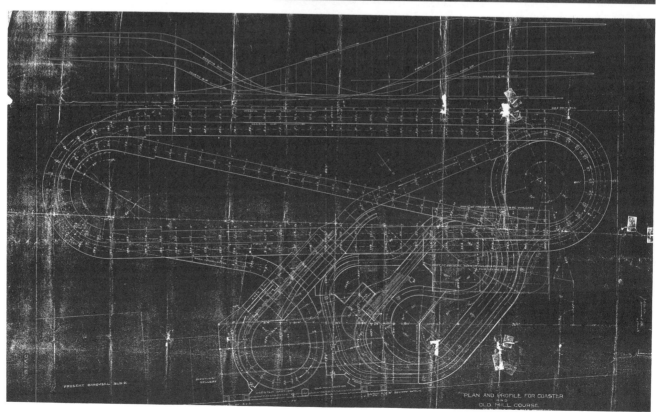

both men sought buyers for the Amusement Center. In 1926, the property was sold to Charles Hamburger and Benjamin C. Sagel, both of Atlantic City. However, it seems that they were not able to keep up with the payments on the property. By 1928, mortgages held by Edward Rhoads, the estate of Gilbert Blaker, and a group of Wildwood business people, were in the process of foreclosure. At this point, Palmer M. Way, Robert J. Kay, and eight other men and women, some of whom were the holders of a fourth mortgage, formed the Cedar-Schellenger Corporation. The corporation acquired the Blaker Block, all of the amusement facilities on the property, and riparian rights to utilize the beach in front of the property. Thanks to the aggressive management of this new company, the property would evolve into the Marine Pier and would become one of the leading amusement enterprises in the Wildwoods.

THE BEACH CONTINUES TO EXPAND

Even as the Boardwalk was being moved eastward to be closer to the sea, the beach continued to widen. The process was accelerated during the 1920s when a jetty built at Cold Spring Inlet to protect Cape May Harbor proved even more of a benefit to the beach at the Wildwoods. The fame of the broad Wildwood beach spread across the country and crowds on the strand reached new highs during the 1920s. On August 23, 1926, the captain of the Wildwood Beach Patrol estimated that more than twenty thousand people were frolicking on the sand beneath a sea of vividly colored beach umbrellas. In order to accommodate the immense crowds that flocked to the beach, there were, in 1920, 2,588 individual bathhouses along the Boardwalk. A large operation, like Sweet's or the Casino, could encompass several hundred of these small changing rooms, as well as showers, hot and cold saltwater baths, and a rental stand for umbrellas, chairs, and other necessities. The number of bathhouses was reduced abruptly in the early morning hours of July 4, 1923, when Sweet's Baths were totally consumed by fire. Considered the "Finest Bath House on the New Jersey Coast," the loss of this large facility was estimated at $100,000.

Over the years, the beach patrols had become vital to public safety. With the great increase in beach usage, the size of the beach patrol in each of the three communities was expanded, salaries for lifeguards were

twenty-four years. Tough, demanding, and dedicated, Hoffman made the beach at Wildwood among the safest in the world. He tolerated no violation of rules among bathers and showed no mercy for a lifeguard that shirked his duties. As a result, Hoffman became a legend in Wildwood and all along the Jersey Shore.

The beach patrols, assisted by the police forces when necessary, were responsible for enforcing the rules established for the beaches. As the years went by, the list of rules became longer and, in 1926, included: No spooning or objectionable conduct; no bathing in unacceptable attire; no alcoholic beverages permitted on the beach; no intoxicated bathers permitted in the water; no

increased and, in Wildwood, an Indian motorcycle was purchased to speed guards to trouble spots. Indicative of the growing crowds and the difficulties to be faced in controlling large numbers of people, the Wildwood Beach Patrol grew from a captain and eighteen guards in 1920 to a corps of fifty-two guards in 1927.

It was during this period that Wildwood's most famous lifeguard, Frank "Dutch" Hoffman, came to the resort. He was just fourteen when he first served as a lifeguard in the Philadelphia area. He then attended the Pennsylvania Military College, and played professional football for the Frankford Yellow Jackets. Hoffman passed the test for lifeguard at Wildwood in 1925, became a lieutenant during the 1930s, and was promoted to Director of the Wildwood Beach Patrol in 1938, a position he held for

Incinerated Boardwalk stores that disappeared in the Sweet's Bath fire.
– Wildwood Historical Society

automobiles, bicycles, or motorcycles on the beach. Dogs were permitted, but only if muzzled and leashed, and ball playing was restricted to roped areas. The provisions dealing with alcoholic beverages gave evidence to the fact that prohibition laws were not always followed at the resort. The lifeguards were proficient at enforcing the beach regulations strictly, but there were constantly new challenges for the beach patrols and the police. In 1929, residents began to complain about people who were branded "gypsy bathers." These were people who parked their cars near the beach, changed into bathing attire in the cars, scattered the remains of

A restaurant, shooting gallery, and other Boardwalk stores wiped out by fire.
– Wildwood Historical Society

picnic lunches near the strand, and, in most cases contributed little or nothing to the economy. The police approached the problem by posting notices that dressing in parked cars was illegal and began arresting anyone caught changing clothes in vehicles. This issue continued to surface for the next two decades.

Another beach-related controversy arose in 1925, when the mayor of Wildwood was informed that many residents, visitors, and merchants were offended by people who strolled the Boardwalk dressed in nothing but their bathing suits. Despite the fact that men were not permitted to be bare-chested on the beach or on the Boardwalk, many found the bathing suit too improper for the Boardwalk. The mayor ordered the police to enforce a law that required proper coverings to be worn over all bathing suits when on the Boardwalk or city streets. One issue which the mayor's decree could not solve was the oil that began to wash up on the Jersey Shore in 1922. The substance was being dumped at sea or pumped out of bilges on oil-burning and oil-carrying ships. For the first time, the communities had to deal with the problem of oil that killed fish and birds, and fouled the shoreline. Unfortunately, this was only the beginning of pollution concerns that would increase in severity in the decades ahead.

ACCOMMODATING CONVENTIONS

The growth of the Wildwoods after the war and the relative prosperity of the decade brought increased numbers of conventions and one-day excursions to the resort. The one-day excursions, still arriving mostly by train, were an important part of the summer economy in the Wildwoods. In 1928, fifty-nine major outings sponsored by corporations, labor unions, and fraternal organizations selected Wildwood rather than Atlantic City, Asbury Park, or any of New Jersey's scores of amusement parks for their summer outings. The number of smaller excursions, including those of churches and schools, went uncounted. In 1926, the Westinghouse Electric and Manufacturing Company of Philadelphia brought 2,500 employees and their families to Wildwood, while during a period of just a few days in early July, 1927, more than twenty thousand enjoyed one-day outings. These included such diverse organizations as the Green Street Methodist Episcopal Church, The Grand Fraternity of Philadelphia, the Colwyn Fire Company, the Eddystone Manufacturing Company, and the Polish-American Society, that alone counted for more than 6,000 of the visitors.

These day-long excursions were usually favored by the Boardwalk merchants, but understandably, held little interest for the hotel and restaurant owners. These business people depended on the multi-day conventions that filled hotels to capacity and created long waiting lines in front of restaurants. Typical of the conventions seen in 1922 were the New Jersey Hotel Association, the New Jersey Movie Men's Association, the Odd Fellows Lodges, the Daughters of Rebecca, and the New Jersey American Legion. The latter convention was won away from Atlantic City and Ocean City when representatives of Wildwood's business community visited the Legion's convention at Lake

Hopatcong and convinced them that Wildwood had more to offer than its neighbors to the north. Many of these events were huge and sometimes taxed even the extensive facilities of the Wildwoods. In 1927, the Odd Fellows from three states established their headquarters in the Hotel Dayton and entertained more than twenty thousand lodge members and their families.

Competition among the Jersey Shore resorts for these large conventions was keen, and Atlantic City, with its massive hotels, always had some advantage over the other resorts. Aside from a lack of large hotels, Wildwood's major disadvantage was not having a suitable convention hall facility. Large conventions found it difficult to conduct major meetings, and convention sessions had to be planned in ballrooms, hotel meeting rooms, and even in the fire stations. By 1926, it was clear that Wildwood needed to either construct a convention hall or lose business to Atlantic City and Asbury Park. Mayor Edward Culver appointed a committee of five businessmen to select a site for a hall and begin the necessary planning. There was, however, the matter of cost and the issue of how the city was to finance this large undertaking. At this point, Edward Fagan proposed that his Holly Beach Realty Company construct the building and lease it to the city for $12,000 per year. This proposal met with everyone's approval, and late in 1926, the realty company obtained a building permit, began architectural drawings, and in early 1927, started selling $500 shares in a $150,000 trust mortgage. By mid-winter, architect Lynn H. Boyer had completed drawings for the building and a local contractor, C. J. Scully & Sons, began work on the facility at Spencer and Young Avenues.

A group of young ladies visiting the resort in 1922 pose on the steps of the Wildwood Manor Hotel. – Cape May County Historical and Genealogical Society

Finally completed at a cost of about a half million dollars, the hall was built on pilings much like the amusement piers. The building was designed to seat four thousand, and included a clear-span auditorium, a completely equipped stage, and a balcony. In order to help offset some of the cost, eighteen stores were built on the front of the structure facing the Boardwalk and in the entrance arcade. These were quickly rented to merchants. Measuring 200 feet wide, the completed hall was supported by a modern steel superstructure and stretched 321 feet onto the beach. The Scully organization finished the hall in time for the first convention to use the facility on June 24, 1927. Finally, the Wildwoods were positioned to attract the largest of conventions and were able to compete on a fairly even scale with Atlantic City, Asbury Park, and Ocean City.

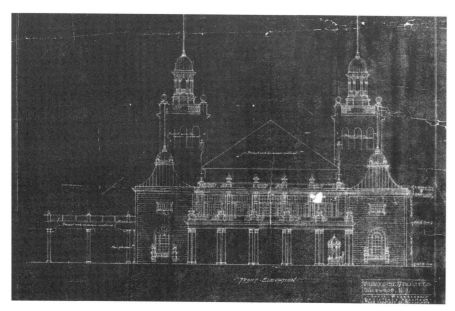

Blueprint of 1927 Convention Hall
– Wildwood Historical Society

The new Convention Hall immediately after construction had been completed. By this time, the Boardwalk was much wider than it had been during the early 1900s. – Robert J. Scully Collection

Viewed from the south, it is obvious that the Convention Hall was designed along the lines of an amusement pier. – Lake County (IL) Museum/Curt Teich Postcard Archives

The Boardwalk entrance to Wildwood's Convention Hall, showing the stores that helped provide revenue for the costly new showcase of the resort. – Lake County (IL) Museum/Curt Teich Postcard Archives

Above: Architect Lynn Boyer's rendering of the new Convention Hall. – Ron Franks Collection

CONVENTION ACCOMMODATIONS

The new Wildwood Convention Hall was a boon to the hotel business, but few hotel proprietors had reason to complain even before the hall was constructed. In fact, the hotel business was generally very good from 1919 through the 1929 season. Most hotel owners took advantage of excellent business conditions to expand and recondition their hostelries. In 1921, the Hotel Dayton, still one of the resort's most prominent lodging houses, was expanded from seventy-four to eighty rooms. In addition, sixteen private baths were built, and, for the first time, the old hotel installed an elevator. When the Wildwood Manor opened for the 1923 season, the resort's largest hotel had spent $100,000 for a facelift of the exterior, refurbishing of the porch, and remodelling of the lobby and guest rooms.

There were also new hotels built at the resort, like the elegant Hotel Seville constructed in Spanish-style on the Boardwalk at Maple Avenue. Advertised as "The Commercial Man's Hotel," the entire structure was finished in stucco. There were tiled roofs on the towers, and each room was shaded with striped awnings. The entrance was ornamented with attractive gardens and near the doors, carefully arranged plants spelled "Seville." In 1927, Manager Edward McGarry opened the swank Castillian Room at the Seville. Music was provided by Club Seville Toreadors, imported from Hollywood, and the suave, Bohemian atmosphere of the new supper club attracted many Broadway stars and theatrical greats who made the Seville their summer headquarters.

As opulent as the Seville may have been, Wildwood still could not offer any hotel that rivaled the massive Boardwalk hotels of Atlantic City or even the new Hotel Flanders in Ocean City. The Flanders in particular rankled the promoters of the Wildwoods. The Flanders had not been financed and built by a large corporation, but rather was the result of a civic effort by 1,072 people who subscribed $856,000 for the construction of the hotel.

Hotel Fenwick was a typical small resort hotel of the 1920s. Located opposite the Pennsylvania Railroad station, the Fenwick offered a dining room and reasonable rates.
– Cape May County Historical and Genealogical Society

Hotel Seville on Ocean Avenue was the first hotel in the resort to employ an architectural theme. Forty years later, such motifs would be common on motel facades.
– Wildwood Historical Society

Everyone in the Wildwoods agreed that the resort's desperately needed a large, ocean-front hotel and the community was overjoyed during the summer of 1925 when the Wildwood Hotel Corporation announced plans to build the 300-room Hotel Philip Baker at Wildwood Avenue and the Boardwalk. The hotel was to be open by Memorial Day of the following year. By early in 1926, the corporation held title to seven tracts of land, including 154 feet of Boardwalk frontage and corresponding riparian rights. At this point, however, things began to unravel. The number of rooms was reduced from 300 to 250, and plans for the swimming pool were scrapped. When Memorial Day of 1926 arrived, construction had not even begun, and by mid-season of 1926, it

was clear the Wildwood Hotel Corporation could not obtain the financing necessary to proceed. Now, the example of Ocean City and Hotel Flanders surfaced, and a civic committee was formed to subscribe enough money to build the Hotel Philip Baker. By late August, the committee claimed that $481,600 had been pledged to the project. Unlike Ocean City, however, Wildwood was never able to obtain enough pledges to make the hotel a reality. Within a few years, the real estate boom in the Wildwoods would collapse, and all hope for a grand, fire-proof hotel faded into memory.

DEALS ON WHEELS

Most of those who came to stay in Wildwood hotels during the early 1920s still arrived by train from Philadelphia and other cities. However, automobiles, buses, and even trucks were steadily cutting into railroad patronage. The State of New Jersey and its counties spent large amounts of money to improve the local highway system, and in 1924 the new Grassy Sound Bridge connected the northern section of the island's roads with Ocean Drive. By late in the decade, the automobile had taken control of travel. On the last weekend of July, 1928, 14,000 people arrived on trains, while 25,000 automobiles transported 100,000 visitors. Over Labor Day of that same year, 37,000 passengers stepped off trains, while 175,000 arrived in cars.

The railroads, however, still offered passenger service throughout most of the 1920s. The Reading Railroad set new records for numbers of passengers taken to the New Jersey coast from Philadelphia in 1920. Over the July 4th holiday, the road carried 74,533 passengers to the coast (8,000 to Wildwood), and on Labor Day weekend, ticket sales reached 78,669 (Wildwood was second only to Atlantic City, with 12,000 passengers destined for Five Mile Beach). Special one-day excursions hit a new high in 1923 when, between June 25 and September 9, 295 trains transported 177,084 people to the Wildwoods. Excursions ran from as far away as Pittsburgh and New York City, and the three dollar ticket from New York was considered an outstanding bargain.

Responding to a 1924 business climate that was still solid, if not quite what it had been around 1910, the Reading Railroad opened the new Camden Terminal. Built especially for seashore service, the terminal included four ferry slips and a train shed and connected the railroad with the Delaware River Ferry Company's ships, making service from Philadelphia easier. The monies spent to build the terminal were apparently well spent. On one Sunday in 1925, there were 243 coaches on the sidings waiting to take passengers back to the cities after a big summer weekend. As evening approached, there was always a mad scramble for seats on the returning trains, and as often as not, there was nothing but standing room when the train pulled out of the station. Sometimes crowds dashing for the departing trains led to tragic accidents, as happened in 1921, when a boy fell beneath the wheels of a passenger coach and was killed.

The resort's business community constantly begged for more railroad service, and the railroads did their best to assign engines and passenger coaches to the shore routes. Over Labor Day of 1927, the rail services were sorely taxed when 32,000 people took the Reading route to the shore, while another 15,000 bought tickets for the Pennsylvania Railroad. And that was only a fraction of the total number of visitors that visited the shore that weekend. After it was all over, 1927's Labor Day weekend was declared the best in the resort's history, or at least in the past twenty-one years. All tolled, the resort's businesses deposited more than one million dollars in the banks after Labor Day. Douglass Candies and Hunt's Theatres set new records, and hotel operators claimed to have had the best weekend in resort history. The railroads brought 47,000 people, but this was probably less than twenty-five percent of the people who came to the resort that Labor Day weekend. The biggest problem for the two railroads lie in the fact that they were forced to share an ever-declining number of passengers. It was clear that as ticket sales continued to slip, both railroads would lose money. Realizing this, the Reading Railroad and the Pennsylvania Railroad began holding joint meetings in 1929 to discuss the possibility of consolidating their services to the shore and eliminating redundant stretches of track and stations.

While the railroads and new highways made travel from the north and the west easier and faster during the 1920s, visitors coming from Washington, Maryland, Virginia, Delaware, and various southern states were forced to make a long trip north before turning east. By 1925, merchants in the Wildwoods began to realize that the travel distance between southern cities and Cape May County could be substantially reduced by operating a passenger and automobile ferry line from Lewes, Delaware, to Cape May. Although the dream of a ferry connection would resurface regularly, it would be almost forty years before enough financing could be found to make the dream a reality.

REAL ESTATE BOOM AND BUST

If one factor would define the Wildwoods and Cape May County in the 1920s it would certainly have to be the real estate boom that lasted for most of the decade. Those who bought and sold real estate at the shore often made great profits in just a short period of time. In fact, so profitable was the real estate business that some bootleggers complained there was more money in selling land than in selling illegal liquor and beer.

One of the most active land investors was William Lipkin, new owner of the Ocean Pier and the builder of Sportland. Lipkin bought one block of land in 1923 for $115,000, and sold it a year later for $135,000. In 1922, he bought the Wildwood Manor Hotel for $20,000 and sold it six years later for $175,000. Lipkin also purchased 1,200 acres on Two Mile Beach for $450,000. In 1925, he sold much of his property for $700,000.

There was no shortage of buyers for the land offered by the real estate agents. In 1923, John Ackley's annual August real estate auction grossed $500,000. Two years later, Ackley's and Day's real estate auctions reported combined sales of $4,000,000. By 1925, the real estate boom was at its zenith. One tract of land sold for $150,000 in 1923 and $350,000 in 1925. Within days, it was back on the market with a price tag of $500,000. The Sagel Block sold for $330,000, the block between Pine and Maple Streets for $500,000, and the Biltmore Hotel for $175,000. A tiny piece of land on Pacific Avenue sold for $12,000 a foot! In an effort to create even more land, thirty-seven acres of ocean front was dredged and filled in to create eight new city blocks near the Hotel Ottens.

Exploiting the increase in land values, owners of Boardwalk properties raised rents dramatically. One Boardwalk merchant paid $550 to rent his store in 1922. In 1923, he returned from a winter in Florida to find that his rent had more than doubled to $1,250. Some merely tolerated the increases, but this merchant promptly sold his fixtures and stock and left the resort.

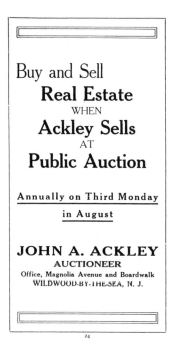
Like the one in Florida, the Cape May County land boom could not last forever. Eventually, prices became so inflated that buyers disappeared and land owners were saddled with over-priced land they could not unload. It was 1926 when the land speculation in Cape May County finally peaked, tottered, and collapsed. Along the Boardwalk, land maintained a high commercial value through 1929, but mostly, values plummeted rapidly. In one authenticated story, a plot of land along the coast that was purchased for $75,000 before 1926, sold for a mere $750 after the market collapsed. Ackley's auction for 1929 reported dismal results. Most real estate men blamed investors who had placed too much money in the stock market, but, in fact, the artificially inflated land values along the coast had simply gone as high as the market would bear before beginning to slide. In some ways, the great economic decline that pervaded the country in 1930, actually began for many Wildwoods' businessmen late in 1926.

WEATHERING THE STORMS

The collapse of the land boom, however, was not the only tragedy to plague the resort during the 1920s. As always, vicious weather wreaked its share of havoc. Although a major storm hit the resort on December 3, 1923, the worst weather disaster of the decade came in mid-October of that year when a violent storm slashed into the island. Buildings swayed in the wind and those in danger of collapse were roped off to keep the curious away. The beach was littered with debris, hot dog stands were levelled, benches were swept off the Crest Pier, and broken parts of buildings dotted the Boardwalk.

Even worse than the unpredictable weather was the constant threat of fire on the wooden Boardwalk. Carelessly discarded cigarettes, faulty electrical wiring, cooking equipment, lightning strikes, and even defective neon signs were responsible for numerous Boardwalk blazes. In 1920, alarms brought the fire department racing to the Boardwalk twenty times. The next year, there were twenty-one fire alarms; eighteen in 1922; nineteen in 1923; and an upsetting forty-six in 1924. The Crest Pier, Hotel Ottens, and Hotel Poplars all suffered serious fire damage in 1919. And, the Hotel Dayton, then the dowager queen of Wildwood hotels, sustained $65,000 worth of damage from a fire in 1929. The decade's major blaze came on July 4, 1923, at Sweet's Baths, destroying the baths and threatening the Amusement Center and Blaker's Theatre.

The period from 1919 through 1929 was, in general, an excellent era of growth and prosperity in the Wildwoods. Business was usually good, thanks in part to mostly favorable weather conditions. Money was available to be spent on a new Boardwalk and modern theatres. The Ocean Pier was reconstructed, new piers were added, and Sportland made its debut. The season of 1929 was the best year to date, and became the high water mark against which summers would be judged and evaluated for two decades to come. But the 1920s also had a darker side. The economy was uneven, with wartime shortages extending well into 1919. There was also the post-war recession of 1920-21, the collapse of the land boom in 1926, and occasional dips in the generally strong economy of the era. Some of the resort's greatest early leaders, including two of the Bakers and Gilbert Blaker, died during the decade. The railroads remained profitable through most of the 1920s, but declining ticket sales forecasted the future. Gambling, illegal liquor, and prostitution, were important moral issues, but these same issues were faced by every resort in the country. Off-season unemployment was a concern, but it was no worse than it had been since the 1890s.

Over the next fifteen years, the world would experience an economic depression of astounding proportions and a war that would leave no one untouched. Both the good and the bad of the 1920s would be forgotten in this new era of concerns.

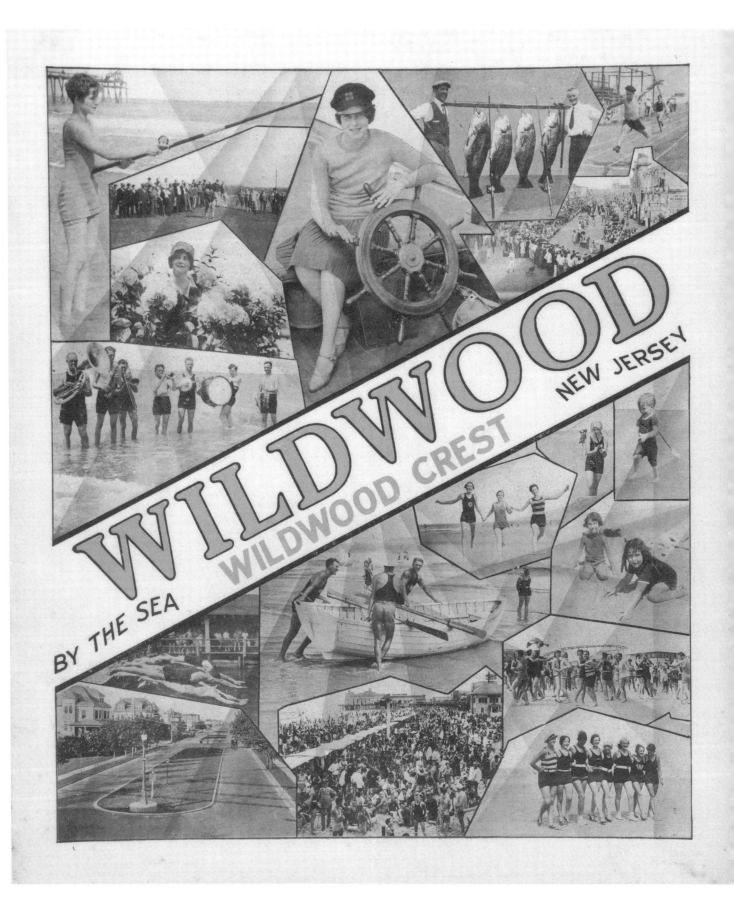

WILDWOOD

WILDWOOD CREST

NEW JERSEY

BY THE SEA

PROPERTY OF WILDWOOD HISTORICAL SOCIETY

A SUMMER RESORT DURING DEPRESSION AND WAR

*T*he Great Depression of the 1930s struck the Wildwoods and the other resorts of the Jersey Shore with particular severity. Because the services provided by a summer resort are non-essential, resorts may suffer only moderate declines during recessions. However, during major economic depressions or panics, such as those of the 1890s and 1930s, resorts face a vicious fight for survival.

CHAPTER 5

In fact, every segment of the amusement industry came near to extinction during the 1930s. Vaudeville, which malingered throughout the 1920s, finally expired. On Broadway, two-thirds of the theatres were dark, and the once-great Shubert theatrical company went into receivership. The motion picture industry had grown steadily throughout the 1920s and finally peaked with a record attendance of 80,000,000 people a week in 1930. However, attendance dropped to 70,000,000 per week in 1931 and to 55,000,000 just one year later. Many radio stations closed, despite the fact that radio receiver sales remained fairly high, even in 1932. Carnivals liquidated rides and many great circuses were forced to strike their tents for the last time. Even the best of the tent shows, Ringling Brothers and Barnum & Bailey, faced such difficult times that John Ringling lost control of the show.

Amusement parks and summer resorts fared no better. Many parks had closed or gone into receivership by 1933 or 1934. Even the most financially stable amusement parks barely survived the first half of the decade.

At Cleveland's Euclid Beach Park, ticket sales fell from 13,666,454 in 1929 to 5,869,654 in 1933. In fact, the park's pre-depression ticket sales would not be reached again until 1942. Correspondingly, the park's payroll fell sharply from almost $237,000 in 1929 to only $83,000 in 1933. With business waning, parks and resorts stopped buying new rides. The Philadelphia Toboggan Company, one of the largest builders of carousels and roller coasters, stopped its construction of carousels forever in the 1930s. During the 1920s, the company had built as many as eleven roller coasters a year; between 1931 and 1934 only two new coasters were constructed.

The Wildwoods began to feel the economic pinch in 1930, when it was noted that the total number of one-day excursions was less than in either 1928 or 1929. In 1931, the Wildwood Title & Trust Company voluntarily closed its doors and the cities began to foreclose on property owners who were unable to pay taxes. Ackley's real estate

Airplane rides were still popular for those who could afford them. Bill James's biplane on the beach about 1930. – Wildwood Historical Society

During the first years of the 1930s, Boardwalk crowds were sparse and spending was a fraction of what it had been during the 1920s. – Lake County (IL) Museum/Curt Teich Postcard Archives

auctions, which had sold millions of dollars worth of property each year during the 1920s, hit a dismal low in 1934 when only twelve tracts sold for a total of $25,000.

The City of Wildwood was desperately strapped for funds. In 1932, eight policemen were cut from the force, while all city employees received a ten percent reduction in salary. At the same time, county workers and local teachers also found their pay envelopes appreciably thinner. The city attempted to raise some funds by imposing a ten cent fee to use the city tennis courts; an action that raised a storm of protest from residents and summer visitors alike.

Wildwood was forced to make unwelcome cuts in every segment of the city budget. Lifeguards' salaries were reduced by twenty-five percent and all expenses related to the beach were eliminated. Boardwalk maintenance appropriations fell from $18,000 in 1930 to $12,000 in 1931. In 1932, there was no appropriation of funds for the Boardwalk, and the condition of the promenade began to deteriorate. Advertising was slashed from $56,000 to $20,000, and funds to pay for a summer concert band were denied in 1932. Unemployment, always a concern during the winter, reached alarming rates even during the summer season. Not surprisingly, Wildwood's population declined for the first time during the 1930s. The decade began with 5,330 residents, by 1940 the number had declined to 5,150.

In 1933, every business at the resort received a letter from Franklin Roosevelt urging them to join the National Recovery Administration and to do their part in restoring confidence in the economy. Some, like Douglass Candies, joined the NRA and made every effort to keep salaries as high as possible. Most, however, could barely keep their doors open. After a disastrous 1933 season, a local newspaper editor made predictions about the coming season: "There isn't any sense kidding ourselves into believing that this year will be another boom year, or even an unusually wonderful one...." In fact, most Boardwalk merchants had little to celebrate until a slow recovery began in 1935.

Most severely affected by the depression were the railroads, both of whom had large payrolls, high maintenance costs, and large investments in equipment. The Reading Railroad and the Pennsylvania Railroad reached an agreement in 1932 when it was decided that consolidation of their seashore service was the only way to survive. As a result, in 1933 the two shore routes were merged to form the Pennsylvania-Reading Seashore Lines. This was accomplished through the Pennsylvania Railroad buying two-thirds of the stock in Reading's Atlantic City Railroad and the assignment of Pennsylvania's West Jersey & Seashore Line to the Atlantic City Railroad. Duplicate right-of-ways were abandoned, and when the new road name was adopted on July 15, the railroad had 413 miles of track, twenty-two steam locomotives, and 216 passenger coaches. Under its new banner, the railroad managed to survive the worst of the depression and continued to provide service to the resorts. One bright spot was the fishing excursions that continued to run from Philadelphia to Five Mile Beach. By 1938, these "Fisherman's Specials" were transporting 50,000 fisherman a year to the Wildwoods and Cape May where the sixty-six boats of the Cape May-Wildwood Party Boat Association gladly provided charter services. Some of these boats augmented their income by serving as fishing boats by day and moonlight cruise vessels by night.

A passenger train with only one coach was evidence of the decline in railroad patronage during the worst of the Great Depression.
– Cape May County Historical and Genealogical Society

The issue of a Cape May-Lewes ferry line surfaced again with the beginnings of an economic recovery. In 1938, the Public Works Administration set aside $2,000,000 for the establishment of the ferry, and three years later Governor Edison signed a bill authorizing the creation of a commission to oversee the ferry operation. Within a few months, however, the United States entered the war and all plans for a ferry system were again shelved.

Despite the continuation of rail service during the 1930s, eighty-five per cent of all visitors to the shore came in automobiles. The streets of Wildwood became dangerously congested and parking spaces were always in great demand. The number of deaths and injuries from car accidents far exceeded the number of deaths from drowning. On one July day, a newspaper reported that there were automobiles on the Wildwood streets from such far-away places as Texas, California, and Canada. Over the three-day July 4th weekend of 1938, an estimated 50,000 cars made the streets of the resort almost impassable.

Those who did not have cars could take a bus to the resort. In fact, it was not uncommon to see as many as 100 buses arriving at the resort in one day. Once there, the streetcars of the Five Mile Beach Electric Railway could take visitors to points of interest throughout the area. Although the company would soon convert to buses, electric streetcars were still a charming reminder of the past. They also played a role in the story of one of the resort's more famous visitors. Alfredo (Freddy) Cocozza, better remembered as Mario Lanza, was a regular visitor to his grandmother's home in the Wildwoods. During the mid-1930s, Freddy and a school-mate, Tony Graziano, obtained jobs on a Wildwood streetcar. With Tony as motorman, Freddy served as conductor, and, according to legend, used his rich and powerful voice to sing the names of approaching streets. Unfortunately, the boys' careers ended abruptly when they took a street car for an unauthorized joy ride.

While resort business owners had little to celebrate during 1932 and 1933, the repeal of Prohibition brought new hope to the communities. As soon as liquor was again legal, Wildwood merchants fell into line to purchase liquor permits. Margaret and Raymond Russo were among the first to obtain a permit. They quickly converted their grocery store into a tavern and within a few years their Golden Dragon Cafe featured a custom-built, fifty-foot mahogany bar and an all-girl band.

Many of the resort's soft drink estab-lishments switched to beer when that bever-age became legal on April 7, 1933. Among the first to open was Herman's Beer Garden at Sportland, where management provided free pretzels, free dancing, and singing wait-ers. Less than a month later, Sportland also featured the Wisteria Room, a higher class night club with no cover charge and Phil Warrington's Revue of "12 Beautiful girls." Not to be outdone, the Casino Arcade con-verted space into a new tap room named the Pirate's Den. At 26th Street, the Hawaiian Island Beer Garden was opened, spotlighting Al Frisco and the Four Waikiki Beach Boys. There was no cover charge, and shore din-ners could be had for as little a fifty cents. So much money was made from the sale of beer that the Italian-American restaurant in the Loreto Hotel could offer a free spaghetti dinner with each stein of Neuweiler's beer, and the El Dorado Hotel promoted a free "Old Fashioned Dutch Lunch" with a ten cent glass of beer. Almost overnight, the Boardwalk and the city streets were dotted with beer gardens including the Grenoble Cafe, the Harbor Inn, the Spanish Cafe, Bennie's Cafe, and near the railroad station, the Terminal Cafe.

THE BRADWAY BOARDWALK BEER BAN

Brewers in Philadelphia and other cities were anxious to distribute brands like Schmidt's Valley Forge Special and Heidelberg beer to the shore, and by May of 1933, S. B. Ramagosa and Ralph Carll, best known as Boardwalk showmen, formed the Cape May County Beverage Company and began dis-tributing beer from the Casino Arcade. Soon, beer flowed in the Wildwoods at an unbe-lievable rate. Of course, with the unrestrained flow of beer came rowdy behavior and an occasional arrest. In 1935, for example, four intoxicated marines were arrested on the Boardwalk after they were refused admission to a dance hall and began a loud protest. Their menacing threats to return to Wildwood with more marines to "clean-up" the town were quickly quieted when they were released to their commanding officer. Drunkenness, improper behavior, and fight-ing appalled Wildwood Mayor Doris Bradway, and the controversial mayor announced that beer would be banned on the Boardwalk in 1934. Said Bradway, "...we want to bring back the appeal it had 20 years ago to conservative, home-loving peo-ple, and the boardwalk is our 'front porch'...." When the sale of hard liquor returned in December of 1933, Bradway declared that no liquor could be served on the Boardwalk, liquor sales would be illegal on Sunday mornings, and women would not be allowed to dispense liquor or even so much as stand in front of a tavern. Bradway's declarations were reinforced by Judge Leroy Loder who ruled that Sunday liquor sales would be confined to the hours from noon to midnight.

By the time the 1934 season opened, it was illegal to sell beer or liquor within 100 feet of the Boardwalk. William Okin, the owner of Sportland, circumvented this law by constructing a new entrance to Sportland's Wonder Bar just about 100 feet from the Boardwalk on 24th Street. The slightly longer walk from the Boardwalk to the bar was only a minor inconvenience for thirsty strollers on the promenade. By 1935, bar and cafe owners were fighting for a repeal of laws that kept liquor sales off the Boardwalk, and, ultimately, alcoholic beverages were again being served on Wildwood's "front porch."

The return of legal beer and liquor sales did much to stimulate the stale economy. It also sparked the beginning of Wildwood's famous night club scene, a significant attraction of the resort for decades to come. At Sportland, the Wonder Bar engaged Earl Denny and his Orchestra, as well as the popular master of ceremonies, Jackie Beekman. Shows were changed weekly and included performers like Maude O'Malley, billed as "the Philadelphia Kate Smith." When female impersonators became popular around 1933-34, Sportland opened the Impersonators' Club, featuring Dee Liddell and his Impersonators' Review and a number of waiters dressed in women's clothes.

Most famous of the new night clubs were the Club Martinique, which opened in 1941 with the Mills Brothers, and Lou Booth's Chateau Monterey (formerly the North Wildwood Yacht Club). An enterprising and popular businesswoman, Lou Booth brought Sally Rand, complete with her famous fan and bubble dance, to the club in 1937 to meet dinner guests and sign autographs. A year later, The Chateau Monterey was totally destroyed by fire. Undaunted, Lou spent $9,000 to remodel the old Henry Otten home and opened a new Chateau Monterey that became the showplace of southern New Jersey. With an oval bar, seating for 250, excellent food, and an unequalled line-up of entertainers, the new Chateau Monterey set the standard for entertainment in the Wildwoods. Lou Booth was largely responsible for the development of a night club industry that blossomed in Wildwood during the 1940s and 1950s.

GAMES OF CHANCE

With the sale of beer and liquor no longer illegal, many former rum runners and illegal liquor distributors turned their attention to gambling. In addition to games of chance on the Boardwalk (which were sometimes considered legal), gambling houses had operated for many years behind closed doors and usually without interference from the police. But, by the 1930s, illegal gambling had come out in the open. Slot machines appeared in respectable stores along the Boardwalk and on party boats used for fishing charters. Bookmaking and other forms of gambling

The Monkey Speedway, which allowed betting on the monkey race car drivers, operated at the Casino Arcade during the 1930s.
– Ron Franks Collection

Ralph Franks's Shooting Gallery in the Strand Block proved to be a popular rifle range during the late 1930s.
— Ron Franks Collection

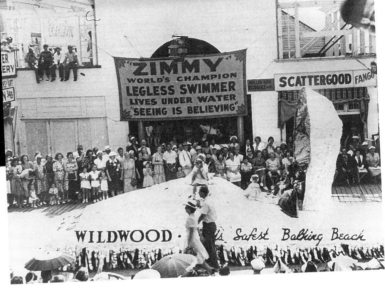

Zimmy provided a unique show at the Casino Pier. Next door is Mrs. Scattergood's Fango game, which was later the centerpiece in one of the many Boardwalk controversies over games of chance. — Richard Ramagosa Collection

became easily accessible, and even the hotels offered gambling of various sorts. Although county and state officers occasionally raided gambling establishments, the City of Wildwood showed little interest in enforcing gaming laws until the crusading Mayor Doris Bradway initiated an anti-vice and racketeering campaign against hotels late in 1933. Declaring that many hotels were nothing more than gambling dens and brothels, she revoked beer licenses at seven hotels. Owners of the hotels such as the old Brighton claimed that Bradway's actions were politically motivated. The feisty mayor's tumultuous administration finally ended in an unfortunate recall election.

Starting in 1930, the cities and the county began to take a hard line on Boardwalk games of chance, while at the same time often ignoring gambling in other areas of town. So-called games of skill could obtain a license to operate, but games of chance were usually denied a permit. However, the city was seldom able to draw a clear line between games of chance and skill. By 1934, county detectives and state police began raiding and closing certain Boardwalk games and arresting the operators. Most heavily targeted were the Pokereno games that awarded cash prizes, expensive merchandise, and large quantities of cigarettes. Sammy's Po-Kee-No, operating in the Convention Hall, was one of two games closed in August at the city convention facility. In North Wildwood, a game operator tried to avoid the law by giving away only tickets as

prizes. These tickets, however, could be redeemed at Ed Morton's cigar shop for cigarettes. Both the game operator and the aging vaudeville star were arrested and had to post bail.

A few years later, the City of Wildwood became more actively involved in the control of games of chance and aided the county and the state in closing questionable games and refusing to grant permits to operate. Claiming they operated games of skill, thirty-two Boardwalk game operators obtained an injunction in July, 1937, restraining the city from closing their games until a hearing could be held. In August, the issue surfaced again when Annie Louise Scattergood, the wife of a respected pharmacist and the operator of Fango games in Wildwood and Atlantic City, was forced to close her Wildwood game. She promptly obtained a temporary injunction, and the city officials were instructed to prove that her Fango game was based on chance rather than skill. A few weeks later, the Chancery Court in Atlantic City refused to grant an extension on the injunction that temporarily protected Scattergood's Fango game and Sebastian Ramagosa's Fortune and Skilo games. Promptly, Ramagosa's games and others that operated on a bingo-like format were raided and closed. The Chancery Court failed to rule on the legality of these games, declared that they were subject to local jurisdiction,

Contestants in one of Bill Hunt's dance marathons, July 17, 1932.
– Cape May County Historical and Genealogical Society

While many of the bands remained the same, there were some subtle changes occurring in the ballrooms of the 1930s. One sad note was the sudden fatal heart attack of Professor Harry W. Roselle just before the 1932 season. It might be said that Roselle's passing coincided with the end of the old order of ballroom entertainment; ballroom owners were now on the threshold of a new, more profitable era.

The genial Sebastian B. Ramagosa was the undisputed "King of the Boardwalk" by the 1930s. – Richard Ramagosa Collection

and the issue of game legality remained unresolved. For the next two decades, the games problem surfaced periodically and inevitably resulted in raids, closings, and controversy. In the meantime, games of chance eventually reopened and, at times, operated unmolested.

SWINGING INTO A NEW ERA

If the return of legal cafes and the rise of illegal gambling brought a renewed excitement to the resort, the ballrooms and dance halls of the 1930s provided a much needed emotional escape from the uncertainty of life during a depression. During the first half of the decade, before the rise of the Big Bands, most of the musical groups were the same orchestras that were familiar to dancers a decade earlier. Among those performing in the Wildwoods were Al Katz and His Kittens; Felix Ferdinando, whose fourteen musicians played a total of sixty-eight different instruments during an evening; Isham Jones, one of the best loved bands of the 1920s; Vincent Lopez and his Hotel St. Regis Orchestra; Slim Marshall and his World's Fair Orchestra, who appeared at the Boon Doggle Derby in the Ocean Pier Ballroom; and Cy Delan and his Kentuckians, who accompanied a Broadway floor show with thirteen dancers and singers. Also popular were special guests like radio celebrity Morton Downey and Helen Kane, the "Boop-Boop-a-Doop Girl," who drew six thousand paying customers to the Hunt's Auditorium-Plaza Ballroom in 1934.

The dance marathon, controversial and often dangerous for its participants, appeared on the ballroom scene during the early '30s. Faced with declining ticket sales during the depth of the depression, almost every major ballroom in the nation hosted marathons to increase business. The point of these marathons was to see which couple could remain standing on the dance floor longest; winners were awarded cash and other prizes. The contestants, who danced to the point of physical exhaustion, sometimes suffered illness, injury and, in a few cases, actually died. As a result, the era of the marathon, although immensely popular, was short-lived.

In the Wildwoods, the impresario of the marathon was S. B. Ramagosa who, in 1931, teamed with Jack Curley, to promote and operate marathons on Five Mile Beach and elsewhere. Over the next three years, Ramagosa operated more than 100 dance marathons from New Hampshire to Florida and from the New Jersey Shore to California. The profit from these contests was huge, especially given the depressed state of the economy. In 1932 alone, Ramagosa and Curley grossed $992,000 from dance marathons.

Wildwood's first marathon began June 25, 1931, at the Casino Danceland, and was notable for its comical young master of ceremonies, Red Skelton. Fifty-six couples took to the dance floor in the hope of winning the grand prize. The dancing continued twenty-four hours a day, although dancers did receive breaks for rest, sleep, and meals. Admission for spectators was twenty-five cents from early morning to early afternoon, and was increased to fifty cents during the prime-time hours. By August 6, the contestants had slowly fallen away until there were only eight couples and one solo girl whose partner had left the floor. The great marathon finally ended on September 14, when Mr. and Mrs. Thomas Day of St, Paul, Minnesota, were the last dancing couple left on the floor. Since they began on June 25, the Days had danced a total of 1,944 hours.

Not to be outdone by Ramagosa, Bill Hunt introduced a second dance marathon at his Auditorium Ballroom. Despite excellent attendance at both marathons, there was a public outcry about the dangers of such exhibitions. In September, 1932, the City of Wildwood passed an ordinance banning further dance marathons in the city.

Another controversy of the early 1930s centered around the opening of the Conventional Hall for dancing. Under the auspices of Doris Bradway, the first female mayor in New Jersey, the Convention Hall was opened to dancers without charge. Manager Ed MacHarg brought major bands to the hall, including Al Katz and His Kittens, McKinney's Cotton Pickers, Snooks and the Memphis Stompers, Will Osborne, Cab Calloway, and Duke Ellington. On Saturday nights, the city covered all operating expenses and admission to the dances was free. Joe Barnes and other commercial ballroom operators complained that the city was engaging in unfair competition, and Boardwalk merchants felt that free dancing drained sales from their businesses during an already bad economy.

At the center of the free dancing controversy was Bill Hunt and his huge Plaza Ballroom, which opened in 1924. Advertised as one of the largest ballrooms in the world, the Plaza could hold six thousand dancers. Under the direction of Hunt and George Coombs, the facility had developed an excellent following by featuring bands such as Ozzie Nelson, Little Jack Little, and Joe Haymes. However, Hunt had the misfortune to become entangled in a political squabble with Doris Bradway. Mayor Bradway was quite a flamboyant figure and far ahead of her time in championing the rights of women, Italian-Americans, and African-Americans. Although registered as a Republican, Bradway supported county Democratic candidates in the 1932 election. This led to verbal attacks on local Republican leaders, including Judge Palmer Way and William Hunt. Her battle with Hunt became very personal, extremely bitter, and, in the opinion of many, a vendetta. At the heart of the vicious controversy was apparently a state supreme court investigation of the city's government brought about while Hunt was a state assemblyman. Whatever the cause may have been, Bradway's response to Hunt was unwise and beyond the proper actions of a mayor. In addition to taking steps against Hunt's theatres, she forbade all lifeguards on the city payroll to attend any dances or events at Hunt's Plaza Ballroom. Those who defied the order were suspended. Most ballroom operators and Boardwalk merchants felt that the establishment of free, city-sponsored dancing at the Convention Hall was a direct attempt by Bradway to injure Hunt's ballroom business and destroy Bill Hunt. In the end result, Bradway's career came to an abrupt end in a recall election, and the free Convention Hall dances were forgotten during the wonderful rebirth of prosperity that ballrooms experienced during the Big Band Era.

The bands that would become the headliners of the Big Band Era began to appear in Wildwood in 1935. The Casino Danceland, Hunt's Plaza Ballroom, and the Ocean Pier Starlight Ballroom played host to virtually every major band in the country, as well as scores of lesser known local and regional bands. Among those featured at these ballrooms from 1935 through the 1941 season were Guy Lombardo, Jimmy Dorsey, Benny Goodman, Artie Shaw, Bob Crosby, Glen Gray and the Casa Loma Orchestra, Woody Herman, Larry Clinton, Ozzie Nelson, Mal Hallett, Ben Pollack, Noble Sissle, Jan Savitt, Del Regis, Will Osborne, Charlie Barnett, Will Hudson, Sonny Dunham, and

Glenn Miller, whose band came to the Ocean Pier in 1938. With these groups arrived some of the great band singers of the age, including the Andrews Sisters, Helen O'Connell, and Bob Eberle.

By 1937, the ballrooms of Wildwood were nationally famous, and Bill Hunt was advertising his dance band entertainment as far away as Pittsburgh. In 1939, the Atlantic Coast Championship Jitterbug Contest which was held on Ocean Pier, and NBC Radio made Wildwood the focus of more national attention when it contracted to carry live broadcasts of music from the Plaza Ballroom on its stations from coast to coast. Other radio stations also carried live broadcasts that were aired in New York City, Philadelphia, and Wilmington. By 1939, The Wildwood area was known as one of the major eastern centers for summer ballroom dancing.

WEATHERING THE STORMY DEPRESSION

The ballrooms that were located along the Boardwalk did bring larger crowds to the promenade, but, in general, the early 1930s were difficult years along the walk. There was little money to spend on Boardwalk repairs and damage done by storms, especially in 1933, a year that burdened the city's resources. Worse even than storms, major fires in 1930 and 1939 damaged the Casino and other buildings while totally destroying the Park Theatre, Park Baths, and a toy store. Each time fire struck the buildings along the Boardwalk, the city was saddled with repairs to the wooden walkway. In 1934, the City of Wildwood was able to increase budget allocations for Boardwalk maintenance, but a year later Mayor Bradway was forced to admit that the city could not cope with the replacement of damaged or rotting boards. Bradway

William C. Hunt (1872-1970) built his empire with movie theatres. In 1935, however, he purchased the failing Ocean Pier for $200,000. – Wildwood Historical Society

turned to the Works Progress Administration in an attempt to obtain $200,000 to completely rebuild the Boardwalk or, failing that, $75,000 for repairs. While the WPA did not approve either amount, it did appropriate $24,619 in 1936. The city contributed another $12,284, and soon a team of eighty-six men were put to work repairing the Boardwalk.

The economy was recovering by 1939, and more WPA funds became available. As a result, $105,000, half of which came from federal government programs, was set aside for the construction of a new Boardwalk from Cedar to Garfield Avenues. Although bad weather and a shortage of skilled carpenters slowed progress and required bringing in extra help from the WPA office in Atlantic City, the new Boardwalk opened on Memorial Day of 1939 and was completed after the close of the season.

Throughout the 1930s, the cities of Wildwood and North Wildwood took a serious interest in enforcing the laws of propriety along the Boardwalk. In 1934, Wildwood's officials worked to ban beer, fortune tellers, and freak shows along the walk. A few years later they banned all barkers and loud ballyhoo in front of games and shows. North Wildwood, in 1936, banned barkers, loud speakers, penny games, gypsies, fortune telling, and mind reading on the Boardwalk, as well as anywhere else in the city. Men who failed to wear shirts on the Boardwalk were arrested, and everyone older than twelve was required to wear proper garments over swim suits when not on the beach. Auction houses, which became very popular during the mid-1930s, were often raided; and those found guilty of operating fake auctions or obtaining money under false pretenses were closed and charged by the police.

One of the more notable new ordinances was introduced by Wildwood Mayor George Krogman in 1938. This law banned the exhibition of dangerous animals in shows throughout the city. Those who supported animal welfare applauded the action, although animal cruelty was not really at issue. The new law was actually the result of a grizzly event that occurred in October of 1938. During the previous summer season, Joseph Dobish and his wife brought two lions to the Casino Arcade to perform with Mrs. Dobish in a motordrome. A lion sat in a motorcycle sidecar, while Mrs. Dobish drove the cycle up the steep side of the motordrome. All went well until an October night when Mr. Dobish attempted to feed the 300-pound Tuffy, who bolted past him and out onto the Boardwalk. Although the

walk was nearly deserted, Thomas Saito, an auctioneer, was attacked by Tuffy and died when the lion's huge paw broke his neck. The lion then dragged Saito's body under the Boardwalk. Fifteen policemen and numerous volunteer firemen began a careful search beneath the walk. Two hours later, Patrolmen John Gares and Millard Campbell came face-to-face with the lion and one well-aimed shot from Gares' service revolver killed the lion. In the aftermath, Tuffy's mate was ordered out of town, Dobish was arrested and charged and Officer Gares became a celebrity, appearing on radio broadcasts and receiving several marriage proposals.

ON THE BRIGHT SIDE

Fortunately, most other happenings on the Boardwalk during the 1930s were more pleasant. The annual Easter frolic continued to draw respectable pre-season crowds, as did the annual automobile shows in April, even if few people had the money to purchase a new car. A new attraction that began in 1931 was the annual mid-summer Mummers' Parade that featured famous string bands from Philadelphia and Wildwood, along with organizations from other cities. Featuring a total of 1,500 musicians, the Mummers' Parade was one of the most colorful events ever held on the promenade.

Free band concerts continued, although there was a great deal of agitation to end them. In 1930, twenty bands bid on the contract and the city again selected Everett Moses, paying him $11,800 to perform from July 22 through September 1. In appreciation, Moses wrote and first performed his "Wildwood- By-The-Sea March" that season. At the end of the season, the Wildwood Merchants' Association passed a resolution calling for an end to free concerts in Wildwood. They cited the fact that band concerts had gone out of fashion and that most resorts were discontinuing them. In addition, they felt that it was unfair to expect the taxpayers to continue to foot the bill for concert bands. The Chamber of Commerce took a similar stand in February of 1931. Ignoring both groups, the city once again accepted bids and hired Moses at a cost of $13,550 for fifty-two days of concerts. In 1932, however, the city eliminated music from the budget and the long-standing tradition of free daily band concerts at the resort came to an end.

Opposite: Everett Moses and his band, based in St. Petersburg, Florida, was one of three bands booked to provide free concerts in 1929. Moses also wrote and dedicated a march to the resort. – Wildwood Historical Society

Despite the widespread shortage of cash, the Boardwalk still attracted patrons. Those who could afford it, bought custom-made jewelry at the Gold Wire Jewelry Company. For those who could not afford to purchase such luxuries, the beach offered other pursuits. Many people searched the sand for jewelry that had been blown onto the beach by firehoses a decade before when Mayer's Jewelry Store burned. Another interesting and inexpensive diversion was created by a shaggy, brown dog that appeared on the Boardwalk every evening at about ten o'clock. He faithfully made the rounds of each hot dog stand until he was satisfied and then disappeared again until the following evening.

While many concession operators were forced to suspend business during the 1930s, a few actually managed to open new Boardwalk entertainments and invest in additional equipment. Sebastian B. Ramagosa, joined by Ralph Carll, rented the Casino Arcade and invested $50,000 in a new Dodgem ride and other attractions. For Ramagosa, who had operated food and game stands for twenty years, it was the beginning of a Boardwalk empire that would expand greatly during the 1940s and 1950s.

THE BEACH AND WHAT TO WEAR WHERE

Those looking for an escape from the grim reality of the depression found the Wildwood beach to be a great bargain. Anyone who could afford the cost of a railroad or bus ticket to Wildwood could enjoy the beach without charge. As the cities sweltered in summer humidity, thousands escaped to the relative coolness of the ocean. In early July of 1934, when the thermometer reached eighty-five degrees, more than one hundred twenty-five thousand people stormed the Wildwoods, and twenty-five thousand of them found space on the beaches! In order to serve the needs of the thousands of bathers, the City of Wildwood opened a Beach Club at Schellenger Avenue in 1935. The new facility included a sun deck, hospital, children's wading pool, beach chair and umbrella rental, showers, volley ball nets, quoit courts, and rooms for physical education sessions and classes. In 1938, a continuing series of special exercise classes was begun, and Knee-Hi, a trained dog who helped to teach beach safety, made his first appearance.

Tuffy the Lion, whose fatal attack on a Boardwalk auctioneer forced a Wildwood policeman to kill the animal. The incident resulted in strict new laws concerning animals on the Boardwalk.
– Wildwood Historical Society

WILDWOOD
BY-THE-SEA

NEW JERSEY

New Jersey's Most
Popular Play Place

Wildwood was the first resort on the Atlantic Coast to hire female lifeguards. The motorcycle was purchased to help speed guards to the scene of an accident. – National Archives

Meanwhile, the lifeguard corps continued to grow. In 1933, Florence Newton and Mae Ottey of Philadelphia, became the first women lifeguards on the Wildwood beach. According to the Associated Press, they were also the first female lifeguards on the entire Atlantic Coast (Atlantic City did not hire female lifeguards until 1975). Two years later, the lifeguard corps organized a "speed patrol" of guards who used surfboards to travel 100 yards in the water in just thirty seconds.

Throughout most of the decade, lifeguards were still enforcing the law that said men must cover their chests when on the beach or in the water. In 1936, Wildwood relaxed the ordinance a bit, although proper attire was still a requirement when not on the beach. Said one newspaper editor, "...there will be no compulsion of male bathers to wear jerseys, yet the display of the manly chest must be kept strictly on the bathing beach." The male bather, he went on to note, "...seems to want to parade his gorilla-like figure before the more or less admiring gentler sex." Obviously, not everyone agreed with the new regulations. North Wildwood refused to allow shirtless men on the beach until Mayor George Redding lifted the historic ban in 1940. Atlantic City did not reverse its policy until 1941, and Ocean City held out until the war was over!

SURF AND TURF WARS

However, the real beach controversy of the 1930s did not center on the issue of shirtless men, but rather a prolonged event called the "Battle of the Beach." The battle actually started in December of 1924, when the Beach Realty Company and City of Wildwood clashed over the use of beachfront property. As a solution, the real company offered to sell the city all of its beachfront holdings for $800,000. As long as the Baker brothers were alive, the city did not need to be concerned about the future of the beachfront land and riparian rights. The Bakers and the city shared common interests. But, with the passing of the civic-minded brothers, the city became increasingly concerned about the future of the beach. By 1930, it was clear that the city intended to acquire all riparian rights and beach land in order to preserve and control the use of the property for the future.

In the first phase of the battle, the city seemed determined to acquire every inch of beach, including the riparian rights deeded to the Cedar-Schellenger Corporation on the old Blaker-Rhoads property. The corporation, led by Judge Palmer Way, vowed to fight, and the city finally relented in return for title to the land directly under the Boardwalk that was owned by Way and his associates. It was just the beginning. Never having acted on the 1924 $800,000 offer, the city now appropriated $300,000 to purchase beach-front land from a total of sixty-six companies and individuals. The landowners refused the offer, and the city raised the ante to $500,000. At this point, local residents and businessmen loudly protested such a large spending of taxpayer dollars during poor economic times. Then, to make matters worse, the United States District Court in Camden declared that the land was actually worth $718,750. In April of 1931, the city declared that $700,000 was an unacceptable price and began the process of repealing the ordinance that had appropriated $500,000. Now, however, the landowners decided that $500,000 was agreeable and obtained an injunction to prevent the city from repealing the ordinance. By July, the landowners were again hoping for $718,750 plus $20,000 in interest. Both interests finally agreed on a price of $425,000, a bond issue was raised, and the city took possession of the beachfront properties. Now the City of Wildwood was in a position to protect the Boardwalk and the beach from undesirable development. Unrestricted building and the construction of any future piers without city approval would be controlled by law.

PIER PRESSURES

The first five or six years of the decade were particularly unkind to the piers and amusement installations in the Wildwoods. Encumbered with debt and large tax payments, these properties were also expensive to operate and maintain. As patronage and spending began to fall in 1930, most of the amusement enterprises faced uncertain and difficult futures. The dilapidated Atlantic Pier was razed in the spring of 1934. As one of the smaller piers, it was never able to compete with the big Ocean Pier, and when the economy turned downward, the Atlantic Pier Company simply elected not to continue a losing business venture. The Crest Pier survived the era, but it was only a shadow of what it had been in the days before the First World War. It still offered dance bands, beauty contests, carnivals, and amateur talent contests, but it had long since stopped trying to compete with the big piers and amusement centers to the north. Even the financially solid Bill Hunt experienced difficulties with his amusement ventures. In 1931, he sold his Boardwalk carousel to a Coney Island ride operator. The ride was moved to the New

York resort, but Hunt had great difficulty in collecting his final payments from the new owner. Hunt's Pier in Cape May, which never enjoyed the same level of business as the Wildwood piers, was in financial trouble by 1931. In that year Hunt stopped paying taxes on the property; three years later, a tax receiver was appointed for the delinquent property. Finally, at a time when all of Wildwood's piers and amusements were struggling for survival, Atlantic City's Steel Pier, a much larger and more famous attraction than anything in the Wildwoods, began advertising aggressively in the Wildwood newspaper. A number of Atlantic City properties, also feeling the pressure of the depression, attempted to augment their slumping business by attracting customers who were staying in the Wildwoods, Cape May, and Ocean City. Able to afford better attractions than the Wildwood facilities, the Atlantic City piers provided a great deal of unwelcome competition.

Sportland, with its rather limited offerings seemed to suffer more than the other facilities in the Wildwoods. In a valiant attempt to compete, Sportland opened the 1930 season with the Hippodrome tent shows, a series of performances that starred fifty entertainers and thirty beautiful girls. Unfortunately, the shows didn't prove to be enough of a draw, and by July of 1930, the owners admitted that they had made a mistake. Claiming that receipts barely covered the taxes on Sportland, they requested their tax assessment be reduced by $100,000.

Not surprisingly, Sportland opened in 1932 under a new manager, Frank Brindell. He proceeded to refurbish the swimming pool, replacing the traditional salt water with fresh water. He also added a seafood restaurant, dance pavilion, and an outdoor ice cream parlor. That year, boxing bouts, wrestling matches, and marathon dances were Sportland's featured events. By August, however, the new company again requested, and was granted, a tax assessment reduction of $57,000 on the property. Brindell gave up on Sportland at the end of the season, and in 1934, it opened under still another manager, Vincent Martino. Martino made a serious attempt to change Sportland from a sports-centered operation to an amusement park. He founded the Sportland rodeo, staring Tex McDaniel and his famous steer, Barker. He also established a pony track, installed kiddie rides, Jungleland, the Prison of Horrors, the Georgia Chain Gang, the Palace of Wonders, the French Village, and other attractions and shows. The pool was again improved, and both boxing and

HUNT'S AFFILIATED ENTERPRISES

GENERAL OFFICES
HUNTS CASINO BUILDING
WILDWOOD, N. J.

Dear Friends:-

The addition of Ocean Pier to Hunt's Affiliated Enterprises in 1934 gave this company an opportunity to develope a new idea in the amusement field....a place of entertainment combining for one admission many note worthy attractions which had, heretofore, been sold as single attractions.

Here you can enjoy motion pictures, ballroom dancing, amusement rides and devices, exhibits, slides and ocean-sun decks--totaling several dollars worth of attractions--at a small fraction of this total under the Ocean Pier plan.

In three years, Hunt's Ocean Pier has gained recognition as one of America's outstanding amusement piers, and the only Pier of its kind in the Country.

Renovations and the addition of new attractions, promise to make your visit during 1938 more exciting than ever--and so we say THIS YEAR-- IT'S OCEAN PIER !

Sincerely yours,

HUNT'S AFFILIATED ENTERPRISES.

W.C.Hunt.
President.

wrestling remained on the bill. Of course, the return of beer and liquor sales also helped. Sportland was one of the first operations to open bars after the repeal of Prohibition.

Sadly, no amount of effort, inspiration, or innovation could make Sportland a paying enterprise. Unable to pay its property taxes for a number of years, the facility was forced into receivership. In 1937, the owners of Sportland, the Commerce Holding Company, asked the Cape May County Tax Board to reduce their tax assessment from $75,000 to $37,500. When this request was refused, Sportland seemed doomed. In 1939, the City of North Wildwood began foreclosure proceedings on the property and, a year later, took control of Sportland. Fortunately, S. B. Ramagosa saw potential in the facility and turned it into a viable business property during the 1940s and 1950s.

At the Ocean Pier, the Wildwood Pier and Realty Company was equally unprepared to ride out the depression. The company attempted to attract more visitors by hiring Rube Nixon's Monkey Circus for the 1932 and 1933 season. Among other acts, the circus featured a group of trained monkeys driving miniature automobiles around a small race track. In 1934, the pier added another circus and a display of Florida alligators; admittance to these attractions was free with the price of general admission to the pier. In spite of these promotions, the pier still failed to make a profit, and in 1935, the Wildwood Pier and Realty Company gladly sold it to Bill Hunt for $200,000, far less than they had paid for the property during the land boom of 1925.

Bill Hunt's theatres had done fairly well through the tough years of 1932-34, and he was probably one of the few men in the Wildwoods who could not only afford to buy the pier but also had the extra funds to improve it. Hunt immediately spent the money to enlarge and renovate the pier, and, when it was ready to open for the 1935 season, New Jersey's Governor Hoffman took part in the dedication ceremony.

Determined to make the Ocean Pier a showplace, Hunt retained Lawrence Johnson, who had managed the pier for twenty-eight years. He also hired William Fennan, who had spent twenty-five years as manager of Tilyou's Steeplechase Pier in Atlantic City and was one of the original founders of the Miss America Pageant. Under the direction of Hunt, Johnson, and Fennan, the facility was rapidly transformed into a first-class amusement pier. The entire facade was revamped and now advertised the fact that forty attractions were offered for a single, forty cent ticket (which, by July, was necessarily reduced to twenty-five cents). On the pier, construction crews built two new theatres and a circus ring, plus a giant Kelly Slide and other stunts for the funhouse. For the first time, amusement rides played a major role on the pier. From the Philadelphia Toboggan Company, Hunt purchased a rebuilt carousel. PTC engineer Herbert Schmeck was to design a roller coaster that would fit in the limited space afforded by the pier. Although small compared to most coasters, the Whirlwind still required $30,047 worth of Douglas fir — a major investment during the depth of the

115

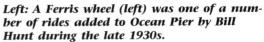

Left: A Ferris wheel (left) was one of a number of rides added to Ocean Pier by Bill Hunt during the late 1930s.
– Philadelphia Toboggan Coasters, Inc.

Middle left: The Ocean Pier's new roller coaster, designed and built by the Philadelphia Toboggan Company. –
Philadelphia Toboggan Coasters, Inc.

A train on the Ocean Pier's new roller coaster climbs the lift hill. On the front of the first car is an illustration of two Teddy bears. – Philadelphia Toboggan Coasters, Inc.

Above: Hunt placed a row of benches along the side of the new roller coaster for the convenience of footsore pier customers.
– Philadelphia Toboggan Coasters, Inc.

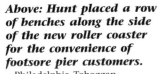

One of Bill Hunt's first improvements for the Ocean Pier was a bold, new facade that announced forty attractions for one price.
– Historical Society of Pennsylvania

Tho' a weird and 'eerie sight
Witches Forest's thrills delight.

On the Jack and Jill
you'll find
Thrills you've sought, of
every kind.

A novel sky-ride, some-
thing new,
Exclusive thrills in store
for you.

For that feeling, deep inside,
We prescribe the Kelly Slide.

Finish of a whirlwind tour,
Safe and sound, at last at moor.

ALL ATTRACTIONS ARE INCLUDED IN THE ONE PIER ADMISSION

depression. Rounding out his array of rides, Hunt installed a Ferris wheel, a Whip ride, and a Custer Car ride.

Pier management also initiated a solid line-up of entertainment that appealed to people of all ages. Direct from Madison Square Garden came Joe Basile and his Canadian Mountie Band, while in the Mickey Mouse Theatre there were continuous showings of cartoons featuring the beloved Disney character. Warren Buck, who had recently returned from Africa with 750 animals, was engaged to exhibit thirty African monkeys, including four newborns. Magician Gordon Alexander revived interest in the spirit of Houdini when he proposed to contact the "other world." Alexander reminded each audience that a Philadelphia bank vault still held $25,000 for anyone who could prove they had contacted the afterworld. Also hired for the 1935 season was Major Casper Nowak, a genial midget who strolled the pier dressed as a policeman. Finally, Philadelphia's "Uncle Wip" was engaged to broadcast his popular children's radio show live from the pier every Tuesday evening during the summer season.

Despite having to lower admission prices in mid-season, Hunt and his team made a success of the Ocean Pier and began a policy of continuous expansion and improvement that was halted only by a fire that destroyed the pier during World War II. In 1936, the new Marine Deck, featuring comfortable chairs and a fabulous ocean view, was constructed. Just two years later, the pier was extended by 200 feet to accommodate the new $20,000 Jack and Jill Sky Slide. Added to these attractions were Bohemian glass blowers, a live bunny and bird village, Parvin's miniature city, an African curio exhibit, Warren Buck's Zoo, the Mystery Maze, the Witch's Forest, Simpleton's Lane, and the largest miniature train exhibit in the world. At the very front of the pier sat Laughing Sal. Many will remember the jolly, rotund mechanical lady who laughed loudly (or frighteningly, depending on your view) and continuously to the delight of customers and the dismay of employees stationed near Sal.

Hunt's entertainment lineup was kept fresh and lively from season to season. Beginning in 1936, the pier promoted an

117

A lady visitor to Ocean Pier's Laff Theatre is surprised by a blast of air that lifts her skirt. – Philadelphia Toboggan Coasters, Inc.

Wildwood lifeguards pull a prize-winning float in the 1939 Baby Parade.
– Wildwood Historical Society

end-of-the-season Mardi Gras complete with confetti, paper streamers, hats, noise makers, and a grand march led by Rex Donnelly's Orchestra. The Ocean Pier Follies, a company of thirty-five talented children, debuted in 1938. Attuned to the power of the air waves, management arranged for a live radio broadcast each Sunday afternoon on the Boardwalk in front of Ocean Pier. People strolling the walk were invited to be interviewed on air, and those who did received a free can of Love Nest Coffee. Through promotion, renovation, and expansion, Bill Hunt and his managers rescued the Ocean Pier from its deep financial abyss of the early 1930s and transformed it into a popular, profitable attraction. By the late 1930s, the Ocean Pier was unquestionably the showpiece of Wildwood's Boardwalk.

Laffing Sal, an animated lady with an endless recorded laugh, greeted visitors to the Ocean Pier's new funhouse and Laff Theatre.
– Philadelphia Toboggan Coasters, Inc.

The fully renovated Ocean Pier at the height of its popularity, about 1939. – Wildwood Historical Society

The Ocean Pier after three years of Bill Hunt's improvements. – Wildwood Historical Society

The large Ferris wheel at Marine Pier was purchased from Ed Rhoads's Carsonia Park in Pennsylvania. – Wildwood Historical Society

Left: A 1930s view of Playland, with Marine Pier in the foreground. – Lake County (IL) Museum/Curt Teich Postcard Archives

MORE RIDES ARRIVE

Ocean Pier was not without rivals, however. Hunt's major competition came from the Cedar-Schellenger Corporation, which had acquired the Rhoads-Blaker Amusement Center. Although the facility was not in good condition when the company took control, they, like Hunt, had adequate funds to renovate and develop the property. While upgrading the original area that contained the carousel, Old Mill, and Jack Rabbit coaster, the company took advantage of their riparian rights in 1930 and announced that it would construct a pier on the east side of the Boardwalk. The new pier section became known as the Marine Pier, while the older westward section was called Playland. After solving the issue of riparian rights with the city, construction of the Marine Pier began in 1931. Adjoining the Casino Pier, the Marine Pier stretched from the Boardwalk to the high water mark on the beach. The company purchased a used Ferris wheel from Ed Rhoads's Carsonia Park, installed a miniature railroad, various refreshment stands, and a

The fast Caterpillar ride was one of the leading attractions on Marine Pier during the 1930s. – Lake County (IL) Museum/Curt Teich Postcard Archives

Mystery Castle was a popular walk-through attraction that was nestled beneath Playland's Jack Rabbit roller coaster. – Wildwood Historical Society

miniature golf course. While the newer thrill rides were most popular, the slow moving boats of the Old Mill still had their place: "There is seclusion in the old mill with peaceful gliding through the canal, and no wonder there is allurement for young men and maidens...." It was one of the few places on the bustling Boardwalk where young couples could steal a few moments of precious privacy.

During the 1930s the company invested most of its money in the new Marine Pier section, but, in, 1938 they also constructed a new, illuminated entrance to Playland and to the Jack Rabbit coaster, greatly enhancing the appearance of this section.

Operated by Carll and Ramagosa, the Casino Arcade also saw expansion once the economy started to recover in 1935-36. In 1935, Ramagosa booked The World of

The inside of the Casino Arcade in 1935. This photograph was taken early in the morning and before the stands opened for the day. – Wildwood Historical Society

Yesterday, Today, and Tomorrow, a collection of curios, relics, and a painting allegedly valued at $250,000, that had appeared at the Chicago World's Fair during the 1933-34 run. By 1937, more money became available and Ramagosa built a short-range shooting gallery, and installed a Thriller ride, Custer Cars, an Auto Skooter, three kiddie rides and a Pretzel dark ride (which had recently been developed by New Jersey's Leon Cassidy). Then he opened a Fun on the Farm attraction for children and designated several days a week as Kiddies Days, when all children received free souvenirs. In 1938, Ramagosa moved the old Casino building westward, decorated it with neon lighting, and installed a Water Dodgem ride. The space where the Casino building had been was decked and used for additional amusements. Clearly, by the late 1930s, Ramagosa was on his way to earning the sobriquet "King of the Boardwalk."

Elsewhere along the Boardwalk, Nixon's Monkey Circus opened near Ocean Pier, and, following the national fad, miniature golf courses sprang up near the walk and elsewhere in the communities. These courses became so popular, and apparently noisy, that in 1931 the City of Wildwood was forced to pass a new ordinance regulating miniature golf operations. All courses were forced to close at 1 A.M. and could not reopen until nine. On Sundays, any course within 150 feet of a church could not open until after services were concluded. Bright lights that shined into homes were forbid-

Roller skating and dancing were major attractions at the Convention Hall during the 1930s and 1940s.
– Robert J. Scully Collection

The shuffleboard courts, located adjacent to the Boardwalk, became very popular during the 1930s.
– David W. Francis Collection

FUN, FOOD, AND FANTASY

The majority of activity was centered around Ocean Pier, Marine Pier, and the Casino Arcade, but many other amusement attractions made the Boardwalk a continuous strip of fun, food, and fantasy. At the Convention Hall, Joe Barnes, Sr., opened a roller skating rink, and by 1940, S. B. Ramagosa was holding roller speedway races there. In these races, two groups of five teams skated over a banked wooden course for a total of 2,500 miles, with the winner claiming a $4,000 cash prize. Also at the Convention Hall was the World Museum, which included a number of static displays, as well as sideshow-style performances.

den, and loud music was prohibited before 9 A.M. and after 9 P.M.

Throughout the 1930s and into the 1940s, there was renewed interest in boxing and wrestling matches. Most of the credit for revitalizing the these sports went to Myer Saul and Charles H. "Turc" Duncan. Saul leased the Convention Hall for wrestling matches in 1935, and Duncan started promoting fights and wrestling at Sportland in 1931. He later moved to the Convention Hall, and, when Hunt's Sports Arena opened in 1937, moved to this new facility. Turc Duncan, a legendary sports promoter, was also responsible for bringing female wrestling to Wildwood for the first time in 1940.

A ticket to the movies could still be purchased for ten cents at the Nixon Theatre on the Boardwalk.
– Wildwood Historical Society

By the 1930s, Hunt had somewhat improved the old Blaker Theatre, but it still retained much of its old appearance. – Wildwood Historical Society

One of the most interesting episodes of the decade occurred at the Convention Hall during a match between Joe Savoldi and a local favorite, Stanley Sokolis. In the audience was Wildwood's outspoken and often outrageous mayor, Doris Bradway. Already a veteran of political battles with powerful Republicans Bill Hunt and Palmer Way, Bradway was not one to hide her feelings or opinions. This day, apparently enraged with some of the wrestling tactics being used by Savoldi, she located a wooden plank, climbed into the ring, and slammed the plank down on Savoldi's head!

RECALLING THE HUNT FOR BRADWAY

The resort's movie theatre industry, very much dominated by Bill Hunt, did not suffer as badly as other entertainments during the depression. Business did decline, however, from around 1930 until after 1935. Despite being elected a state assemblyman in 1933 and a state senator three years later, Hunt had plenty of time to devote to his theatre business. By 1935, Hunt's empire included nineteen theatres in New Jersey and Pennsylvania, the Ocean Pier, the ballrooms in Wildwood, a ballroom in Trenton, and bowling alleys in Wildwood, Cape May, and Pitman. Although the pressures of the economy forced Hunt to curtail billboard advertising in 1931, he continued to aid the community during the tough years of the depression by offering a free Christmas show for children and hosting a number of benefit fundraising events for unemployment relief.

Bill Hunt was very popular with almost everyone except Mayor Doris Bradway. Hunt, a loyal Republican, was troubled by Bradway's endorsement of Democratic candidates in 1932, and Bradway was furious over an investigation of her government instigated by Hunt. The conflict between these two reached a crisis during the 1934 season. Although the city had seldom paid much attention to New Jersey's Sunday closing laws, on May 26, Bradway announced that the law would now be enforced and ordered all movie theatres to close on Sundays. Since her decree was aimed only at movie theatres, and since

Hunt's Regent Theatre operated only during the summer season, while the Casino and Blaker Theatres were kept open throughout the year. – Wildwood Historical Society

122

virtually all theatres on the island were operated by Hunt, the move was viewed as a personal one and a vicious attack on a political foe. There was an instant storm of protest from all corners of the business community. To help save face, the mayor appointed a committee to study the situation and make recommendations. By June, the theatres were again open on Sundays. When Bradway expanded her attack on Hunt's ballrooms later in the season, Hunt brought a suit against the mayor for $50,000 and threatened criminal charges. Defeated in her efforts to damage Hunt, Bradway ended her crusade against him and finished her political career amid the embarrassment of a recall election.

The economy was slowly reviving by the late 1930s, and Hunt began to again expand and remodel his theatres. In 1939, the new Shore Theatre, heated and air conditioned for year round use, opened at Schellenger and Atlantic Avenues. While this new theatre was under construction, however, the old Casino Theatre was destroyed in a $200,000 fire on April 19, 1939. Unfortunately for Hunt, much of the theatre equipment used in the other facilities had been stored in the Casino Theatre. Hunt promptly replaced the burned equipment and contracted with Joseph Scully to construct a new Casino Theatre for the 1940 season. Designed with an ultra-modern exterior, the new theatre was air conditioned and provided seating for 1,200. It opened on April 11, 1940, and six days later premiered the first Cape May County showing of Gone With The Wind. Hunt's close ties to the film industry led to the personal appearance of Shirley Temple in Wildwood in 1940. She came to the resort as part of a special event in which crippled children were treated to an outing at the seashore resort.

FIGHTING TO DEPRESS THE DEPRESSION

The convention and outing business suffered greatly during the 1930s, although there were a few bright spots. In 1932, the New Jersey Fraternal Order of Eagles brought 25,000 to the Wildwoods for a three day conclave, and in 1934, Wildwood was chosen over Atlantic City and several Philadelphia amusement parks to host 4,000 from the Lit Brothers Department Store. In 1936, the General Electric Company held a large outing in Wildwood and arranged for the great German airship Hindenburg to fly over the resort at low altitude. Among the Hindenburg's passengers on this flight were actor Douglas Fairbanks, Jr. and boxer Max Schmeling.

Hunt's Casino Theatre, with Blaker's Theatre visible at the far right. – Wildwood Historical Society

In spite of these few bright spots, convention business was so bad by 1932 that the city asked for rent reduction on the Convention Hall. The Holly Beach Realty Company refused, stating that it was already losing more than $2,000 a year on the facility. Throughout 1933 and the first half of 1934, the city failed to make any rent payments to the realty company for the hall. Then, in July, 1934, when the city failed to make a promised payment of $1,000, the bondholders of the realty company initiated legal action to collect $15,000 in delinquent rent plus interest. The issue was finally settled when Holly Beach Realty agreed to lower rent from $12,000 to $10,000 for 1934, and further reduced that amount to $9,000 for 1935.

Following the destruction of the old Casino Theatre by fire, this new, ultra-modern Casino Theatre opened in 1940.
– Wildwood Historical Society

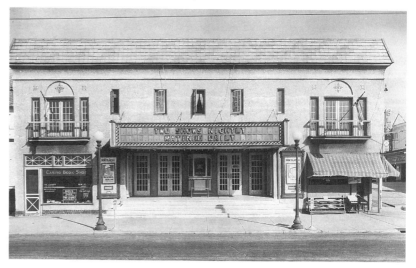

The hotel business, which relied heavily on conventions for its livelihood, struggled through a dismal decade. Nationally, 80% of hotels defaulted on mortgage payments, and many could not meet tax payments or payroll. Occupancy in hotels, which stood at 70% in 1929, fell to 51% in 1932. Large hotels, with their high operating costs, were further injured by the rise of inexpensive tourist camps, of which there were 20,000 by 1935. The burgeoning motel industry also added to the hotels' woes.

Most of Wildwood's hotels survived the decade, although the old Brighton Hotel, as famous for its gregarious headwaiter, Nate, as for its good food, was razed in 1940. The hotels benefited from the repeal of Prohibition, the Hotel Dayton being a typical example. In 1934, the Hotel Dayton Tavern opened, serving mixed drinks, beer on tap, sandwiches, salads, and free deviled crabs.

At this point there were still large numbers of resort visitors that could not afford to stay in hotels. Many of them slept under the Boardwalk in what was jokingly referred to as the Underwood Hotel. This practice was understandably unpopular with hotelmen and, since it was also illegal, the police began arresting anyone found under the Boardwalk after dark.

By 1937, the hotel business was recovering and a new hotel, the Maryland Hall, was built and managed by F. L. Hoskins. Since he also operated the Kenmore Hotel in Bel Aire, Maryland, Hoskins imported Maryland chefs to create southern recipes such as fried chicken and Maryland crab cakes. Prices for these popular dishes ranged from seventy-five cents to a dollar.

Restaurants were not as dependent upon conventions as the hotels were. By lowering their prices during the depression, most were able to survive. At the Sportland Restaurant, a full seafood platter, the "best on the island," was offered for sixty-five cents. And at Lowe's Restaurant, chicken chow mein, served with bread, butter, and coffee, was priced at fifty cents. By 1937, the economy was rebounding for restaurants as well as hotels. The Crest Pier Restaurant was fully redecorated, and Earl Groff could now afford to erect a new building with more kitchen and dining room space at the rear of his restaurant facing Magnolia Avenue. Ed Morton successfully operated his Bit of Broadway Restaurant, and Tauber's menu boasted of forty-eight different kinds of waffles. Still not satisfied with this variety, Tauber, "The Waffle King," offered prizes to any of his cooks that developed new waffle creations.

An advertisement for the 1932 Miss America Pageant. – Wildwood Historical Society

Battling the dismal economy and fierce competition from other seashore resorts, the Wildwoods placed extra emphasis on special events and attractions during the 1930s. Fishing contests, regattas, boat races, and the ceremonious arrival of King Neptune season's opening were all contrived to attract visitors to the island. There was also the annual pet parade that included more than two hundred animals walking or riding on floats. Predictably, the parade, featured a large number of dogs, cats, birds, ponies, and goats, but also parading were pigs, turtles, a prairie dog, a chameleon, and a even a red ant!

Wildwood managed to take advantage of Atlantic City's misfortune in 1932, when the Miss America Pageant came to Five Mile Beach. The inaugural pageant had been held in Atlantic City in 1921, but in 1928, amid charges of immorality, the event was discontinued due to financial losses of $52,000. Although not connected with the Atlantic City committee and never recognized as one of the official Miss America Pageants, the 1932 event gave Wildwood an opportunity to take part in a pageant that was becoming

The cover for the official program for the only Miss America Pageant ever held in the Wildwoods. – Wildwood Historical Society

The logo for Wildwood's Miss America Pageant was, unfortunately, only needed for one year. – Wildwood Historical Society

Some of the hopeful contestants for the title, "Miss America, 1932." – Wildwood Historical Society

a national institution. The pageant took place during the first three days of September and attracted thirty-seven contestants vying for an array of prizes including $2,000 in gold. Held in the Convention Hall, the pageant was heralded by two Boardwalk parades that drew a great deal of attention. In 1933, Atlantic City attempted to revive its pageant, but it was not until 1935 that the original Miss America Pageant was reborn. Wildwood might have enjoyed being the per-

manent home of Miss America, but the event was destined to be forever linked to Atlantic City. Although the Miss America Pageant slipped through Wildwood's grasp, other beauty pageants and fashion shows took place at the resort. In 1932, a nine-week event was presided over by Miss Sportland, and in 1934, Marion Bergeron, Miss America of 1933-34, appeared with two dance bands in Bill Hunt's Auditorium-Plaza Ballroom.

The 1932 Baby Parade passes the Ocean Pier. In the depth of the Depression, most parents hoped for cash prizes. – Wildwood Historical Society

During the latter years of the decade, Ocean Pier offered a number of events for kids under age ten, including juvenile fashion shows and a Tarzan, Jr. contest. The baby parade, of course, remained Wildwood's major claim to fame. The event was well received in 1931, when girls from forty-five different cities competed for the Queen Oceana crown. In an elaborate coronation ceremony, Catherine Coates of Cleveland, Ohio, was crowned at the Convention Hall before reigning over a well-attended baby parade. Despite a worsening depression, the 1932 event was also very successful. In 1933, however, problems arose. Months before the event, the city announced that it could not afford to subsidize the baby parade. As an alternative, the city searched for a private concern to manage and operate the 1933 parade. The few offers that came in were unsatisfactory, and in early August it was announced that the twenty-fifth Baby Parade was cancelled. It was an unpopular decision, but neither the Chamber of Commerce or any other organization could find enough money to finance the event. The scaled-

At the Casino Pier, Queen Oceana XXIV poses with the founder of the Baby Parade, John Ackley. – Wildwood Historical Society

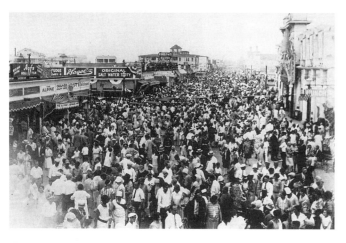

Left: Even with high unemployment and a scarcity of cash, the Baby Parade could still draw huge crowds. – Wildwood Historical Society

Lower left: One of the lucky winners in the Baby Parade's Push Cart and Decorated Float Division. – Wildwood Historical Society

Queen Oceana XXIII (Kathleen Coates of Cleveland, Ohio) and her court of princesses. – Wildwood Historical Society

down version of the Baby Parade was held the following year in conjunction with the annual Pet Parade. Nevertheless, the combined events did manage to entice sixty-five thousand spectators to the Boardwalk. By 1936, adequate financing enabled the Baby Parade to be run as a separate event once again, and eight hundred babies were entered as contestants.

Probably Wildwood's greatest coup of the 1930s was its selection as the site of the 1937 National Marble Tournament. The event began in Philadelphia in 1922, moved to Atlantic City in 1923, and then to Ocean City in 1929. By snagging the event for 1937, Wildwood not only increased its hotel and resort business, but it also garnered a great deal of free national media exposure. Newspaper reporters from forty-three cities, newsreel cameramen, and national radio networks converged on the city to cover the tournament. Virtually overnight, Wildwood became a household name at the beginning of the 1937 resort season.

To play in the Wildwood Marble Tournament more than three million boys and girls competed in smaller events throughout the United States and Canada. Forty-nine

boys and one girl travelled to Wildwood for the finals. During the contest, Hunt's Theatres provided free tickets for the mibsters, as did Carll and Ramagosa for their Playland and Joe Barnes for his skating rink. A banquet was held at the Adelphi-Witte Hotel and fourteen-year-old Bill Kloss from Canton, Ohio, was crowned the 1937 marble champion. The annual Marble Tournament was

One of the resort's greatest promotional coups came in 1937 when the National Marbles Tournament selected Wildwood as the site for the annual event.
– Historical Society of Pennsylvania

The newly added facade and expanded staff of Groff's Restaurant, 1938. – Earl A. Groff

In 1934, when the staff gathered on the Boardwalk for a photograph, Groff's was already on its way to becoming one of the most popular resort restaurants.
– Earl A. Groff Collection

held at Wildwood through 1948 after which time it was moved to Asbury Park. In 1960 the event returned to Wildwood where it remained.

By 1935, the resort was feeling the pleasant effects of a gradually improving economy. That season, Groff's Restaurant reported a twelve percent rise in business, one-day outings increased, and both the rail-roads and the bus companies sold more tick-ets. The City of Wildwood increased its advertising budget from $13,000 in 1934 to $22,000 in 1935. Postcard mailing, a positive indicator of business conditions, went from all-time lows in the 1932-34 period, to 130,000 a week in 1935. Finally, by 1937, bank deposits came close to equalling those of the late 1920s. In 1937, there were still 2,007 unemployed in the county, but for all intents and purposes, the Great Depression had ended in Wildwood. Confident that prosperity was returning, Boardwalk mer-chants no longer felt they had to cut prices to survive. Consequently many of them agreed to raise prices from five to ten cents on certain games, rides, and refreshments. Except for the nickel ice cream cone, five cent price signs quickly disappeared from the Boardwalk.

WINDS OF WAR ... AGAIN

Just as it seemed that things would return to normal, rumors of America's impending involvement in the European war grew stronger and stronger. The Cape May Coast Guard station, which almost had to close during the mid-1930s, was taken over by the navy and opened as a naval air station in September of 1941. Navy patrol planes became a familiar sight over the beaches, and uniformed naval personnel were conspic-uous on the Boardwalk. In 1940, Red Cross booths were set up on the Boardwalk to col-lect money for European relief. The 1941 sea-son experienced the first gasoline shortages due to the U. S. shipping petroleum to England for war use. The government threat of "gasless Sundays" was met with shock and dismay in Wildwood. By the time some twenty-five thousand New Jersey American Legionnaires descended on Wildwood for their annual convention in August, 1941, war was the major topic of conversation. By this time, twenty-seven hundred men from the county were registered for the draft, and overzealous residents were already question-ing the loyalty of local families of German or Italian descent. Fishermen were suspected of providing fuel and food to German sub-marines operating off the coast, and others were thought to be openly sympathetic to the soon-to-be enemy powers.

The traditional Easter Weekend opening of the season brought record crowds to the Boardwalk during the late 1930s and early 1940s. – Historical Society of Pennsylvania

Although the beach looked normal during the summer of 1942, cameras, binoculars, and telescopes were forbidden on the strand. In addition, the beach was closed and patrolled at night. – Lake County (IL) Museum/ Curt Teich Postcard Archives

At twilight, the Boardwalk was a glittering show of street lights and brightly lighted signs. When the war arrived, most of these lights were dimmed or extinguished because of the danger of German submarines operating off the coast.
– Lake County (IL) Museum/Curt Teich Postcard Archives

129

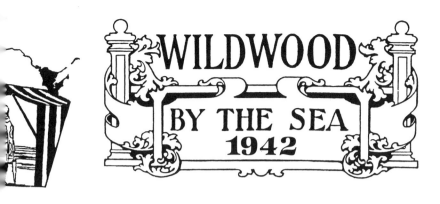

WILDWOOD
BY THE SEA
1942

By the summer of 1942, uniforms were a common sight on the Boardwalk.
– Historical Society of Pennsylvania

A USO canteen in Wildwood entertains a few of the thousands of servicemen and women who passed through the resort from 1942 to 1945. – Wildwood Historical Society

The December 7, 1941, attack on Pearl Harbor caused much concern. A number of area men were stationed there, including one who served as chief radioman on one of the damaged battleships. Within days, the Wildwoods were on a war footing. A coast artillery battery was deployed to Cape May Point, and all of the communities received assistance from Civil Defense offices and the American Legion in planning for air raid drills and the possibility of a seaborne invasion.

On the Wildwood Boardwalk, Japanese businessmen were immediately targeted, and local police, aided by Federal Reserve employees, padlocked four Japanese-owned businesses. Kuchi Oishi, a respected businessman who had operated an auction on the Boardwalk since 1921, openly criticized the Japanese attack and supported a United States victory despite his Japanese birth. Soon, everyone was involved in the war effort. Amos, a Doberman, was the first Wildwood dog to "volunteer" for K-9 service. S. B. Ramagosa offered a hundred dollar reward to any pilot from Wildwood who shot down a Japanese airplane. Fighter pilots William Bunting and Philip Kirkwood both received Ramagosa's bounty.

By early in 1942, life in Wildwood had changed drastically. Many loved ones were now serving in the military, government-imposed restrictions affected every sector, and residents were actually living on the edge of the war at sea. German submarines operating within a few miles of the Jersey Shore sank the first Allied vessel off Cape May County on January 25, 1942. Less than two months later, a U. S. Navy destroyer was torpedoed and sunk just off Cape May. In all, eleven vessels were sunk within sight of the Cape May County shore. In fact, oil from sunken tankers caused serious problems when it washed onto the beaches throughout 1942.

The sinking of ships within four miles of Wildwood led the navy to increase security measures. Telescopes, binoculars, and cameras were forbidden on the beaches, and only on-duty military patrol personnel were permitted on the beaches after twilight and before dawn. A midnight curfew was imposed, and Boardwalk establishments were forced to close much earlier than usual. And finally, in lieu of a full blackout, the navy ordered a "dimout." Then, when tankers fell victim to enemy torpedoes right off the Jersey coast, total blackouts were ordered. Every building was required to comply by turning off or blocking out all lighting within five minutes of the alarm. Late in 1943, the threat of German submarines diminished and orders for dimouts and blackouts were lifted.

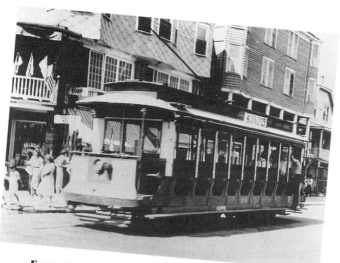

Even during the final years of streetcar operations, the old, open summer cars were still in use. In 1940, tickets were four for twenty-five cents. – Wildwood Historical Society

A Pennsylvania Railroad K4s engine leads a passenger train into the Andrews Avenue Station. With gasoline rationed, trains and buses provided the only access to the resorts for many people. – Wildwood Historical Society

Hunt's Plaza and Starlight Ballrooms were the center of activity during the war years.
– Wildwood Historical Society

131

Guy Hunt, manager of the Ocean Pier and a second lieutenant in the army reserve, was called to active duty, and hundreds of other Boardwalk employees either enlisted or were drafted. Manpower shortages became so acute that Earl Groff was forced to close one of his two dining rooms. Food rationing proved an even greater hardship on restaurants. Coffee rationing began late in 1942, and such necessary foods as eggs, sugar, meat, and butter were almost impossible to obtain on a regular basis. By the 1944 season, restaurants in the Wildwoods were constantly running out of food and were forced to apply to the War Price and Rationing Board for more rations. Most were allotted more food items if they could prove that their business had increased twenty percent or more since the last rationing period.

More trouble came in May, 1942, with the announcement that the Pennsylvania-Reading Seashore Lines could not spare the engines or passengers cars for special excur-sion service to the resort. However, the railroad did maintain regular line service at prewar levels. At the same time, the government also placed restrictions on bus transportation. The cuts in available passenger transportation resulted in a loss of about one hundred thousand visitors to the Wildwoods during the 1942 season.

It was also during the war that a decision was made that would change the streets of Wildwood forever. In 1944 the electric railway company announced it would terminate all streetcar service in Wildwood. The tracks were removed from roadways and streetcars were replaced by buses, bringing an end to a Wildwood institution that dated back to the turn of the century.

Regular railroad and bus service helped to ease the impact of wartime gasoline rationing, but the Office of Price Administration was still concerned about gas consumption for pleasure driving, and it considered forbidding the rental of summer homes for the 1943 season. Wildwood's mayor fought the issue, and the threat never became a reality. By the next year, the government began to relax its many travel restrictions.

The hotel business was also very much affected by the war. In Atlantic City, and, indeed, in all major resorts, many of the major hotels were taken over by the military and converted to use as hospitals, barracks, and recreational facilities. In Wildwood, Hotel Davis was acquired by the army and remained under military control until the end of the war.

The war even had an effect on Wildwood's ballrooms. While dancing was still very popular, many of the top bandleaders had enlisted in the armed forces. As a result, there was something of a shortage of the major bands that had appeared at the resort from 1937 through 1941. At the Ocean Pier Starlight Ballroom and the new Starlight Ballroom that opened in 1944, Bill Hunt booked mostly local bands from the Philadelphia area. These included Charlie Black, Len Mayfair, and Joy Caylor and Her All Girl Orchestra. At Danceland in the Convention Hall, bands were replaced by recorded music, and management acquired a collection of 1,500 records. On Thursday nights, all servicemen and women were admitted to Danceland free, and a token admission fee of only twenty-five cents was charged on all other evenings.

Except for the problem of oil washing ashore in 1942 and the restrictions on cameras, beach activity was generally unaffected by the war. The sand continued to build-up at an incredible rate, and, in 1943, the city offered 500,000 tons of sand to anyone who would haul it away. It was even suggested that residents should keep buckets of beach sand to use as fire extinguishers. With many servicemen and their families in the area, crowds on the beach increased, forcing Dutch Hoffman to raise his lifeguard staff from thirty in 1942 to forty-two in 1943. Hoffman also initiated daily flag raisings and evening flag lowerings, a tradition that was still observed long after the war ended.

In spite of labor, food, and maintenance material shortages, cut-backs in transportation, gasoline rationing, and blackouts, Boardwalk businessmen managed to cope with the problems of operating a summer resort during a war. Of course, some concessions were necessary. In 1942, Ocean Pier opened on Memorial Day weekend and then closed again and did not reopen until the regular summer season began in late June. New rides and equipment were not available, but the Hunts made up for this inconvenience by booking a Junior Miss America Pageant, Mariana and her marionettes at the Kiddie's Theatre, Alf Loyal's Dogs, Kay and Karol's juggling act, George Downey's pantomime routine, and the Four Earles, a "Thrilling, sensational cyclone on wheels." Hunt also continued to offer wrestling matches, as did the Convention Hall, where wrestlers like the Masked Marvel, Jim Austeri, and Maurice Lachappelle were big hits.

S. B. Ramagosa, now known to everyone as "Ramey," acquired Sportland in 1942, and began making whatever improvements he could without the usual supplies of lumber and paint. The pool was reopened, and, in 1945, he debuted the first Watercade, a sort of circus in the pool. Produced by Dick Edwards and accompanied by Gillard's Orchestra, the Watercade featured water clowns, comedy divers, Olympic swimmers executing intricate routines, and the fifteen Aquabelles performing a water ballet. The Watercade was a major success and Ramagosa expanded on the show after the war years.

Popular on the Boardwalk throughout the war years were any exhibits that focused on the war and America's enemies. At the Convention Hall, a wartime exhibit included wax figures of Hitler, Mussolini, and Hirohito, as well as a twenty-foot Japanese midget submarine, and a collection of photos from the Pacific war zone.

During the war, Baby Parade entrants often selected patriotic or military themes.
– Temple University, Urban Archives

The traditional Memorial Day ceremonies took on new meaning during the war years. – National Archives

Lifeguards launch a floral boat in memory of naval heroes on Memorial Day. – National Archives

The interior of the Douglass Candies store in 1942, with Joseph Douglass behind the far counter. Later, the store was greatly enlarged. – Douglass Candies

Hunt's Strand Theatre entered the war years with an appearance little changed since the 1920s. – Wildwood Historical Society

On Christmas Day of 1943, the wonderful Ocean Pier was completely destroyed by fire. – Wildwood Historical Society

In contrast to these more or less violent exhibits, the Boardwalk also carried a message of hope and peace. In 1944, the Orthodox Presbyterian Church wanted to reach the thousands of Boardwalk patrons with prayers, sermons, and religious music. When a Boardwalk store came on the auction block, the church managed to raise $2,950 and purchased the property. Under the direction of Leslie A. Dunn, the Boardwalk Gospel Pavilion, or Boardwalk Chapel, offered inspirational music, sermons, slide presentations, counseling, and literature to the three thousand or more people who passed the chapel on a busy evening.

During the war years, the Wildwood Boardwalk lost some of its most famous pioneers. Charles Douglass, the founder of Douglass's Candies died in 1941. He was replaced in the business by his brother, Joseph, who died in 1942. Following Joseph's death, control of the great candy concern fell to Joseph's wife, Minerva, and their three children, June, Charles, and Harvey.

One of the new entrepreneurs to arrive in Wildwood during the war was Angelo Nickels. The Nickels family had operated games and fortune telling concessions at Chicago's White City Park until that amusement enterprise closed in 1934. Searching for another location for their business, they settled on Wildwood in 1944, opening concessions that provided readings, ball games, and "Guess Your Weight" stands on the Boardwalk. Over the years, the Nickels family would play an important role in the future of the Wildwood Boardwalk.

Although both Wildwood and North Wildwood had taken action against gypsy fortune tellers on the Boardwalk during the 1920s and 1930s, by 1941, a number of them had reappeared. Operations like Mme. Renee's Temple of Knowledge provided advice on love and business and flourished throughout the war years. In 1945, the city again banned fortune telling, but some of the gypsies opened legitimate photographic galleries and then defied the law by telling fortunes in the back rooms. The battle to keep Boardwalk attractions above board while at the same time meeting the public's demand for amusement raged on throughout the 1940s.

By the mid-point in the war, the sale of beer and liquor had been legal for a decade, and the profits from bars, taverns, and night clubs prompted an increasing number of people to open clubs that offered both refreshment and entertainment. By 1942, there were 125 night spots in the Wildwoods. Some, like Lou Booth's, were carry-overs from the 1930s, while others, including Marty Bohn's famous Nut Club, opened during the war. After the war, the Nut Club became known as a legendary comedy club. Bohn, who was well known for his charity work, began his comedy career in 1925. Later he worked with the Three Stooges and as a straight man for Bud Abbott. He first appeared in the Wildwoods during the 1930s at the Orange Grove and at Pop Moore's. When he decided to settle in the Wildwoods, he became a leader of the postwar night club scene.

135

Even in 1945, after years of resort growth, the north end of the Boardwalk was largely undeveloped. – Wildwood Historical Society

Rubble was all that remained of the famous Strand Theatre after the fire of August 12, 1944. – Wildwood Historical Society

When the Wildwood Manor Hotel reopened in 1944 (it had been closed since 1940), a major goal of the new owner, John Tempest, was to revitalize the property with a lavish night club. Accordingly, Tempest debuted the Bamboo Room in 1945. The new club featured good dance bands, talented organists, and a selection of excellent comedians. The development of major night clubs during the war years was merely a setting of the stage for Wildwood's evolution into "Little Las Vegas" during the two decades that followed.

With maintenance and construction materials in very short supply, natural disasters caused more concern during the war than ever before. The great Atlantic City Hurricane of September, 1944, ravaged the Jersey Coast, causing $25,000,000 in damages and totally destroying nearly 700 homes and buildings. Atlantic City lost part of its Boardwalk, as did Sea Isle City and Stone Harbor. Although some of Wildwood's streets were inundated with five feet of water and there was considerable wind damage, the wide beach of Five Mile Island lessened the devastation that occurred at the other resorts.

During the war, two of the resort's most damaging fires occurred. On Christmas Day of 1943, it took a million gallons of water to fight the roaring blaze that levelled more than thirty businesses and claimed the life of a firefighter and the Ocean Pier night watchman. When the fire was finally extinguished, gone was the million dollar Ocean Pier, the Surfside Hotel, Nixon's Baths, Sagel's candy store, twelve apartment houses, and two

dozen smaller businesses. An explosion heard at sea prompted speculation that the pier had been shelled by a German submarine, but subsequent federal investigations could find no evidence of enemy action. Two years later, on August 12, 1944, a $250,000 blaze between Maple and Pine Streets destroyed the Strand Theatre, Julius Koester's salt water taffy stand, a shooting gallery, apartment houses, and five other businesses. For most of these businesses, wartime restrictions and shortages made rebuilding impossible.

Early in 1945, the entire coast became alarmed when it was reported that robot bombs from Germany might be dropping along the shore. However, as the war moved toward conclusion, the threat of enemy action along the shore decreased. Rules forbidding cameras on the beach were withdrawn in June of 1944, and gasoline restrictions for motorists and boaters had eased by early 1945. That same year, curfews and dimouts faded into memory as islanders anticipated an end to the war.

Victory in Europe came before the regular season opened, but by V-J Day there were 100,000 summer visitors in the Wildwoods. Upon hearing that the war was over, thousands of sailors and marines from the nearby base flocked to the Boardwalk in jubilation, hugging and kissing all the available women in a scene that was repeated from coast to coast. After a highly emotional victory parade on the Boardwalk, everyone looked forward to 1946 as the first normal year at the resort since 1929. A new age of growth and prosperity for the resorts was just around the corner.

Except for the business recessions of 1948-49 and 1957-58, the years between the end of the war and the end of the Eisenhower Administration were relatively carefree, bringing record crowds and unequalled growth to the Wildwoods.

After the war, Wildwood's publicity department began an aggressive campaign to promote the resort. Included in the many photos sent to newspapers was this shot of eight attractive girls standing in front of Wildwood's illuminated directional sign.

– Wildwood Historical Society

CHAPTER 6

POSTWAR PROSPERITY AND RESORT GROWTH

The Boardwalk of the late 1940s and 1950s was clean, crowded, and very much family-oriented. Although dress codes were relaxed, dresses, suites and sport coats were still a common sight. – Temple University, Urban Archives

Concerns of the period ranged from the serious polio epidemics to the far less serious 1952 potato shortage that affected restaurants and Boardwalk French fry stands. Cape May County experienced an overall population increase throughout the postwar years, although Greater Wildwood actually lost 913 residents during the 1950s. Nevertheless, population density in the area grew from 220 people per square mile in 1900, to 828 in 1930, and 1,169 per square mile in 1956. Compare these figures to the 72 people per square mile on South Jersey's mainland.

The decline in Wildwood's population, probably due in large part to wintertime unemployment, was more than offset by the growing numbers of summer visitors. Research conducted in Philadelphia in 1946 revealed that thirty-one percent of vacationers went to Atlantic City, eighteen percent to the Wildwoods, and just five percent to Ocean City. In terms of gross revenues, the summertime spending of vacationers along the Jersey Shore rose from $400,000,000 in 1946 to $1.7 billion ten seasons later. In 1951, 900,000 people visited Wildwood and parted with an estimated $78,000,000. These attendance figures placed Wildwood in third position, behind Atlantic City (16,000,000 visitors), and Asbury Park (4,000,000). At the same time, Ocean City attracted a modest 600,000, and Cape May, just 250,000. From 1951 on, the number of visitors to the Wildwoods increased nearly every season. Crowds of more than 150,000 on holiday weekends were not uncommon, and during the July 4, 1952 holiday, officials counted 50,000 automobiles and estimated the crowd at 300,000. Boardwalk concessionaires seconded the estimate, after tabulating hot dog sales at 300,000!

There were still other indicators of growth at the resort. On one July day in 1952, the Wildwood Post Office set a new record of 129,000 cancellations, mostly postcards. And, after the July 4th weekend of 1958, local businesses deposited almost $3,000,000 in the Wildwood banks. After fifteen years of depressed economy and wartime restrictions, prosperity had returned to the seashore in a big way.

During the period between 1946 and 1960 Wildwood merchants had some incredibly profitable years as well as a few they would rather forget. The seasons of 1946 and 1947 were fairly good, but in 1948 sales declined by about twenty-five percent and remained in a slump for 1949.

The Ship Ahoy, built by Ben Schlenzig at Taylor and Ocean Avenues, was one of the resort's pioneer motels.– Wildwood Historical Society

During the post-war era, 1957 was probably the best in terms of resort popularity and profitability. Bank deposits through Labor Day totalled $67,000,000, an increase of $16,000,000 over 1956. And on one day, July 10, 1957, the Wildwood Post Office processed 83,328 pieces of mail, primarily postcards. By August, the resort's hotels and motels had occupancy rates of ninety-eight percent. The following year, partially due to a wet, cold June, patronage suffered a noticeable decline, and business dipped about twenty percent.

Weather was always an important factor in the success of each season. In addition, the nation's economy also played a deciding role. Other factors, too, affected business, such as the August, 1953, water line break that closed all of the hotels and motels for a few days. That same season, business suffered because rumors of a polio epidemic in Wildwood aired on radio stations as far away as Cleveland.

The July 4th attendance count was always a good barometer of the season's success. Nineteen forty-six was the first season that fireworks were available after the war, and that year the holiday crowd was estimated at 125,000. A season later, the number swelled to 200,000, with 140,000 arriving by train or bus. Then, after a few dismal seasons, the 1951 holiday crowd again reached 150,000, with an estimated 90,000 bathers jamming the beach.

Motel construction boomed starting in the late 1940s. Two of the small, early motels were the Sun Deck and the Sun Dial.
– Wildwood Historical Society

MOTELS MOVE INN

Naturally, such immense crowds strained Wildwood's overnight accommodations to the limit. Replacing the traditional hotel, new motels became a symbol of resort growth during the 1950s, and several companies specialized in the construction of motels at the resort.

The modern motel was the product of twenty years of evolution, starting with tourist camps, cottages, auto camps, and motor courts. By the time the war ended, motels were popping up all over the country. Gasoline rationing was a thing of the past, and more and more families were taking motor vacations, stopping at motels instead of hotels. Part of the attraction of the motel was the casual atmosphere, park-at-the-door convenience, playgrounds and swimming pools, and maybe best of all, no doormen or bellboys to tip! By 1948, there were 26,000 motels and motor courts in the United

Above: The Skylark Motel, built during the winter of 1955-56, was one of the new generation of resort motels. – Wildwood Historical Society

Below: The Carousel Motel, in Wildwood Crest, was one of the many 1950s motels designed with a theme. – Wildwood Historical Society

The Ebb Tide Motel offered its guests television, air conditioning, a sun deck, and only a short walk to the beach. – Wildwood Historical Society

States; another 15,000 were constructed between 1949 and 1952. The Wildwoods played a major role in the growth of the motel industry. In fact, by 1956, the Wildwood Hotel Association had changed its name to the Wildwood Hotel and Motel Association. Wildwood had become a model resort for the motel industry. Businessmen travelled from Asbury Park and Long Branch to learn the secret of Wildwood's success with this new mode of overnight accommodation.

In 1950, Wildwood motels like the Holly Court and Lantern Lane caught the fancy of vacationing families, probably because they offered playgrounds, ping pong tables, kitchenettes, and could make arrangements for golfing. Many new motels were modelled after designs seen in Florida. The Sandy Shores Motel and Jay's Motel, both built during the early 1950s, featured Florida styling, stucco walls, Jalousie windows, and baths finished in ceramic tile. Several motels, like the Sea Cove Court, were built as close to the beach and the Boardwalk as possible. Many featured air conditioning, music in all the rooms, daily maid service, free ice, a recreation lounge with a television set, shuffleboard courts, card tables, billiards, swimming pools, and coffee shops. In 1957 alone, twelve new motels were ready to open by the July 4th holiday.

To help meet the demand for all the new motels, several companies, most notably the Morey brothers, specialized in the design and construction of the modern, attractive buildings. The Capri, the San Souci, Knoll's Motel, and the Castaways, were all built by the Morey brothers. Each in its own way represented the new, postwar style in motel design.

Initially, all motel construction was limited to Wildwood and North Wildwood, because Wildwood Crest zoning regulations did not permit the erection of motels. By 1953, landowners and construction firms were agitating for a change in the laws, and one contractor noted that five motels he had recently built on the northern end of the island could have been built in the Crest. Under extreme pressure, the commissioners altered the zoning code in 1954 to permit motels east of Atlantic Avenue and at various other locations served by sanitary sewers. By 1956, most of the land adjacent to the Wildwood Crest beach area was open to motel construction.

Hotel owners were less than happy about the rise of motels, especially since their own investments were tied to aging, wooden hotels with limited parking space and no room to expand. They were equally troubled by stricter hotel safety regulations that were imposed by the state beginning in 1947. Included in the new requirements were iron fire escapes above the second floor, rope ladders in every room above the second floor, and alarm systems with gongs on all floors. Additional laws that took effect in 1950 required fire detection systems, sprinklers, and a watchman for hotels with twenty or more rooms. Such safety improvements were costly, especially for hotels that were starting to lose their clientele to modern motels. Nevertheless, they were forced to either meet the safety requirements or remain closed. Even before the 1950 season, four Wildwood hotels were warned that they must either

close, install proper fire alarm equipment, or face fines of $100 a day for each day they defied the law.

Most hotels accepted the inevitable and contracted to install the appropriate safety equipment. In many cases it provided the hotelmen a good excuse to modernize their aging properties in an attempt to compete with the motels. Sarah Binns, veteran owner of Hotel Binns on Atlantic Avenue, expanded her Florida-style hotel by adding seventeen new rooms on a new second floor complete with wall-to-wall carpeting and luxurious furnishings. Valentino Lanoce transformed the Hotel Hof Brau into a year-round facility, adding fifteen bedrooms, thirty baths, heat for fifty rooms, and a new clover-shaped bar. At the Hotel Lincoln, Harry Steele, Jr. put a bath and radio in every room, installed a ninety-five foot bar (the longest in the resort) and opened the new Mirror Room, "The newest and most beautiful cocktail lounge in Wildwood." The old Oceanic, a thirty-five room hostelry, was actually moved a short distance, then expanded with a thirty-eight-room fire-proof addition, and parking for sixty-six cars.

Throughout the late 1940s and into the 1950s, every hotel attempted to keep its clientele and attract new customers by presenting a unique image. The King Edward was advertised as Wildwood's "Leading Jewish Hotel," while the Hotel Dorsey was a strict temperance house that catered "...to a Refined Clientele." The Hotel Adelphi-Witte boasted of smooth service, warm hospitality, spacious porches, sensible rates, and an

Harry Steele's Hotel Lincoln was one of the first hotels in the resort to be constructed using fireproof materials. – Wildwood Historical Society

Inside the Hotel Lincoln was the Mirror Room, outfitted with one of the longest bars in the resort. The Mirror Room was remodelled several times during the flush post-war years. – John Williams Collection

Harry Steele, Jr., Mayor of Wildwood (1948-56) and the owner of two resort hotels, was known as the "Flying Mayor."
– Wildwood Historical Society

Holliday's Restaurant, owned by the Zaberer family, was a favorite Boardwalk eatery of the 1950s. – Wildwood Historical Society

Holliday's Restaurant after extensive remodelling. – Wildwood Historical Society

A line of hungry visitors wait for a table at Groff's Restaurant. At the height of the season, these lines stretched well down Magnolia Avenue. – Earl A. Groff Collection

unsurpassed cuisine centered around such local delicacies as bluefish, clams, crabs, sea trout, sea bass, and flounder. The Grandview Hotel claimed that every room had an ocean view and added a new sun deck for those that did not want to venture as far as the beach for a suntan. The Cromwell claimed to be exclusive but not expensive, while the old Hotel Dayton simply stated that it was the largest and the best. The Dayton's Bolero Supper Club was an added attraction. Despite motels, business remained good at the old hotels throughout the 1950s, and the fact that the old Hotel Sheldon sold for well over $100,000 in 1953 proved that hotels were still viable business ventures.

PLENTIFUL PALATABLES

Closely linked to the hotel-motel business in the Wildwoods were scores of restaurants, coffee shops, sandwich stands, and bars that satisfied the hunger and thirst of the millions of people who visited the resort. The end of the war eliminated most food and employee shortages, and the return to prosperity gave restaurant owners reason to rejoice. With the end of wartime price controls, the five cent ice cream cone disappeared to be replaced by cones ranging in price from seven to fourteen cents. With sugar now readily available, the candymakers thrived. Sagel's store at the Casino Arcade received a new facade of stainless steel and stone, while Minerva Douglass moved her famous candy store to a new location at 3300 Boardwalk. By 1950, Douglass Candies was using forty tons of sugar a year, a sure indication that the tough years of the 1930s and 1940s were over.

145

Groff's Restaurant set a new record in 1946 when 260,000 customers were served. However, long lines waiting to enter the restaurant caused many complaints from nearby Boardwalk merchants, so beginning in 1947, the entrance lines were moved to the Magnolia Avenue dining room and the Boardwalk dining facility was closed. When Groff's closed the Boardwalk dining room, the vacant building was acquired by Ed and Charles Zaberer, who opened Holiday's Restaurant. In 1950, the Zaberers remodelled the restaurant in colonial style. The revived establishment seated 150 and attracted diners with tanks of live lobsters in the window.

Numerous other new restaurants began appearing by the late 1940s. In 1950, S. B. Ramagosa & Sons acquired a franchise for a Howard Johnson's, and opened the new restaurant on the Boardwalk. The first major franchise restaurant on the walk, Howard Johnson's served twenty-eight flavors of ice cream, fried clams, and a famous barbecue sandwich. Other new restaurants that became popular included Gerace's Bar and Restaurant, operated by "The Three Vets," Henry Loo's Chinese Restaurant, which served meals until five in the morning, and the Sea Spray Terrace, which claimed to offer forty-nine different kinds of sandwiches. In 1952, there were 340 eating establishments in the Wildwoods and most were so well managed that only five failed to pass the inspection for sanitary standards.

On the Boardwalk, pizza, then called Tomato Pie, was tempting hungry visitors by 1947. Most famous of the pizza parlors were Mack's and Joe's, although by the 1950s, pizza restaurants were numerous. Some of the best remembered Boardwalk eating places of the 1950s included Taylor's Pork Roll Sandwich Shop, Dick's Tropical Drinks (specializing in orange, grape, grapefruit, and lemon-lime flavors), Odger's Restaurant

(famous for crab cakes), Pierre's Restaurant (best known for blueberry pancakes), Read's Steak House, Franks's Nut House, Nate's Famous Hot Dogs, Alpine Fruit Drinks, Johnson's Popcorn (the oldest popcorn vendor on the Boardwalk), Zaberer's Hot Dogs, Snow White Hot Dogs, Planter's Peanuts, Schaeffer's Hot Dogs (thought by many to be the best hot dog along the shore), Kohr Bros. Frozen Custard (regarded as the best in the nation), Rick's Lime Rickey, and Scully's Beach Grill. Each of these, open only from May through September, thrived in the postwar years, and some were still operating along the Boardwalk forty years later.

A legendary restaurant was founded in the resort in 1954 when Ed Zaberer purchased the small, forty-eight seat Eldorado Hotel and Restaurant. The restaurant had been less than successful and had gone through a succession of nine owners. Zaberer, however, was an experienced restaurateur whose grandmother had operated the Glenwood Hotel, with its 175-seat dining room. Ed Zaberer and his brother had also been involved in restaurants, hot dog stands, and waffle houses on the Boardwalk. Ed embarked on an almost never-ending expansion of what became Zaberer's Restaurant. Eventually, he offered 12 dining rooms with seating for 1,600, 6 bars requiring a staff of 35 bartenders, and 10 lounges. Each night, Zaberer served 4,000 people. Among those who frequented the famous eatery were Ronald Reagan, Richard Nixon, New Jersey Governor Richard Hughes, Jimmy Durante, Don Rickles, and Muhammad Ali.

The secrets to Zaberer's success were atmosphere, quality, and fair pricing. To obtain the best prices, he bought in quantity. He placed the largest order to date with Kraft Foods when he ordered 80,000 pounds of cheese, and he used a freight car load of Idaho potatoes each week during the sum-

Rudy's Dog House (which at one time was also Nate's) operated in the shadow of the Jack Rabbit roller coaster and had changed its appearance very little since the 1920s.
– Wildwood Historical Society

This Boardwalk lunch stand featured two of Wildwood's most popular foods...Burk's hot dogs and Welch's grape juice. Both were standard fare on the promenade for decades.
– Temple University, Urban Archives

mer season. On a daily basis, Zaberer served 300 pounds of Maryland lump crabmeat, 1,400 fresh chicken breasts, and 1,500 pounds of prime beef. The term "to Zaberize" came into usage for anything that was done in a big way.

Zaberer was highly successful, but a number of restaurant owners were not as fortunate. In 1952, a $60,000 fire took one person's life while destroying the Elmira Cafe and another restaurant. Four years later, a spectacular $200,000 blaze that could be seen from as far away as Cape May, decimated Ricci's Restaurant and the Patio Restaurant. Throughout the history of the Wildwoods, fires, usually started in the kitchens, were the bane of the food service industry.

POSTWAR BOARDWALK BOOM

The postwar years, except for a dismal 1958 when business was down thirty to forty percent, comprised a gilded age on the Boardwalk. With crowds in abundance, money readily available, and wartime shortages over, Boardwalk merchants beamed as they carried cash bags to the banks. In 1949, the Wildwood Boardwalk Merchants

Association was formed to improve conditions along the promenade and to help promote summer business. Many merchants responded to the postwar prosperity by installing new facades of glass block, brick, or stone, as well as new lighting, signage, and many coats of colorful paint. William Weiner built four new Boardwalk stores, a modern bathhouse, and a beach grille at 26th Street. Even the Boardwalk Chapel, with no interest in Boardwalk economics, prospered, bringing gospel music and Elvin Bjornstad, a tenor with the Metropolitan Opera, to the crowds that strolled the wooden way.

In 1949, S. B. Ramagosa purchased a number of passenger trams that had been used at the 1939 New York World's Fair. He then formed the Tram Car Amusement Company, and hired eighteen young ladies to drive the trams and collect the ten-cent fare. For the first time, tired boardwalkers

Wildwood

The Sightseer trams, now a Boardwalk land-mark, were brought to the resort in 1949 by S. B. Ramagosa. – Wildwood Historical Society

Gilbert Ramagosa assumed control of the Ramagosa amusement empire after the death of his father in 1953. Among the seventy-six enterprises owned by Ramagosa were the Casino Arcade and Sportland. – Richard Ramagosa Collection

Even before the summer season opened, the Boardwalk and the Marine Pier was used for the annual spring automobile show. After the war, boats and airplanes were added to the show. – Wildwood Historical Society

could hop a tram and ride from one end of the Boardwalk to the other. Today, nearly fifty years later, the Sightseer trams are still running every few minutes — much to the relief of weary Boardwalk strollers.

It seemed that there was something new and exciting to see along the Boardwalk, such as the 1953 snake exhibit sponsored by the American Legion. A number of species were on exhibit and ten Eastern Diamond-back rattlesnakes were milked for venom by noted herpetologist Warren Fletcher. The automobile shows, which had been suspended during the war, were reinstated in 1947, but now included all types of boats and even airplanes.

As with any amusement institution, the Boardwalk also saw its share of unpleasant and even tragic episodes. In 1949, a young shooting gallery attendant accidentally

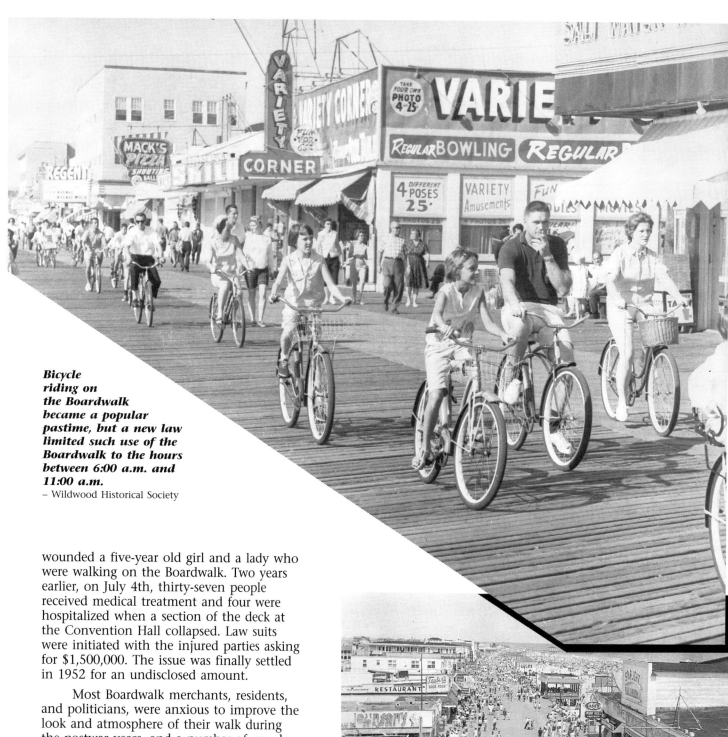

Bicycle riding on the Boardwalk became a popular pastime, but a new law limited such use of the Boardwalk to the hours between 6:00 a.m. and 11:00 a.m.
– Wildwood Historical Society

wounded a five-year old girl and a lady who were walking on the Boardwalk. Two years earlier, on July 4th, thirty-seven people received medical treatment and four were hospitalized when a section of the deck at the Convention Hall collapsed. Law suits were initiated with the injured parties asking for $1,500,000. The issue was finally settled in 1952 for an undisclosed amount.

Most Boardwalk merchants, residents, and politicians, were anxious to improve the look and atmosphere of their walk during the postwar years, and a number of new laws were passed to help them attain their goal. Picnicking, which often left unsightly litter, would no longer be permitted on or near the Boardwalk. And, there was yet another movement to ban the fortune tellers who had reappeared along the walk. Once again, there was an effort to dictate dress codes on the Boardwalk. In North Wildwood, a new ordinance prohibited bathing suits or shorts on the Boardwalk after six P.M., and in Wildwood Crest, men still could not leave the beach without wearing a shirt. In Wildwood, a number of organizations asked for legislation that would prohibit women from appearing on the Boardwalk in bathing

The Boardwalk, looking north, on a pleasant summer day in 1954. – Newark Public Library

149

suits, shorts, or even slacks. One newspaper writer noted that, "The question is not merely one of indecent exposure, but also repulsive exposure." The mayor responded that a 1934 law already covered the issue of proper dress, and he instructed the police to enforce dress codes along the Boardwalk, as well as on city streets.

WAR GAMES

The Boardwalk was also a battleground for the war between the State of New Jersey and the games operators, but most visitors to the Boardwalk were oblivious to the controversy that lasted for almost a decade. It began quietly in 1951 with the state attorney general's announcement that efforts would be made to close games of chance such as wheels of fortune, and perhaps even bingo parlors at seaside resorts. The issue did not attract much attention until June, 1956, when the New Jersey Supreme Court ruled that the long-standing issue of skill versus chance was no longer a factor in determining whether or not a game would be considered gambling. Suddenly, games in greater Wildwood and other resorts were inspected and closed simply because they gave away money or other valuable prizes. This action, supported by the

high court, might have cost the New Jersey amusement park and summer resort industry an estimated $10,000,000 in losses a year. In response, S. B. Ramagosa & Sons' legal counsel succeeded in obtaining a restraining order on the closing of the games, and State Senator Charles Sandman and Assemblyman Robert E. Kay introduced a bill that would make certain games of skill fully legal. The Sandman-Kay bill passed but was subsequently vetoed by Governor Robert Meyner. Soon after, the state resumed shutting down games.

In an effort to test the laws, Gilbert Ramagosa and others refused to close their games, were arrested, and released on bail. The issue was serious; in Cape May County there were seventy games operators who paid rents of $210,000, taxes of $31,000, and who paid 140 employees a total of $75,000 a season.

Moreover, the games were very popular with summer visitors because they awarded more than $500,000 in prizes each season. Not surprisingly, many started working toward a voter referendum on the games issue, and in 1957, Sandman again introduced a bill to legalize certain games of skill. At this point the Supreme Court again entered the fray, ruling that any game that could be lost by a player was illegal. At this point Sandman dropped his bill and started to work toward constitutional reform. A state-wide Skill Games Operators Association was formed in 1957 to agitate for favorable

The interior of Ralph Franks' Sportland Arcade. On the left is a line of the popular, and sometimes controversial, Pokereno games. – Ron Franks Collection

Ron Franks, a future Boardwalk businessman, stands in front of Ralph Franks's Sportland Arcade. – Ron Franks Collection

150

state legislation. In the meantime, the courts found Gil Ramagosa and the other arrested games operators innocent and ordered their games reopened. According to the judge, their games met the criteria of a legal game.

True to his word, Senator Sandman worked to pass new laws permitting the operation of most games, although there would probably be a certain measure of state control. Early in 1958, he called for a state-wide voter referendum that would legalize many games of chance but would still count roulette wheels, dice, and slot machines as illegal games. The referendum did not materialize, but a year later Sandman introduced two bills that established a licensing program for games operators and limited wagers to twenty-five cents and prizes to a value of fifteen dollars. The bills passed, were signed by Governor Meyner, and went before the voters in November of 1959. Across the state, voters gave their approval, and in Cape May County the bills passed by a very comfortable margin of 11,859 to 5,312. When the 1960 season started, games of chance were back on the Boardwalks, but were strictly monitored by the state, the county, and local officials.

BEACH BATTLES

While the Boardwalk was waging its battles with new laws and dress codes, the beach was addressing other problems. Most disconcerting was the oil discharged from tankers at sea which rolled up on the beach as a sticky, tar-like substance. Bathers were more than upset about the pollution and Dutch Hoffman quickly took the matter to the Coast Guard and the Army Corps of Engineers. Unfortunately, this was only a preview of the pollution problems that would arise in future decades. There were also problems with beach peddlers, mostly ice cream vendors, who insisted on selling their products on the beach without the formality of a permit. Wildwood finally took action in 1950 when the law limited the number of beach peddlers to fifteen (compared with the 100 permitted by Atlantic City's new law). The city also required a licensing fee, clean white uniforms, and health department inspections. Bowing to the demands of Boardwalk merchants, the peddlers were prohibited from selling within 100 feet of any permanent food stand or on the Boardwalk. Another controversy that would continue for years arose in 1954 when lawmakers allowed communities to charge for using their beaches. Although many New Jersey seaside towns did initiate beach fees, the Wildwoods steadfastly refused to charge for use of the strand.

Right: Captain Frank "Dutch" Hoffman with some of the 1957 beach patrol and medical staff. To Hoffman's right is Lieutenant Rom Nardi, and to his left, Lieutenant John Capacio. – Rom Nardi Collection

151

The beaches of the Wildwoods were pleasant and inviting during the postwar years, and they attracted a number of interesting people, like Warren Malkin, a lifeguard at Wildwood Crest. Warren became known as the "Arthur Godfrey of the Patrol," because he often brought his ukulele to the beach and led the other guards in singing on rainy days. And there were the animals like Oscar, an injured sea gull that guards nursed back to health and adopted as the mascot of the Wildwood Beach Patrol. Oscar was fond of tomato and lettuce sandwiches, but was equally happy digging for crabs in the sand.

Many beach visitors congregated with others from their neighborhoods, hometowns, and even native countries. Italian-Americans often met at Rio Grande and Hand Avenues, Irish-Americans at Magnolia Avenue, and African-Americans at Garfield Avenue. Kids from South Philadelphia gathered at Hand Avenue, those from west and southwest Philadelphia at Pine Avenue, and those from the northern section of the city at Magnolia Avenue (this area became known as Jitter Bug Beach).

Single day crowds on the beach routinely reached 25,000 and placed a great deal of strain on the lifeguard patrols of the three communities. In 1951 alone, the Wildwood Beach Patrol handled 294 rescues, 731 lost children, and administered first aid to 4,606 at beach hospitals that were staffed by doctors and nurses. To assist the lifeguards, Dutch Hoffman formed a beach police unit. Dressed in their white uniforms and sun helmets they patrolled the beaches in search of rule violators. But, Hoffman didn't stop there. He scanned the beach with his binoculars and quickly dispatched a lifeguard or even the police when anyone dared to bring beer or liquor onto his beachfront. Hoffman also installed a 75-foot flagpole at beach patrol headquarters which became the main place to meet up with friends or to find a lost child. "Meet me at the flagpole" became a common resort phrase after 1950.

Far left:
A typical, crowded day on the beach. Note the lifeguard's surfboats just off shore.
– Temple University, Urban Archives

Left:
Wildwood lifeguards Paul Misura and John Capacio man the oars in surfboat #10, 1956.
– Temple University, Urban Archives

BROADWAY MELODY

GOLDEN YEARS FOR THE SILVER SCREEN

The movie theatre industry remained very strong in the Wildwoods during the postwar years, and, after decades in the business, Bill Hunt had established a nationwide reputation. In 1948, on the occasion of Hunt's forty-second year in the industry, Jesse Lasky and a group of Hollywood stars including Leo Carrillo, Ruth Warrick, Lizabeth Scott,

Charles Coburn, and Rhonda Fleming, visited Wildwood. Lasky was designated honorary mayor and Carrillo became honorary police chief at a reception hosted by Governor Alfred Driscoll. When Hunt celebrated a full half century in the film industry, he was overwhelmed with letters and telegrams of congratulations from Bob Hope, Jane Russell, Clark Gable, Marlon Brando, John Wayne, Barbara Stanwyck, Harry Warner of Warner Brothers Studios, and scores of other silver screen personalities. In fact, Hunt had become so respected in the film industry that in 1952, 20th Century Fox Studios selected the Strand Theatre for the world premier showing of What Price Glory, staring James Cagney. Hunt was quick to capitalize on the honor and dubbed the Strand, "Home of World Premieres." Other promotional coups for Hunt included a visit by the Goldwyn Girls in 1946, the selection of the Strand as host of the Esther Williams Neptune's Daughter Beauty Contest in 1949, and a visit by the cast of the Mickey Mouse Club in 1958.

Constantly fighting competition from television and drive-in theatres (the Wildwood Drive-in Theatre opened in 1951), Bill Hunt and his two sons made sure that the com-

Hunt's Strand Theatre and the newly constructed Strand Shops.
– Wildwood Historical Society

Hunt's Shore Theatre, at Atlantic and Schellenger Avenues, was located behind the Jack Rabbit roller coaster.
– Wildwood Historical Society

pany's theatres were kept modern, comfortable, and safe. The original Strand, which had been lost to fire in 1944, was replaced for the 1947 season. With 1,800 seats, the new Strand was the largest theatre constructed in the United Sates since the war. It was fire-proof, with attractive decorations and glass Hurculite doors. In 1953, Hunt spent $25,000 to purchase the first stereophonic sound system in New Jersey and the first RCA Synchro Panoramic screen in the world. The latter gave pictures a wider appearance and was hailed as the first major innovation in the film industry in more than twenty-five years. Even though he was now eighty years old, Bill Hunt continued his career as showman and innovator.

Bill Hunt's sons, Bud (left) and Guy (right) with Wildwood Mayor Charles Masciarella at Zaberer's Restaurant.
– Robert J. Scully Collection

OCEAN PIER REAPPEARS AS HUNT'S PIER

Movies were far from the only thing on the minds of Bill Hunt and his sons, Guy and Bud. The loss of Ocean Pier to fire during the war had delivered a financial blow to the Hunt organization. The lack of building materials due to the war prevented immediate reconstruction of the pier. Then, when the war was over, an uncertain economy forestalled rebuilding the pier. By the mid-1950s, however, materials became available

More than a decade after the Ocean Pier was destroyed by fire, the Hunt family built Hunt's Pier during the winter of 1956-57. Some of the surviving pilings from the Ocean Pier are visible on the beach in front of the new pier. – Charles J. Jacques, Jr. Collection

and the resort economy was thriving, giving the Hunts the impetus to build a new pier on the site of the old Ocean Pier. The first phase of Hunt's Pier began in 1955 and centered on construction of a ten unit commercial complex on the west side of the Boardwalk between Poplar and Juniper Avenues. By now Hunt was extremely cautious about fires and so had his new facility built of steel and concrete. Initial tenants included game operators, a drug store, a novelty store, and a jeweler. Later, Skyline Miniature Golf Course was constructed on the roof, and a large pylon advertising Hunt's Pier was erected on the front of the complex.

The actual construction of Hunt's Pier began on October 14, 1956, and came under the immediate supervision of Harry S. Witte of Hunt Theatres, Inc. The pier, as initially built, covered about 55,000 square feet and cost approximately a quarter of a million dollars. Specifications called for predominately fireproof materials, and the entire deck area was made of a lightweight concrete. The largest single investment was $41,667 budgeted for the new Flyer roller coaster. Designed by John C. Allen and built by his Philadelphia Toboggan Company, the structure rose 36-feet high and operated two sixteen-passenger trains.

Philadelphia Toboggan also supplied eight Panther sports cars and 1,710 feet of track at a cost of $8,549.50. The new pier featured a merry-go-round, ten gasoline Hot Rod cars, a Scrambler, and a miniature passenger train painted in Pennsylvania Railroad livery. For the youngsters, there was a turtle ride, buggies, boats, and a helicopter ride. The Flyer coaster was given its first test run on May 24, 1957, and it was open for

The new Flyer coaster provided riders with a great view of the beach and the Boardwalk.
– Charles J. Jacques, Jr. Collection

Right: At the Boardwalk entrance to Hunt's Pier were a merry-go-round and several other new rides. – Charles J. Jacques, Jr. Collection

155

A new roller coaster, the Flyer, was the featured ride on Hunt's Pier in 1957. – Wildwood Historical Society

156

Hunt's Pier in 1957, looking toward the Boardwalk.
– Charles J. Jacques, Jr. Collection

Hunt's new miniature train, painted in Pennsylvania Railroad livery.
– Wildwood Historical Society

Jungleland, part of the Hunt family's aggressive expansion of their pier.
– Photograph by Charles J. Jacques, Jr.

The entrance to the new Hot Rod ride on Hunt's Pier. – Photograph by Charles J. Jacques, Jr.

business on Memorial Day along with four other rides. The entire pier opened in late June, and Zippy the Chimp, who played Cheeta in the Tarzan movies, performed on the pier three times daily.

At the end of a very successful season, the old Ocean Pier pilings were removed, new ones were sunk, and construction began on a pier addition for 1958. That season, the "Oceanic Wonderland" installed two new rides: a German-built Satellite (the first in the U. S.) and the new Crazy Cups (or Crazy Dazy) ride built by the Philadelphia Toboggan Company. Both rides attracted so much attention that amusement park operators from all over the Eastern United States travelled to Wildwood to see them in

operation. Again in 1958 the pier reported an excellent season, prompting the Hunts to plan another great attraction for 1959. Covering 6,000 square feet, Jungleland featured fourteen passenger boats that floated past animated scenes including charging crocodiles and rhinos, a fight between a cock and a native boy, a family of friendly rhinos, an island of monkeys, and even some Gooney birds. The new ride opened in late June and by mid-August it had already carried more than a hundred thousand riders.

Jungleland was the most impressive ride built at Wildwood to date. But still the Hunts were unwilling to rest on their laurels. They added another 16,000 square feet to the pier at the end of 1959 and began to plan for expansions that would go on for more than a decade to come.

WILDWOOD RIDES AGAIN

Other amusement operators, most notably Sebastian Ramagosa and Joe Barnes, Jr., also had their sights fixed on expanding their amusement facilities. The Ramagosa interests were led by Sebastian until his death in 1953, at which time his son, Gilbert, assumed leadership of the seventy-six different enterprises controlled by the family. Like the Hunts at their pier, the Ramagosas concentrated on installing new amusement rides at the Casino Arcade (considered the world's largest kiddieland) and at their North Wildwood Kiddieland at 24th Street. Postwar expansion of the Casino Arcade started in 1949 with the purchase of a fleet of Scoota Boats and other rides including the Auto Skooters, a Bubble Bounce, Roto Jet, Round-Up, a two-story dark ride, and numerous kiddie rides. Among the non-ride attractions were a major railroad exhibit, the Florida Seminole Indian Village, complete with nine-foot long wrestling alligators, and the Great Marcello, who rode a motorcycle in the "Suicide Globe." The Ramagosas also added eight new bowling alleys, but most of their investment dollars were slated for rides and the more traditional Boardwalk games.

Ramagosa's Sportland focused on staging the annual Water Follies event that had been initiated in 1945. Each season the talent became a little more exciting and daring, culminating in Billy Outten, the Human Comet. Soaked in gasoline, Outten plunged 115 feet from a platform into a tank of water covered with a surface of burning fuel. Some of the less dangerous acts included Freckles, an actor in the Our Gang comedies, Sioux City Sue and her sister (billed as Gene Autry's Yodelling Sweethearts), Ann Howe, "the Body Beautiful," and Charlie Chaplin protege, Joan Barry.

One of the outside row horses on the marvelous Philadelphia Toboggan Company carousel at Playland. – Photograph by Charles J. Jacques, Jr.

Also competing in the amusement business were the aggressive and innovative owners of Playland and the Marine Pier. In 1948, the Cedar-Schellenger Corporation's entertainment fare included the Jack Rabbit coaster, the Old Mill, the grand Philadelphia Toboggan carousel, the Caterpillar, Cuddle Up, Auto Skooter, Swooper, Roll-O-Plane, Ferris wheel, miniature railroad, kiddie rides, funhouse, and miniature golf. Like the Hunts and the Ramagosas, the owners of Playland and Marine Pier constantly added new rides. By the end of the 1950s, their facility offered twenty amusement rides plus two excellent miniature golf courses.

The Playland carousel building after modernization. On the corner is a Kohr Bros. frozen custard stand. Archie Kohr invented frozen custard in 1919 and his tasty product came to the Wildwoods a few years later.
– Wildwood Historical Society

For a decade after the war, when the major dance bands were still in vogue, Hunt's Starlight Ballroom was the center of resort night life.
– Wildwood Historical Society

Although he had operated a Wildwood skating rink for many years, Joe Barnes, Jr. was a relative newcomer to the amusement pier industry. Late in 1957, Barnes, who also operated concessions at Philadelphia's Willow Grove Park, acquired a long term lease on the old Convention Hall pier. Many shops and the arcade were demolished, a new entrance to the Convention Hall was built, and enough deck space was constructed to handle about twenty amusement rides and a miniature golf course. Although Fun Pier was barely underway by the late 1950s, it became a major Wildwood attraction during the following decade.

Last among the entertainment piers of the postwar years was the Crest Pier. Totally land-locked by 1948, Crest Pier no longer offered amusement rides and was used mostly as a community center. In 1948, an effort was made to improve the pier's location and appearance by moving it 300 feet to the east. Dances, community sings, amateur contests, and flower shows were the events that attracted the most people to Crest Pier in those days. Near the Crest Pier, the Crest Fishing Pier was extended by 229 feet in 1950, giving it a total length of 500 feet and a new, 27-foot fishing platform at the ocean end.

DANCING TO DIFFERENT BEATS

In the years immediately following the war, the resort's musical entertainment was centered close to the amusement piers. The Convention Hall still offered a few concert bands, such as the United States Army Field Band, but both the Convention Hall and Hunt's Starlight Ballroom concentrated on big band dancing. Vaughn Monroe, Tex Beneke, Woody Herman, Charlie Spivak, and a score of other famous bands were booked into both the Convention Hall and the Starlight Ballroom during the late 1940s and 1950s. In fact, in 1948 Tex Beneke's band broadcast live from the Starlight Ballroom to an estimated sixty million radio listeners. Big band broadcasts from Harry Steele's Lincoln Hotel also attracted a large audience in New Jersey and Pennsylvania. But the era of the big band was winding down and dance attendance declined each season. The Wildwood area ballrooms found it increasingly difficult to compete with the large dance floors of Atlantic City's Steel Pier and Million Dollar Pier. Hiring only the top bands, these piers spent huge sums of money on advertising, making it even harder for the Wildwood ballrooms to make a profit with the traditional dance bands. Nevertheless, the Convention Hall ballroom was totally redecorated in 1957 and greeted the season with a new name, the Neptune Ballroom.

*Charlie Spivak leads his orchestra on the
stage of the Starlight Ballroom, about 1948.*
– Wildwood Historical Society

Even as one era ends, another begins.
As the managers of Hunt's Starlight Ballroom
soon discovered, rock and roll was waiting in
the wings to bolster profits throughout the
1950s and 1960s. In 1956, Philadelphia television disc jockey Bob Horn moved his
Bandstand Show to the Starlight Ballroom for
the summer. Playing records instead of hiring
live bands, Horn hosted six shows a week
in a format similar to that of his Philadelphia television show. After returning to
Philadelphia, Horn encountered problems at
his station and was replaced with the soon-
to-be rock and roll icon, Dick Clark. During
the summer of 1957, Clark held record hops
in the Starlight Ballroom that were broadcast
on a local radio station nightly from Tuesday
through Saturday. Until this time, Clark's
popular show had been known only in the
Philadelphia area, but on August 5, 1957, the
first national broadcast of Dick Clark's
American Bandstand was aired live on ABC-
TV from the Starlight Ballroom. The show
took off like a rocket, and Dick Clark's career
was launched right along with it. Within a

year, both American Bandstand and Dick
Clark were enjoying phenomenal success,
and Wildwood could proudly boast "It all
started here!" Of course, it was now out of
the question for Clark to return to Wildwood
as a summertime disc jockey, and he was
replaced at the Starlight Ballroom by "Old
Shoe" Lawyer. Even without Dick Clark, the
Starlight's popular record hops still managed
to attract more than six thousand teenagers
a week.

Those who enjoyed a more adult sound
could find their favorite entertainers in the
many bars, night clubs, and supper clubs
that sprang up within a few blocks of
Wildwood's amusement zone. Clubs had
been popular in the 1930s and 1940s, but it
was in the two decades following the war
that Wildwood became known as "the" place
for great live entertainment. In fact, in
October, 1955, a Newark newspaper reported
that entertainment booking agents had
begun to refer to Wildwood as "Little Las
Vegas." Indeed, the Wildwoods ranked second only to that western gambling mecca in
both the quantity and the quality of the
entertainment it offered.

A capacity crowd at the Starlight Ballroom.
– Wildwood Historical Society

WATERSON
BERLIN
&
SNYDER CO
Music Publishers
Strand Theatre Bldg
Broadway at 47 St.
NEW YORK

Teenage idol Dick Clark returned to Wildwood on Friday, June 19, 1960, to spin records.
– Wildwood Historical Society

When it came to music, Wildwood offered something for everyone: big band, jazz, R & B, swing, rock and roll, and even country and western music. For example, in 1954, one could enjoy Julius LaRosa at the Club Avalon, Louis Prima at The Riptide, or Bill Haley and the Comets at the Starlight Ballroom. In addition, there were shows featuring the Ames Brothers, Mills Brothers, Buddy Greco and others. For country-western fans, Nebraska Joe and His Circle J Ranch Boys were appearing at Harry Genson's Lyndhurst Bar.

Tony Bennett, who performed in the Wildwoods a number of times, credited the resort as the birthplace of rock and roll. While other cities may argue the point, it is factual that several major rock and roll performers launched their careers in the Wildwoods. Chubby Checker, who drove to the Rainbow Club in his silver Jaguar XKE, was booked into resort clubs early in his career and actually developed his hit the "Twist" in the Wildwoods. Bill Haley and the Comets were resort regulars, playing at the Starlight Ballroom, the Hof Brau Hotel, and other locations. According to local witnesses, "Haley started the rock n' roll craze in Wildwood at the Hof Brau and followed the

162

beat to its height." Most importantly for his career, Haley's clever manager, Lord Jim, rented a house in Wildwood Crest and invited important disc jockeys to spend a rent-free vacation at the house. When they returned to their hometowns, the air waves were filled with the sounds of Bill Haley and the Comets.

The line-up of stars playing the Wildwoods by the early 1950s was impressive. The lavish, new $200,000 Bolero Club debuted in 1951 and offered a bill of performers that included Peggy Lee, Patti Paige, the Mills Brothers, Rosemary Clooney, Little Richard, Screamin' Jay Hawkins, Sam Cooke, and the Andrews Sisters. In 1952, the Bolero Club's owner booked curvaceous television star Dagmar, who inspired one of the bartenders to invent a new drink, the Dagmartini. By the time the Bolero was destroyed by fire in 1959, it had an annual summer entertainment budget of more than $150,000.

Setting its sights on the quiet dinner trade was the Manor Supper Club that opened in the remodelled Wildwood Manor Hotel in 1955. Along with full course dinners starting at $1.50 and the danceable music of the Frankie Mayo and Mike Francis orchestras, the Manor Supper Club offered top shelf talent such as Tony Bennett, the Four Aces, Frankie Lane, Pat Boone, Peggy Lee, Liberace, Georgia Gibbs, Patti Paige, the Maguire Sisters, and Jerry Lewis. Similar to the Manor Supper Club was Lou Booth's Chateau Monterey that provided a full band, an emcee, and two complete floor shows of six or seven acts each. A veteran club operator, Booth also brought in many name performers, including Rosemary Clooney and crooner Art Lund, "...who sings like melting vanilla ice cream."

The list of Wildwood's important talent and successful night clubs was truly impressive. At the Beachcomber on Schellenger Avenue appeared the Ames Brothers, Tony Bennett, Sarah Vaughn, the Three Suns, Mel Torme, June Christy, Don Cornell, and Billy Eckstine. Patrons of the Club Martinique danced to the house band of Steve Gibson and His Original Red Caps, and listened to the music of Louis Armstrong, Earl Hines, Arvell Shaw, Velma Middleton, Jack Teagarden, Dizzy Gillespie, Bob Eberle, and the Four Aces. Ella Fitzgerald performed at the Surf Club and future Las Vegas headliner, Freddie Bell, were booked into the Riptide. Those seeking "hot" shows patronized the Creole Follies and the Harlem Revue at Issy Bushkoff's Club Esquire. With stars performing in scant bikinis, the Harlem Revue was advertised as "...the Hottest Show in Wildwood."

The exposure that entertainers received in the Wildwoods often benefited their private as well as their public lives. For example, while performing in Wildwood in 1958, singer Al Martino met a local girl, Gwen Wenzel. A year later, they were married by Mayor Ralph James.

In addition to the strictly musical clubs, there were several that combined music and comedy. One was Marty Bohn's popular Nut Club which was greatly expanded in 1950 to accommodate the crowds that roamed Wildwood's streets late into the night. Another was the Club Avalon, operated by ex-boxer Eddie Suez. During the early 1950s, Suez booked a young Philadelphia banjo player and comedian, Cozy Morley. Late in 1958, Morley managed to scrape together $15,000 for a down payment and bought the club from Suez. Morley changed the club little. Seating eleven hundred at tables and chairs that had seen better times, Morley's club had a ceiling covered in burlap and sold little or no food. There was no cover charge, no air conditioning, and no heat for cool nights. But Morley's great talent and his excellent line-up entertainers drew capacity crowds every night for a three-hour show that began at ten o'clock. During the 1960s and 1970s, Morley's Club Avalon was known as the leading comedy and entertainment facility in the area.

WILDWOOD OUTINGS OUTDO THEMSELVES

By now, business at the resort was booming, and the communities made every effort to ensure that the prosperity would continue by advertising extensively. In 1948, newspaper ads for the resort were seen in Cleveland. In 1950, an aggressive billboard campaign was launched, and in 1954 the Information Bureau distributed 62,000 pieces of literature and handled 10,000 written inquiries about the resort. Of course, by this time, television was also playing an important role in the marketing of Wildwood. When business took a decline in 1958, the Wildwood Public Relations Bureau provided motels and hotels with 20,000 color postcards to mail in an attempt to bolster business in August. The resort left no stone unturned in its marketing program. When it was found that Canadians loved Wildwood and enjoyed the favorable currency exchange rate of the period, much of the resort's ad budget was directed at Eastern Canada, especially Quebec.

Finally, in 1956, the city constructed a new Tourist Information Center on the Boardwalk at Schellenger Avenue. Here the public relations staff fielded both written and

Although not summer resorts, amusement parks in New Jersey and Pennsylvania competed aggressively with the Wildwoods and other seaside resorts for single day excursions or group outings. Palisades Park, across the river from Manhattan, was a particularly strong competitor.
– New Jersey State Archives

Cape May, with stately old hotels like the Colonial, also vied for a share of the summer tourist trade. – New Jersey State Archives

Wildwood's major competitor in the 1950s was Atlantic City, which offered larger amusement piers, grander hotels, and a good beach.
– David W. Francis Collection

in-person inquiries, assisted with motel and hotel reservations, distributed information on activities and special events, and found the parents of approximately two thousand lost children each summer. By the 1950s, the Public Relations Bureau was humming like a well-oiled machine, distributing news stories and photographs to hundreds of newspapers, producing effective advertising campaigns, and attending many important trade shows and conventions throughout the Eastern United States. Through the efforts of this department, most of the United States and Canada were reawakened to the many pleasures of the Wildwoods.

Although not as important as they had been, special events were part of the entertainment package that drew millions to the seashore during the 1950s. In the tough times just before World War I and throughout the 1930s, these events were used to draw crowds to the resort. By the 1950s, they were often merely added attractions. The annual Baby Parade remained popular, with 250 entrants competing in 1946. That year, Elaine Richman was crowned Queen Oceana XXXVI. Richman was no stranger to baby parades, as she had won first place in the Wildwood parade of 1929, second place in 1932, and first place in a Cape May contest. The Baby Parade of 1951 was declared the greatest in the history of the events, drawing 261 contestants, 65,000 spectators, newsreel camera crews, and media representatives from numerous cities and the wire services. The only glitch in the baby parades of the post-war years came in 1954, when the 44th annual parade was cancelled due to heavy rains and wind. After several delays, it was determined that too many costumes and floats had been damaged by the weather, and the Baby Parade was called off.

Wildwood was never able to recapture the glory of the Miss America Pageant held there during the early 1930s, but a number of Miss America finalists did visit the resort on their way to Atlantic City, sometimes making an appearance at one of the busy night clubs. And, starting in the mid-1950s, the Miss New Jersey Contest was held in Wildwood each June as a preliminary to the Miss America Pageant in Atlantic City.

The National Marble Tournament seemed at home in Wildwood after the war and continued to be a great publicity vehicle for the resort. Then, unexpectedly, the tournament left Wildwood for Asbury Park in 1949, where it remained until wooed back to Five Mile Beach for the 1960 event.

The old Convention Hall was still the center of most of the indoor sporting events at the resort, with Turc Duncan's wrestling matches as popular as ever. The facility's

Vivian Parsons is crowned Queen Oceana during the 1953 Baby Parade.
– Temple University, Urban Archives

roller skating rink had something of a rebirth in 1946 when Duncan's attractive, soft-spoken daughter, Louise, signed a contract to manage the rink. In addition to traditional skating sessions, Louise Duncan brought in roller hockey games that featured some of the best teams in the East. Duncan also added a soda fountain to the rink and opened the skating facility for matinee sessions on rainy afternoons when the beach and the Boardwalk were too wet for most visitors.

The Convention Hall was now an aging facility, mostly inadequate for the needs of large conventions. By 1954, Public Relations Director Jack Kay and others were lobbying

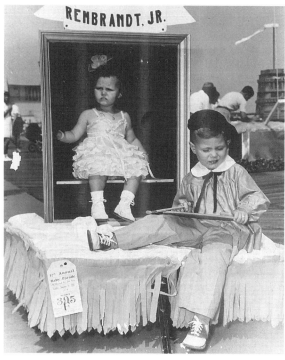

A typical float in the annual Baby Parade of the post-war years. – Wildwood Historical Society

for a new facility, estimating it would cost some $215,000 to build. That figure was just a fraction of what the new building would cost when it was finally built more than a decade later.

Meanwhile, Wildwood businessmen continued their aggressive bidding for conventions and one-day excursions. So zealous were they that a group of Atlantic City promoters, led by pier owner George A. Hamid, complained that Wildwood was out to steal all of the business from its northern neighbor. Indeed, some major conventions selected Wildwood over both Atlantic City and the equally popular Asbury Park. In 1946, Wildwood hosted 25,000 New Jersey Veterans of Foreign Wars, and in 1951, the 33rd Annual State Convention of the American Legion drew 25,000. Smaller groups were also welcomed by the resort. These included the United Spanish War Veterans and the New Jersey Circuit No.2 of the Jehovah's Witnesses who found the ocean surf ideal for baptizing eighty-three members of the faith.

THE AUTO SIDETRACKS THE TRAIN

Convenient access by automobile was a major reason for the popularity of the Wildwoods during the 1950s. By now most families were taking vacation trips in their own automobiles. Responding to this fact, most highway systems had been improved to the extent that the once-remote Jersey Shore was far more accessible than ever before. In 1950, the Rio Grande Bridge was replaced with the new George Redding high-level bridge, and a year later, the Delaware Memorial Bridge at Wilmington opened, providing direct access to the seashore. The most important highway development, however, was the high-speed Garden State Parkway. By the beginning of the 1955 summer season, the Parkway stretched from the New York State line to Cape May. It was estimated that the new expressway would bring an additional 349,000 automobiles to Greater Wildwood each season. Inevitably, this great influx of cars resulted in increased numbers of traffic accidents, congestion on the streets of the resorts, and a serious shortage of park-

ing spaces. As early as 1949, the City of Wildwood, already reeling from the costs associated with increased automobile traffic, authorized the installation of 404 parking meters which managed to generate about $19,000 in new income during the first year of metered parking. Although the city began construction of additional parking lots, the problems associated with traffic congestion and limited parking would not be easily solved.

To avoid traffic tieups, many began to use the inter-city buses instead of the family car. Recognizing the importance of the opportunity, S. B. Ramagosa acquired control of the Five Mile Beach Electric Railway Company (now totally a motor bus line) in June, 1951. Ramagosa purchased new buses, improved service, and added open-air buses for sightseeing use. For out-of-towners, the Public Service Interstate Transportation Company ran buses every twenty minutes from Philadelphia to Wildwood during the summer season. To accommodate more buses, the City of Wildwood built a new bus parking lot in 1947, and, a year later, the Public Service firm built a $150,000 bus terminal at Oak Avenue.

Another mode of transportation to the shore became available with the opening of the Cape May County-Wildwood Airport in May, 1949. All American Airways immediately offered service to twenty-four cities, and bandleader Vaughn Monroe flew his private plane into Wildwood when appearing at the Starlight Ballroom. By the mid-1950s, Allegheny Airlines was providing efficient, regular service to Wildwood from as far away as Cleveland, Pittsburgh, Washington, and New York City.

The Pennsylvania-Reading Seashore Lines continued to play an important role in passenger transportation during the summer season. Immediately after the war, the line's service and the quality of the equipment used were marginal at best. Resort residents pleaded with the railroad to make improve-

The Andrews Avenue railroad station. As automobile traffic increased during the 1950s and 1960s, the area around the station was the scene of frequent traffic jams.
– Wildwood Historical Society

ments. With equipment still scarce following heavy wartime usage, the company did begin to improve its service in 1946. But the railroad was not the indispensable entity that it had once been, and residents of Wildwood Crest began to complain loudly about the smoke, soot, and noise that was created by steam engines as they passed through the town. Partial relief came in 1950 when diesel-electric engines began to replace the old steam engines. Then, in 1951, the line assigned its new Budd RDC (Rail Diesel Car) units to the Wildwood route. Streamlined, clean, quiet, and fast, the new Budd cars could easily cruise at seventy miles per hour and could be operated as single units or coupled together as a train.

Even with new, modern equipment, the fortunes of the Pennsylvania-Reading Seashore Lines declined rapidly in the 1950s. In 1946, the line transported 9,117,403 people to the coastal resorts. Seven years later, the number had dropped dramatically to only 2,131,000. In 1955, the line suffered a $2,777,000 deficit in passenger operations, and total losses of $3,500,000. The railroad was forced to curtail service, and during the winter season, trains to the coast were few and far between. The railroad also terminated daily excursions to the resort, but in 1954, Mayor Steele and Public Relations Director Kay convinced the line to again offer excursions from Philadelphia. The excursions were advertised heavily, but the first train left Philadelphia with just 173 people onboard. Clearly, the era of the passenger railroad was almost over. Desperate for parking space, the cities worked with the railroad to relocate stations and remove tracks, replacing the right-of-way with parking lots. Then, in 1958, the rail spur into Wildwood Crest was abandoned, and only two trains ran daily from Camden to Wildwood in winter.

TRYING TO CUT CORNERS

After the war, the idea of a ferry line from Lewes, Delaware, to Cape May resurfaced. In 1947, costs for the construction of two ferries and the needed shore facilities were estimated, and plans were made for a $5,000,000 bond issue. In 1951, Governor Driscoll signed legislation enabling the establishment of a ferry line, and, with the Garden State Parkway providing a solid link from Cape May to the north, a number of private firms expressed interest in operating the ships. However, once again, plans stagnated, and although everyone seemed to want the ferry line, no one really spearheaded the effort. As a result, the concept languished all through the 1950s and did not become a reality for another decade.

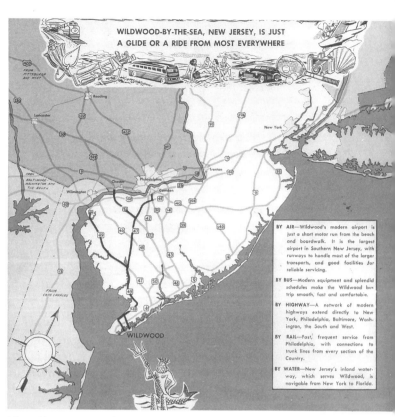

Travel routes to the Wildwoods. (From a postwar brochure).
– Wildwood Historical Society

A distant cousin of the transportation business was the resort's party boat and cruise boat industry. During the early 1950s, more than one hundred party boats offered fishing charters from Wildwood piers, and in 1950 alone, these boats entertained fifty-six thousand anglers. There were also a number of passenger sightseeing boats, several capable of handling more than two hundred passengers per trip. With the war over, several navy surplus motor torpedo boats came on the market, and several of these were successfully converted into passenger vessels by Allen Warren, Otto Stocker, and other boat operators. Both daytime and evening cruises were extremely popular with families vacationing in the Wildwoods during the 1950s.

MORE GROWING PAINS

The tremendous growth of business during the 1950s brought many problems for the cities of Wildwood, North Wildwood, and Wildwood Crest. To serve the needs of only 22,000 people in winter and 250,000 in summer, a flexible water supply was vital. Such a system required twenty-four artesian wells supported by modern pumping facilities. Then there was the age-old war with the tiny mosquito, an on-going battle that required the aerial spraying of 3,000 gallons of DDT in 1951 alone. Other perennial concerns included the cost of maintaining the Boardwalk, staffing the beach patrols, and sufficiently expanding the police force in summer.

The Wildwood Yacht Basin was the center of pleasure boating on Five Mile Island.
– Wildwood Historical Society

In the 1950s, Wildwood's commercial fishing fleet was still among the largest on the Atlantic Coast. – Wildwood Historical Society

One of Wildwood's most famous sightseeing cruisers.
– Wildwood Historical Society

A war surplus air-sea rescue boat was converted to Captain George Sinn's eighty-five foot sightseeing boat that operated from Wildwood Crest during the 1950s.
– David W. Francis Collection

Of more serious concern was the increase in rowdyism and crime that came with the influx of people and the rise of the night club districts. As early as 1949, the Wildwood Police found it necessary to assign a dozen officers to special night duty around the clubs. Drunken driving, fights, under-age drinking, and gambling all occupied the police and strained their resources. Over Labor Day weekend in 1956, 81 people were arrested and fines totaling $2,040 were levied. Fines, which totalled $9,910 during June and July of 1958, swelled to $24,550 during the same two months in 1959. Many blamed the one-day bus excursions that often carried intoxicated passengers to the resort, and an attempt was made to curtail or eliminate bus charters. Many one-day excursionists also brought their lunches and left the beach and Boardwalk strewn with litter. In addition, many were caught changing from street clothes into swimsuits under the Boardwalk. But, bus charters were only part of the problem. In fact, Greater Wildwood's resorts, like most resorts, had grown to the point where public disturbances and law breaking were becoming routine. The communities made a noble effort to curb rowdy behavior, arrest gambling operators, enforce decency laws, and even to reinstate the Sunday closing laws. Curfews on beach usage from late night to early morning helped, as did increasing Wildwood's police force by twenty-five officers for the summer of 1953, but the problems inherent with increasing crowds and relaxing moral standards would persist throughout the turbulent years of 1960s.

the *TURBULENT* *60s*

Nineteen-sixty heralded not only the beginning of a new decade but also the start of a whole new era in American history. Unlike the conservative, mostly benign years of the preceding decade, the 1960s were marked by political liberalism, radical movements, anti-war demonstrations, campus unrest, urban riots, and the increased use of drugs among teenagers. In many ways, the cultures and countercultures of the 1960s manifested themselves in the seaside summer resorts.

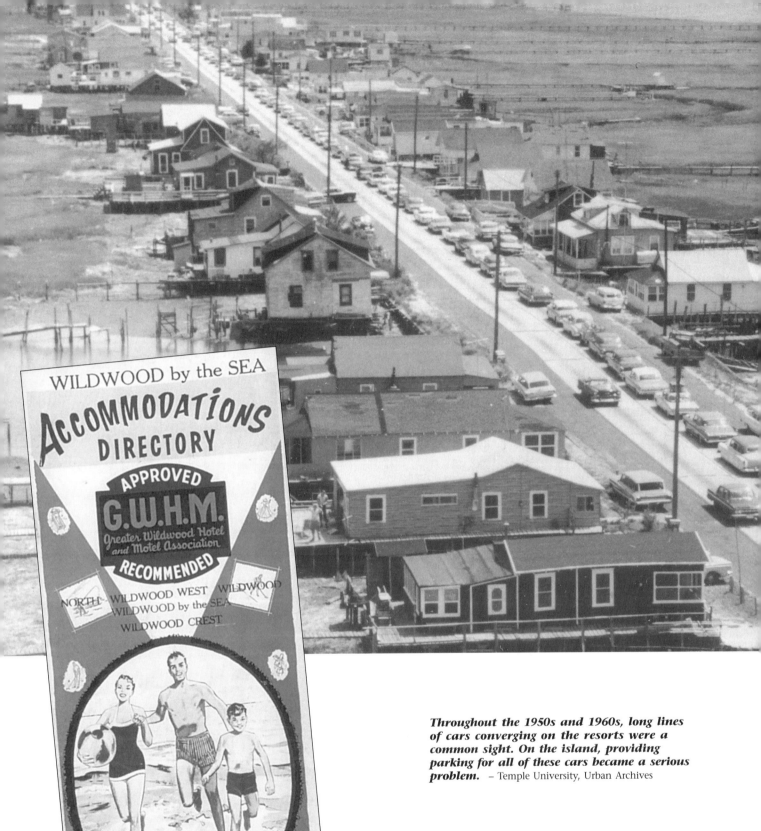

WILDWOOD by the SEA

ACCOMMODATIONS
DIRECTORY

APPROVED
G.W.H.M.
Greater Wildwood Hotel
and Motel Association
RECOMMENDED

NORTH WILDWOOD WEST WILDWOOD
WILDWOOD by the SEA
WILDWOOD CREST

NEW JERSEY

Throughout the 1950s and 1960s, long lines of cars converging on the resorts were a common sight. On the island, providing parking for all of these cars became a serious problem. – Temple University, Urban Archives

Previous page: The Riptide was among a dozen night clubs that earned the Wildwoods the nickname, "Little Las Vegas" in the 1960s and 1970s.
– Temple University, Urban Archives

CHAPTER 7

The favorable business climate of the 1950s continued into the 1960s, but many merchants were discovering how hard it was to survive on the profit from a four-month business season. As a result, numerous retail stores went out of business during the 1960s. During the winter, unemployment levels at the seashore rose to new heights and were usually the highest in all of New Jersey. With no answer to the problem of how to find jobs for people when the resort was not open, Wildwood's population declined from 5,475 in 1950 to 4,690 in 1960. During this same period, North Wildwood experienced very slight growth, while Wildwood Crest, by now considered the elite section of the resort, showed a substantial population growth. As the resort's central and largest community, Wildwood suffered most from the problems of seasonal unemployment. Attending the loss of jobs were decaying neighborhoods and vacant buildings just waiting to be vandalized. The city showed all the signs of becoming a real eyesore. Fortunately, by the late 1960s, urban renewal plans were underway in Wildwood; many of the old, derelict buildings were repaired or replaced and neighborhoods were gradually revitalized.

The '60s were profitable for most resort businesses; this, despite the sparse crowds due to poor weather in 1961 and 1967 and the stiff competition for Canadian trade from the Montreal World's Fair. In 1960, it was estimated that the Wildwoods entertained as many as 2,000,000 people a year, and the July 4, 1966, crowds numbered an incredible 400,000. In terms of actual revenue, the Wildwood resorts took in $139,387,000 in 1964, a figure that rose to $176,000,000 just three years later. By comparison, Ocean City had an annual resort income of $136,000,000, and Cape May took in $21,000,000 in 1967. Still the leading resort south of Atlantic City, the Wildwoods represented about fifty percent of the total resort business in Cape May County.

The resort communities had many concerns during the 1960s, but most disturbing was the rise in crime and rowdy behavior that came with large crowds and increasing numbers of teenagers and young adults. Robberies on the beach and the Boardwalk were common, and numerous Boardwalk stores were looted during the night. Arrest lists grew longer and longer, and the big holiday weekends proved particularly difficult. Over July 4, 1966, there were 222 arrests (compared to only 50 in 1959). Although those arrested comprised a very small part of the total crowd of 400,000, the constant reports of crime and disorder were damaging to the family resort image of the Wildwoods. After a particularly bad Labor Day weekend

The tennis courts and playground at Fox Park. – Wildwood Historical Society

in 1962, the local newspaper reported that, "...a major crime wave seemed to hit Wildwood over Labor Day weekend... robberies, assaults, fights, drunk and disorder and climaxed by the murder of a 22 year old woman on the North Wildwood beach...." Three seasons later, the newspaper lamented, "All Hades Breaks Loose in Resort." Ninety-six people were arrested, five men attacked two policemen, and a police officer found it necessary to fire his revolver in an incident on the beach.

With the reputation of the resort and the economy of the island at stake, the communities were forced to take action. The Wildwood Police Department, which numbered twenty-three officers during the winter months, was expanded to seventy men in summer. Recognizing that most of the trouble stemmed from teenagers consuming alcoholic beverages, the City of Wildwood passed an ordinance in 1962 establishing a curfew; no one under nineteen could be on the streets between 1 A.M. and 6:00 A.M. during the summer season. Some months later, Wildwood Crest invoked a similar ordinance. Further efforts to curb the growing rowdiness included limiting the number of licenses for coffee houses, dance halls, and other places where trouble was likely to start. Clearly it would not be easy to keep the resort safe for family visitors and at the same time cater to a younger generation that was eager to spend money.

Even on the beaches there was turmoil. In 1962, the North Wildwood lifeguards threatened to leave their posts unless they received a pay increase. Both the city and the news media were outraged, but, faced with little alternative, salaries were increased. Five years later, the North Wildwood guards staged two wildcat walkouts, which again forced the city to raise salaries or provide bonuses. Witnessing the lifeguards' success, the resort's summer police followed suit and also requested higher pay.

Wildwood by the Sea, N. J.

The Wildwood Boardwalk of the 1960s, with Hunt's Pier in the distance.
– David W. Francis Collection

Despite everything, the beach patrols in all three communities remained dedicated and highly capable. In 1965, it was reported that 1,176,020 people used the North Wildwood Beach between late June and early September. Utilizing Jeeps and lifeboats, the patrol made 164 rescues that season. A year later, the Wildwood Beach Patrol conducted 119 rescue operations, again often using the traditional heavy wooden lifeboats. In 1968, the patrol was equipped with the first lightweight, fiberglass lifeboats that proved to be faster and easier to handle. In light of the heavy crowds that descended on the beaches, the sometimes rowdy behavior of some of the bathers, and the difficulty of keeping alcoholic beverages off the beach, all three lifesaving services did a marvelous job of making the island's beaches among the safest in the nation.

THE BOARDWALK – THE MAIN THOROUGHFARE TO FUN

Adjacent to the beach, the Boardwalk enjoyed a continuation of the post-war business explosion. By 1960, the Boardwalk boasted no less than five major amusement centers. Together, these operations offered 116 amusement rides, the largest concentration on the East Coast, and perhaps in the world. The $60,000 in maintenance required each season to keep the Wildwood section of the Boardwalk in top condition was nothing compared to the revenues and tax base generated by these outstanding operations. And, while the big amusement operators were expanding and raking in great profits, many smaller investors were also finding the

Boardwalk to be a money-maker during the 1960s. National Tumbletown, U.S.A. of Cleveland installed three trampoline centers for the 1961 season. North Wildwood's facility was situated near the beach and consisted of thirty trampolines. Miniature golf continued to be immensely popular with families and Lou Costar installed a new golf course at Schellenger Avenue for the 1968 season. At Sportland, an entirely new Aqua Circus, which had toured arenas around the country under the direction of Norma and Bob Maxwell, opened in 1966. This new show included the beautiful Aquamaids, the Comedy Aquamaniacs, and Acapulco cliff divers who plummeted 130 feet into a tank of water.

Laura's Fudge Shop in its new building just off the Boardwalk. Laura's advertised its candy as "The Cadillac of all Fudge."
– Laura's Fudge Shops

Above: The interior of Zaberer's Restaurant, showing the Tiffany-style lighting that was a Zaberer trademark. – Ed Zaberer Collection

Below: Ed Zaberer's Restaurant became a seashore landmark and the haunt of many famous visitors during the 1960s.
– Ed Zaberer Collection

WILDWOOD MUNICIPAL CONCERT SHELL

In 1962, the City of Wildwood built a new band shell at Young Avenue, but it was moved to Montgomery Avenue a year later to appease Boardwalk business owners.
– Wildwood Historical Society

Good indicators of Boardwalk business were the food operations, and at Douglass Candies the nationally-known confectionery was selling as much as a ton and a half of taffy and an equal amount of fudge per day. Tastes were changing, however, and during the 1960s, fudge replaced salt water taffy as the favorite candy on the Boardwalk. By the end of the decade, two pounds of fudge were being sold to every one pound of taffy. All up and down the Boardwalk, restaurants, hot dog stands, and the increasingly popular pizza shops were enjoying the excellent business climate of the 1960s.

Band concerts returned to the Boardwalk during the 1960s when the fourteen-piece Wildwood Community Band was formed in the winter of 1961. A band shell was built at Young Avenue, and, directed by Jack Ferro, the band began presenting free concerts during the summer of 1962. The Sunday evening concerts drew more than a thousand listeners, but, not surprisingly, Boardwalk merchants were less than enthusiastic about the musical diversions. Just as they had decades before, the shop owners insisted that concert audiences congested the Boardwalk, interfered with business, and kept their wallets firmly closed. Under a great deal of pressure from the merchants, the city moved the band shell to Montgomery Avenue, which was considered the terminal end of the business district. Despite the negative reaction from businesses, the return of free concerts to the Boardwalk was a popular move.

Meanwhile, disorderly behavior and outright crime was becoming more and more prevalent, compelling the communities to be even more diligent in the enforcement of laws and moral codes along the Boardwalk. In the early 1960s, undercover police once more targeted fortune tellers, some of whom were extracting large sums of money from gullible visitors. In one case, a fortune teller was fined $200, given a three month suspended sentence, and ordered to leave Wildwood. Games also fell under the watchful eye of the law, and a North Wildwood ordinance was passed that required all games to be licensed. Officers from the state Office of Amusement and Games Control spent a great deal of time monitoring games to ensure that they were operated fairly and legally. In 1965, the officers closed three wheels of fortune because of stopping devices that permitted the operator to control where the wheel stopped. Unfortunately, the disclosure of such closings in the local newspapers cast a shadow on the many operators who ran their games fairly and honestly. In related instances, Boardwalk patrons were also starting to complain about auction houses that cheated buyers and sold questionable merchandise. However, it was not until the 1970s that any action was taken against the auction houses.

Hunt's Pier at the height of its popularity.
– Photograph by Charles J. Jacques, Jr.

Hunt's Pier in 1960. Ramagosa's Sportland
Pier is immediately north of Hunt's Pier.
– Charles J. Jacques, Jr. Collection

175

The Golden Nugget Mine Ride, Hunt's highly successful investment for the 1960 season.
– Photograph by Charles J. Jacques, Jr.

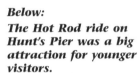

The new Iron Horse miniature railroad and its station. – Photograph by Charles J. Jacques, Jr.

By this time, the amusement piers and night clubs formed the entertainment nucleus of the Wildwoods. Generally acknowledged as the finest amusement pier in North America, if not the world, Hunt's Pier defined the Wildwood of the 1960s. Thanks to yearly improvements funded by the Hunt family, their pier had become an entertainment showcase. In 1960, the Hunts contracted with John Allen and his Philadelphia Toboggan Company to construct the eight-car Golden Nugget Mine Ride. The enclosed, coaster-like device featured an interior with both audio and visual effects. The Golden Nugget proved an immediate success, and in 1962, John Allen was called upon to design another ride, the Skua, a walk-through pirate ship funhouse. With unique special effects

Christening the new Skua Pirate Ship attraction in 1962. – Charles J. Jacques, Jr. Collection

Bill Hunt (left), now past his ninetieth birthday, inspects the Skua. – Charles J. Jacques, Jr. Collection

Although in 1967 old hotels still filled the side streets, Hunt's Pier and the new shop complexes give the resort a modern appearance.
– Wildwood Historical Society

developed by industry leaders Bill Tracey and Messmore and Damon, the ship rocked and swayed as patrons gingerly picked their way through darkened tunnels, a cavern, a mirrored room, a maze, and a tilted room. Throughout the adventure, the hapless riders were accosted by a variety of menacing mechanical pirates. By 1963, Hunt's Pier was 650 feet long and completely packed with amusements. So, in 1964, the Hunt family added another 80 feet of green-pigmented concrete pier to accommodate 1965's newest additions: an Iron Horse miniature train, Himalaya thrill ride, and a new Boardwalk theatre. At decade's end the Hunts were again looking for a major attraction to help their facility retain its place as America's finest amusement pier.

The menacing pirate face that served as the entrance to the pirate ship.
– Photograph by Charles J. Jacques, Jr.

Fun Pier at the height of its popularity during the 1960s. – Pete Barnes Collection

Beneath the Ski Lift, Joe Barnes installed a Tilt-A-Whirl and the Spook's Hide-Away dark ride. – Wildwood Historical Society

Business boomed during the 1960s, and Marine Pier was lengthened by 60 feet in order to accommodate more rides. – Wildwood Historical Society

Miniature golf was a favorite pastime throughout the resort, and the Marine Pier offered one of the best courses on the island. – Wildwood Historical Society

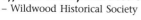

One of the exquisitely carved chariots on the Playland carousel.
– Photograph by Charles J. Jacques, Jr.

The rounding boards of the Playland carousel still looked just as they did when they left the Philadelphia factory fifty years earlier. – Photograph by Charles J. Jacques, Jr.

The Wild Mouse on Marine Pier (foreground) was one of dozens of new amusement rides to appear in the Wildwoods during the busy 1960s. – New Jersey State Archives

Although Marine Pier constantly received new rides and attractions, the old Ferris wheel was as popular as ever.
– Wildwood Historical Society

As Hunt's Pier expanded, the other Boardwalk amusement piers followed suit. At Fun Pier, Joe Barnes, Jr., added numerous rides and attractions, including a monorail, observation tower, ski lift ride, and a dark ride called the Spook's Hide-Away. In the meantime, the Cedar-Schellenger Corporation lengthened its Marine Pier by 60 feet and added rides like the popular Wild Mouse, Tilt-A-Whirl, and the Haunted House walk-through. The Ramagosa family, now famous for their European-built rides, also continued to expand the Casino Arcade, Sportland, and their kiddielands. In 1964, however, their Casino Arcade's Mars ride was struck by a tragic $150,000 fire that took the lives of three children. The ruins of the Mars ride, a miniature golf course, and a photo stand were quickly cleared and the site was converted into a parking lot. After the tragedy, Gil Ramagosa seemed to lose his enthusiasm for developing the Boardwalk amusement piers and he dedicated more time to his other enterprises.

THE WILDWOODS – AN ENTERTAINMENT MECCA

Nineteen sixty-three marked the first time that the Boardwalk piers experienced any serious competition from outside their ranks. Located far from the Boardwalk, the new $150,000 Fort Apache opened in Rio Grande. Designed and built with a Western theme, Fort Apache offered stagecoach, burro, and covered wagon rides, a passenger train pulled by a steam locomotive and a Mississippi River steamboat ride. There was also continuous entertainment that included Sioux war dances, can-can dancers in the Silver Dollar Saloon, and cowboy shoot-outs in the streets. A saloon, bank, hotel, barber shop, restaurant, confectionery, stable, and other period structures made up a main street straight out of the Old West. But, even though Fort Apache offered an exciting array of out-of-the-ordinary diversions, it didn't really have much impact on the Boardwalk patronage.

Another 1960s business venture, although interesting, never really got off the ground. In an attempt to convert an old Hudson River ferryboat into an entertainment complex, the owners removed the stacks and some deck houses and towed the 200-foot ship into the Wildwood Yacht Basin in August, 1960. Plans called for the ship to be used as a floating pier that would include dancing, dining, retail stores, and more. The project was never completed, however, and the frequently vandalized old ship stood forgotten for more than a decade. Another concept involved construction of a North Wildwood municipal pier complete with recreational facilities and forty stores. Proposed in 1960, this plan never proceeded beyond the discussion stage.

Although the Hunt family spent a fortune expanding Hunt's Pier, they never neglected their thriving movie theatre empire. In 1965, the Hunts acquired additional theatres in Stone Harbor, which meant they now owned ten theatres in Cape May County. That same year, the Ocean Theatre opened in the Hunt's Ocean Center complex across the Boardwalk from Hunt's Pier. Then in 1968, their Casino Theatre was totally remodelled and modernized. In addition to showing movies in their theatres, the Hunts used the facilities for a number of special events. In 1968, the Regent Theatre housed the national finals of the Little Miss North American Hemisphere Pageant, hosted by Philadelphia television personality Sally Starr.

The Hotel Wildwood and its well-known Glass Bar. The Glass Bar was one of the resort's famous night spots for name entertainers and Go Go dancers.
– Wildwood Historical Society

Continuing their success of the 1950s, the night clubs located west of the Boardwalk were still booking the kind of big name entertainment that earned Wildwood the nickname "Little Las Vegas." The industry's most famous names appeared at the Surf, the Hurricane, the Beachcomber, the Rainbow, and the Manor Supper Club, but numerous smaller clubs also flourished throughout the resort. Within a four-block area of Atlantic Avenue, fifteen clubs were in full-swing by 1960. By the mid-1960s, the country was wild for "go-go" entertainment and Wildwood happily provided it. There was Joe Cavalier's Frenchee A-Go-Go Review at the Hurricane East and Giselle's International Go-Go Review at the Rainbow Club. The Club Esquire advertised, "Our Own Sepia Go-Go Girls." Suddenly, the resort was inundated with teenagers doing the Monkey, the Frug, the Jerk, and the Freddy. The same dances also showed up at the nightly record hops held at the Starlight Ballroom on the Boardwalk. The record hops were hosted by Jack "Old Shoe" Lawyer, until he was replaced in 1964 by Philadelphia disc jockey Ron Diamond. Although no longer affiliated with American Bandstand, the events were still called the Bandstand Record Hops.

The list of performers who were booked into the clubs of the Wildwoods during the 1960s reads like a Who's Who of stardom. The Manor Supper Club concentrated on attracting the dinner crowd with such top notch entertainment as Connie Francis, Paul

The Beach Hotel was operated by ex-mayor Harry Steele, who also owned the larger Hotel Lincoln. – John Williams Collection

Anka, the Lennon Sisters, Jerry Vale, Jimmy Dean, Joni James, Jackie Wilson, Theresa Brewer, Phyllis Diller, and Al Martino. The club's one concession to teen-oriented music was Wildwood's perennial favorite, Chubby Checker, who played the Manor in 1963. Among the other headliners booked into the Wildwoods were Wilson Pickett at the Rainbow Club; Dion at the Starlight Ballroom; Fats Domino (who arrived in splendor in a lavender Cadillac), Brook Benton, The Drifters, and the Shirelles at the Hurricane; the Isley Brothers, Dinah Washington, Gary U. S. Bonds, and the Platters at the Beachcomber; and Rick Nelson and Bobby Rydell (whose grandmother lived in Wildwood) at the Surf Club. Wayne Newton and Kaye Ballard appeared in Wildwood, and the Riptide Club brought in Bo Diddly and his band. The Riptide also promoted their Creole Frolics, starring, "20 Swinging Sepia Beauties," plus Ceceila Cooper, Miss Cannes of 1959. Without doubt, there was something to please everyone's musical taste in the Wildwoods of the 1960s.

INCREASED "STAYING" POWER

Of course, with such a wealth of attractions and entertainment, Wildwood's hotel and motel industry burgeoned during the '60s. If the impressive crowds needed some place to sleep, the resort's hotel, motel, boarding-house, and cottage owners were equal to the challenge by providing rooms for up to two hundred thousand people per week! By the early 1960s, the resort's motel community had developed its own unique personality. Just a glimpse of their facades pulled visitors into another world of fun, sun, and excitement. There were the bright pink walls of the Pink Champagne Motel and the even brighter yellow of the San Souci, the stuccoed walls and coats of arms of the Ivanhoe, the plastic palms and donkeys at the Rio, and the Tempo's neon sign with its musical notes. And there were still others with names as exotic as their decors: the Roman Holiday, the Casa Bahama, the Sea Shell, and the Pink Orchid. During the mid-1950s, a twenty-five unit motel could be built for around $300,000 and since that time entrepreneurs had spent more than $8,000,000 on new motels at the resort. Within just a few years, sixty-nine new motels had been built in Wildwood, sixty-five in North Wildwood, and fifty-two in Wildwood Crest. The number of available rooms swelled to 3,238 (1309 with air conditioning and 1730 with television sets), and 47 swimming pools competed with the ocean for bathers. During the busiest part of the 1960 season, the new motels were expected to handle 380,000 visitors at rates ranging from eight dollars to twenty-five dollars a day for two people. By 1963, 2,000 more motel rooms had been added in the three resort communities.

Evidently, the new rooms were greatly needed, for in July and August of 1963, virtually every motel and hotel in the Wildwoods had their "No Vacancy" signs switched on daily.

Most of the motels built in the late 1950s and the 1960s were classed as "Miami Beach-type", usually no more than two stories high. However, starting in 1960, taller, hotel-style structures began to appear, especially along the shore in Wildwood Crest. In that year, Palmer Way, Jr. and Will Morey built the luxurious Port Royal Hotel, and Morey followed this in 1964 with the $600,000 Pan American Hotel. Initially offering sixty rooms, the Pan American was designed to be expanded to twice that size. The deluxe facility featured television in every room, oceanview balconies, a coffee shop, sun deck, swimming pool, and convenient parking. It was hotels like the Pan American that set a new tone of luxury and comfort in the resorts. The new Diamond Beach opened in 1967. Promoted as a complete family resort, it included an Olympic-size swimming pool, the Colonial Dining Room, Mediterranean Lounge, shuffleboard, miniature golf, tennis courts, playground, and horseback riding stables.

Such phenomenal growth was bound to have its downside, and by 1965, motel burglaries had become common. In just a two-day period, more than $5,000 was stolen from five North Wildwood motels. Around this time, one of the few cases of racial discrimination in the resorts surfaced. In 1963, the NAACP staged demonstrations in front of several motels and hotels, saying that blacks had been denied accommodations on a number of occasions. A bi-racial committee was established by the Wildwood Hotel and Motel Association and the matter was quickly brought to a satisfactory conclusion.

While most investments were in new motels, the old hotels still prospered. The fifty-four room Adelphi-Witte sold for $99,000 in 1965, and many area hotelmen spent freely to modernize their old structures. The Hotel Roosevelt received a whole new facade and added five new rooms, while the Hotel Dayton was thoroughly redecorated and reopened as the New Hotel Dayton. Sadly, a few of the resort's old historic hotels disappeared during the 1960s. The Hotel Biltmore burned totally in 1960, and the resort's largest traditional hotel, the 168-room Wildwood Manor, was also destroyed by fire in 1968.

The Pennsylvania-Reading Seashore Line's new Budd RDC cars, as well as some old pre-war passenger coaches, at the Wildwood passenger station, 1964. – Wildwood Historical Society

After decades of conversation, the Cape May-Lewes Ferry became a reality in 1964.
– Delaware Bay & River Authority

183

Commissioners of the Norfolk-Cape Charles Ferry Commission meet to consider selling their surplus ferries to the new Cape May-Lewes line.
– Ed Zaberer Collection

FERRY SERVICE – A REALITY

Throughout the 1960s, the highways leading to the Wildwoods were jammed with cars and buses. On weekends, it was estimated that as many as three hundred thousand people were using the Garden State Parkway to get to the resorts. On one day in July of 1967, seventy-four charter buses were counted in the public parking lot. The Garden State Parkway provided a smooth, fast access route from the north, but there was still a need for better access to the resort from the south. Inevitably, the concept of a ferry line linking Cape May with Delaware was again brought up. By now, the idea had been around for fifty years, with only limited meaningful action taken during the 1940s and 1950s. Finally, in 1962, restaurateur Ed Zaberer, then chairman of the Cape May County Economic and Industrial Development Commission, prodded New Jersey Governor Richard Hughes into action. A committee of twenty-five business and community leaders formed the Cape May-Delaware Ferry Committee. It just so happened that the four ships of the Cape Charles-Norfolk line came on the market at that time and Governor Hughes sent Zaberer to Virginia to bid on the ships. Despite strong competition from Hawaii and Alaska, the vessels were purchased by Zaberer to service the Cape May-Lewes route. Renamed the Delaware, New Jersey, Cape May, and Cape Henlopen, the ships began the long awaited service between Cape May and Lewes, Delaware, on July 1, 1964. Each vessel had the capacity to handle 120 automobiles and

1,200 people. An immediate success, the service ferried 38,353 vehicles and 151,929 people in August, 1965, and by the following July, the line recorded its one millionth passenger.

While the ferry line grew in popularity, the Pennsylvania-Reading Seashore Line was not so fortunate. Despite a state subsidy of $276,000, the line reported, in 1960, that it had not shown a profit since 1943 and that during the past year it had lost $6,000,000. That year the railroad asked the Public Utility Commission for permission to terminate service to Wildwood, Ocean City, Cape May, and Atlantic City. The commission did not grant the request, but a year later it did permit the line to eliminate fifteen weekly trains, seventeen Saturday trains, and eleven Sunday trains. The railroad attempted to drop service to the resorts again in 1962 and 1967, proposing that rail transportation be replaced by 520 buses operating year-round to handle both vacationers and commuters who used the trains. Again, permission was denied, and in 1968, when the Pennsylvania Railroad and the New York Central merged to form the ill-fated Penn Central, the new line became owner of two-thirds of the ailing Pennsylvania-Reading Seashore Lines. A bit of railroad nostalgia was sparked in 1968 when the line ran a rail fan trip from South Camden to Cape May using old steam locomotive #127 and a 1912 parlor car. However, this did little more than reinforce the notion that the railroad was rapidly becoming a hopelessly outdated form of transportation to the Jersey Shore.

Some of the contestants in the 1965 Miss New Jersey Pageant in front of the Information Bureau. – Wildwood Historical Society

185

SPECIAL EVENTS ARE STILL SPECIAL

Throughout the 1960s the resort was so busy that it was not really necessary to stage special events to draw the crowds. Nevertheless, the annual Easter event (which still attracted 50,000 people in 1968) was held, as were the Miss New Jersey Pageant, golf tournaments, the National Marbles Tournament, a kiddie fishing rodeo, the Baby Parade, a boat parade, sailing regattas, fireworks, parades, and band concerts.

The fiftieth anniversary Baby Parade was held on August 4, 1960, with 250 entrants, 11 bands composed of 1,000 musicians, and 16 former event winners. Among those present was the oldest living Queen Oceana, Alice Hendee Stauffer of Rochester, New York, who was crowned in 1915. All 16 former queens rode on a large float escorted by four Wildwood lifeguards. Covered by Philadelphia television stations, the 1968 Baby Parade story was picked up by both the CBS and NBC national news.

The National Marble Tournaments also generated a great deal of publicity for the resort. In 1961, radio and television star Arthur Godfrey was on hand to crown that year's champs, Augustus "Ace" Millen of Yonkers, New York, and Anita Danyluk of Niles, Ohio, both of whom later appeared on the Ed Sullivan Show. Ed McMahon was the celebrity guest at the 1963 Tournament, and that year the winner appeared with McMahon on Johnny Carson's "Tonight Show."

Three championship mibsters prepare to compete in the 1963 National Marbles Tournament. – Wildwood Historical Society

During the mid-1960s, Wildwood was ranked as third most popular convention site in the state, right behind its old rivals, Atlantic City and Asbury Park. Conventions were worth about $2,000,000 a year to the resort, and it was computed that the average conventioneer spent twenty-one dollars a day while in the Wildwoods. The island continued to attract large groups, including the American Legion, the Eagles, the Veterans of Foreign Wars, the Elks, the Italian-American Veterans and the 28th Division Reunion. The Elks alone brought more than sixty thousand people to the Boardwalk.

Wildwood still did not offer adequate convention facilities for groups of more than a thousand people, and this failing was made even more apparent with the 1966 opening of Cape May's new 12,000 square foot convention hall. The Greater Wildwood Hotel and Motel Association began calling for a new convention hall in 1960 when the Miss New Jersey Pageant had to be held at Wildwood High School to accommodate the contestants and the audience. Plans for a new hall languished for a number of years, occasionally resurfacing, as they did in 1966. Originally, most people believed that all three seashore communities should join together to build a Greater Wildwood convention facility. North Wildwood was indifferent to the idea, and Wildwood Crest flatly refused to be part of the plan, announcing it would build its own civic center with 1,400 seats (although voters rejected this proposal in the 1968 election). Undaunted, the Wildwood City Commissioners elected to move ahead alone and in 1968 appointed a seven-person Convention Hall Authority to oversee the planning and construction of the hall. Although there were still many obstacles to overcome, Wildwood was on its way to having a new, modern convention facility.

For the most part, the weather of the 1960s was pleasant and comfortable at the Jersey Shore. Of course, there were a few notable brushes with severe storms. In 1960, hurricane Donna, the worst storm to hit Cape May County since 1944, did $150,000 in damage, mostly in broken windows and neon signs along the Boardwalk. The big storm of March, 1962, however, was far more severe. According to the local newspaper,

Mayor Ralph James of Wildwood crowns the champions of the 1964 National Marbles Tournament. – Wildwood Historical Society

"Ringer Bowl," with six playing rings, at the National Marbles Tournament.
– Wildwood Historical Society

"Greater Wildwood in the last two days experienced the most disastrous period in its history...." High tides and vicious winds swept water into the towns, flooding the streets. More than one hundred fires were caused by electrical shorts. Fire trucks were useless on the flooded streets, and firefighters had to battle the flames and evacuate victims in small boats. National Guardsmen and firefighters came from as far away as fifty miles, and the federal government declared the Jersey Coast a disaster area. More than five hundred people needed immediate shelter, and when a relief loan office was established on the Boardwalk, requests came in for nearly two million dollars in assistance loans. Cape May lost its entire boardwalk in the storm, and Seaside Heights suffered damage to much of its wooden walkway. In West Wildwood, ninety-two of the community's four hundred homes were washed off of their foundations. Resorts are accustomed to such disasters, however, and the ever-resilient Wildwoods worked tirelessly to clean up the debris and rebuild as much as possible before the traditional Memorial Day season opening. Amazingly, when the holiday arrived, it was business as usual in the Wildwoods.

The 1960s were profitable years for most businesses in Greater Wildwood, but the economic boom that had begun in the late 1940s could not last forever. By the late '60s there were definite signs that the glory days of the past two decades might be coming to an end.

Drum and Bugle Corps competition at the annual New Jersey Veterans of Foreign Wars convention. – Wildwood Historical Society

Officers and men from the Cape May Coast Guard Station take part in the annual parade at the Veterans of Foreign Wars convention. – Wildwood Historical Society

DECLINE and RENAISSA of the RESORT

*T*he period from the mid-1960s through the 1980s was a difficult one for America's summer resorts and traditional amusement parks. Due to a number of factors, many resorts and parks began a long, painful decline. Some, like the Wildwoods, survived and recovered. Others, like New York's Coney Island, never really rebounded after the closing of its last original amusement park (Steeplechase Park) in the mid-1960s.

CHAPTER 8

Throughout the country, amusement parks that had prospered for decades were forced to close after several losing seasons. Two of the country's greatest amusement parks, Chicago's Riverview Park and Cleveland's Euclid Beach Park, were closed and razed during the latter 1960s. While many parks continued to squeak by financially, the really successful facilities of the era were the new super-parks located across the country. Enormous investments were made at such parks as Cedar Point, Magic Mountain, the Disney facilities, and the Six Flags parks. Literally millions were spent on advertising, bigger and faster coasters, and a wealth of other attractions. Smaller traditional parks simply could not compete with the emerging giants of the amusement industry.

CE

Across the country, seaside and summer resorts suffered a similar fate. After years of neglect, many of the once-great resort hotels fell into disrepair, were closed, and demolished. Among the unfortunate victims was the legendary Traymore, one of Atlantic City's best, which succumbed to the wrecking ball in 1972. Along the Jersey Shore amusement piers were beginning to look shabby, and boardwalks suffered from a lack of proper maintenance. In spite of urban renewal projects, neighborhoods near the boardwalks deteriorated into avenues of boarded up store fronts and abandoned homes. Atlantic City and Asbury Park, Wildwood's old competitors, had become depressingly worn out by the 1970s.

Things weren't much better in the Wildwoods. Business suffered greatly due to the nation-wide decline of summer resorts and parks and a new generation of vacationers in search of bigger and better thrills for their money. But these were not the only reasons for the near demise of the Wildwoods. The raising of the legal drinking age to twenty-one certainly helped to eradicate most of the clubs that catered to the youth crowd. Atlantic City inflicted immeasurable damage to Wildwood's entertainment industry as the big names in show biz flocked to the glitzy new gambling casinos. There was simply not room for two "Little Las Vegas" resorts. And, finally, the Wildwoods had begun to look their age. For more than two decades, owners had extracted enormous profits from their resort businesses. While people like the Hunts and the Ramagosas continued to re-invest in their properties, many did not. Having no reason to believe that the business boom of the 1950s and 1960s would end in the near future, they saw no reason to revamp or improve their properties. Motels that were

Despite many concerns about pollution, the beaches remained crowded throughout the 1970s. – Wildwood Historical Society

quite pleasant in the 1950s had become hopelessly outdated and inadequate by the 1980s. By the time most resort business owners realized that the Wildwoods were in decline, it was obvious that the road to recovery would be a long and difficult one.

The entire Jersey Coast was also beset by other problems. A 1969 survey revealed that 100 percent of the one million visitors to the shore over the July 4th weekend named the ocean and beach as the resort's primary attractions. These natural assets, however, were suffering from a flood of negative publicity about pollution. Oil and other refuse had been dumped into the ocean for decades. Beginning in 1922, Cape May County officials had tried in vain to obtain federal assistance to end off-shore dumping. And the situation only worsened with time. The cities of New York, Philadelphia, and Camden were dumping their sludge into the ocean, to this sewage was added medical wastes, chemicals, industrial by-products, land run-off from heavy rains, and the constant flow of oil discharge and spillage from ships. Beaches were becoming horribly fouled, wildlife was threatened, and the fishing industry was being destroyed. Finally, a glimmer of hope was seen when seaside communities were ordered to build new sewage treatment plants, and both federal and state governments began to take aggressive action against pollution. But, the clean-up of the Jersey Shore would take time, and in the ensuing years, thousands of vacationers elected not to visit resorts with contaminated beaches.

Another blow to the resort business came with the passing of the so-called Old Guard. Those industrious men and women who had guided the resort, some since the early 1900s, had either died or sold their businesses. Bill Hunt, the undisputed Amusement King of the Wildwoods, passed away on July 12, 1970, at the age of ninety-eight. Five years later, his son, Guy, died unexpectedly after ulcer surgery. Management of the family's huge amusement empire fell to Guy's brother, William "Bud" Hunt. Although Hunt continued to administer the business for a number of years, the future of Hunt's Pier and the Hunt Theatres was in doubt. Joe Barnes, Jr., who had developed Fun Pier, opted for semi-retirement in 1969, leaving the operation of the pier to others. And, although Gilbert Ramagosa lived until 1995, he now concentrated more on his ride importing business, eventually selling the Casino Arcade, Sportland, and the Sightseer trams. The Wildwoods resort could ill-afford to lose so many important amusement operators, especially at a time when the economy was already burdened by declining business and bad press.

As they had at various times in the past, economic downturns played havoc with the resorts. The recession of 1973-75 injured business and left Wildwood with an unemployment rate of nine percent. But the worst was yet to come. In 1990, the City of Wildwood was embarrassed by an unemployment rate of nearly nineteen percent, the highest along the southern New Jersey shore. Per capita income was a mere $10,079, and 27 percent of the city's residents lived below the poverty level. Population fell from 4913 in 1980, to 4484 in 1990. While both North Wildwood and Wildwood Crest fared somewhat better than Wildwood, both of these communities suffered from high unemployment rates, and only North Wildwood managed to show a slight gain in population.

NEW LEADERSHIP LEADS BACK TO THE BOARDWALK

Amid the economic crises and disastrous publicity of the 1970s and 1980s, there was one small ray of hope. While the once-bustling night club district had succumbed to poverty and decay, the center of activity in Greater Wildwood was shifting slowly back to the Boardwalk. But it would take a great deal of effort and cooperation during the 1970s, 1980s, and 1990s, to effect a renaissance in the Wildwoods. The battle to halt the decline of the resort and bring it back to its former glory was undertaken by the Morey, Nickels, and Catanoso families, as well as a host of others. With an unshakable belief in Wildwood's potential these modern-day amusement pioneers invested their time and money, working tirelessly to revive the dying resort.

One big problem that had to be overcome was crowd control. After a particularly unruly Memorial Day weekend in 1971, the local newspaper editor reported that, "...our first big weekend saw an invasion of wild, dirty, sleazy young animals that, prompting more than revulsion, prompted primarily sympathy." He went on to claim in disgust that, "...the stockyards of Chicago have more class...." There were 105 arrests that weekend, most for under-age drinking and use of illegal drugs. At the end of the season, over the Labor Day weekend, police from the three resort communities had made a total of 252 arrests, a record for the resort. But disorderly

By 1984, the Wildwood Boardwalk was again the center of activity. – Richard F. Hershey Collection

The future of Wildwood's Boardwalk was determined in 1969 when The Morey family installed a giant slide on a small pier.
– The Morey Organization

conduct, no matter how widespread, paled in comparison to the resort's more serious crimes such as burglary, car theft, and even murder.

Tired of the negative publicity and unlawful, belligerent visitors, the communities of Five Mile Beach took action to return the Wildwoods to their previous status as a great family resort. Landlords who rented low-cost rooms to students during Senior Week each June were taken to court by residents and forced to stop renting to youths

who drank and had loud parties. Night clubs hired burly bouncers, and police patrols were increased around favorite night spots. Trained police dogs were brought in for the Wildwood Police Department's new K-9 unit, and in 1971, the police began patrolling the Boardwalk in Jeeps. New laws were passed to deal with problems created by a number of "nuisance groups." Any group deliberately blocking pedestrian or vehicular traffic could be dispersed and arrested. In 1970, it was declared illegal to consume alcoholic beverages on public property (including the Boardwalk, city streets, and the beach), to play any musical instruments on the Boardwalk or the beach, or to drive vehicles on the beach or the Boardwalk. Of course, there were still problems, but the city governments and the police made it clear that the law would be enforced and order maintained.

Another issue that came to the forefront during the 1970s was the control of auction houses along the Boardwalk. These establishments were nothing new, but during the 1960s and 1970s, the public began to complain about the loud, amplified voices of the auctioneers, the unethical practices of some of the auction houses, and the fact that some auctions sold objectionable or even pornographic merchandise. Responding to scores of complaints, the City of Wildwood tried to deal with the problem. While it was difficult to control the auction houses, the city made it illegal to operate behind closed doors, forcing the auction procedure to be fully visible from the Boardwalk.

GAMBLING WITH LEGALIZED GAMING

The age-old problem of illegal gambling at the resort took a new turn in 1970 when it became clear that Atlantic City might become the East Coast Las Vegas. At first, fearing that the aura of gambling would engulf the entire Jersey Coast and further jeopardize the Wildwoods already shaky image, virtually everyone in the Wildwoods opposed the legalization of gambling in Atlantic City. Others believed that Atlantic City, Wildwood's long-time competitor, would siphon off the majority of summer business, thereby ruining the local economy. In self defense, some business owners favored a new law that would permit cities other than Atlantic City to introduce legal gambling if their economies were threatened. As it turned out, gambling was legalized for Atlantic City, while other communities were not given the option to initiate gambling. But the effect of this decision was not as disastrous for the Wildwoods as had been feared. In fact, the legalization of gambling in Atlantic City actually gave the Wildwoods an opportunity to rebuild their reputation as a traditional family-oriented summer resort.

ENTERTAINING IDEAS

Even though the big gambling casinos regularly booked major entertainers, their impact on nightlife in the Wildwoods was minimal. The night club district on Five Mile Beach was already in an advanced state of decline before the first Atlantic City casino was constructed. Possibly, raising the drinking age to twenty-one played a major role, but so did the increasingly high cost of booking top-flight entertainers. Many club owners discovered that their patrons were not spending enough to cover the cost of big name entertainment. The extra expense of hiring bouncers and security personnel only added to their economic woes. During the 1960s and early 1970s, the Surf Club might spend as much as $20,000 a week for talent. After presenting Gladys Knight and the Pips and the Buddy Rich Orchestra in 1971, the Surf Club eliminated all big name entertainment. The Hurricane East also tried some solid acts in 1971, but its owners recognized that the night club era had come to an end and they suspended bookings of all major entertainers.

Even so, there was still some musical entertainment to be found in the Wildwoods. Cozy Morley's Club Avalon, which catered to a mature crowd, became the leading night spot at the resort. Cozy did much to bring the Big Bands back to the resort, booking groups such as the Glenn Miller Orchestra,

and Les and Larry Elgart. Along with his own comedy act and a troupe of house singers and musicians, Morley also presented the Four Lads, the Four Aces, Don Cornell, Bob Eberle, Julius LaRosa, Helen O'Connell, and comedian Joey Bishop. Cozy Morley's dedication to bringing back the glory days of traditional entertainment attracted a large and loyal following for the Club Avalon. The old club was finally razed after being closed by building inspectors in 1989, but the amazing Cozy Morley went on to become a big hit in Atlantic City during the 1990s.

After the construction of the new Convention Hall in 1971, and to the dismay of many financially-troubled night club owners, the Convention Hall Authority decided to enter the entertainment business. The Convention Hall's management signed a contract with Larry Magid and the Spivak Brothers, who had presented successful concerts at Philadelphia's Spectrum. The promoters set up a top-notch schedule of performers including the Carpenters, Neil Diamond, the 5th Dimension, the Osmond Brothers, Tony Bennett, Elton John, Steppenwolf, Black Sabbath, David Cassidy and the Partridge Family, the Four Seasons, and some rock festivals. Many of these same artists had appeared at the resort a decade earlier but this time they were performing on the Boardwalk instead of in the night club district.

The Boardwalk benefited from some unexpected national publicity in 1971, when actor Robert Mitchum and a Hollywood cast filmed the movie Going Home in Wildwood. Movie viewers were treated to scenes featuring the largest amusement midway in the world. At that time the resort could boast of 125 amusement rides located at six major amusement centers (Hunt's Pier, The Marine Pier, Fun Pier, Surfside Pier, Sportland, and the Casino Arcade). The amusement piers were well maintained and active, but many visitors in the 1970s noticed that the Boardwalk itself was in dire need of repair. After all those years, the Boardwalk had become a serious financial burden on the cities and quite often repairs had to be delayed. In fact, Wildwood was so strapped for funds that in 1972 Commissioner Charles Masciarella proposed that visitors should be charged a fee for strolling the twenty-eight blocks of the Wildwood promenade. Predictably, this idea met with massive resistance. Nevertheless, with many residents unemployed or living below the poverty level it was clear that the communities were having an increasingly difficult time paying for Boardwalk maintenance.

In the spring of 1973, engineers determined that repairs to the Wildwood Boardwalk would cost $900,000, a significant portion of which was needed to rebuild the concrete supporting structure. Unable or unwilling to spend this much money, the city appropriated only $200,000 in May and another $175,000 in October. In the meantime, the Wildwood Boardwalk got some unexpected help from Washington, D.C. Following President Nixon's inauguration, Senator Harrison A. Williams, Jr. arranged for the city to acquire $400,000 worth of lumber used in the inaugural reviewing stands for only $60,000. This lumber was shipped to Wildwood and used as replacement planking on the Boardwalk. When the restoration was completed in May of 1973, the walk was re-dedicated as "Inauguration Walk" and the

final nail was driven with a simulated gold hammer. Two years later, the city was able to set aside another $430,000 and a major section of the Boardwalk was stripped to its concrete ledgers and replanked. While the cities were busy trying to maintain and upgrade the Boardwalk, fires were working against them. A $400,000 fire in 1973 destroyed a restaurant and three other businesses, and this was followed with other serious Boardwalk conflagrations in 1976, 1978, and 1982. As always, the resort recovered from the fires, rebuilt as needed, and opened for business soon after.

SOMETHING OLD, SOMETHING NEW

In spite of all of the negative publicity of the 1970s and 1980s, businesspeople continued to invest their precious time and money along the Boardwalk and the neighboring streets. New businesses appeared such as Mack's Pizza and Lou Costar's Giant Slide. Claude and Evelyn Bradshaw bought the Laura's Fudge operation and continued the same standards of quality that had been established many decades before. Hankins's Candy Store, which had been at the resort since 1946, was still selling candy at the rate of 20,000 pounds a season. The resort's oldest Boardwalk food vendors, Douglass Candies and Kohr Brothers Frozen Custard, were both thriving, while newer stores, like Franks's Nut Hut, helped boost the Boardwalk's revival.

Many new promotions sprang up along the Boardwalk, including an art show sponsored by the Union Trust company that featured works by more than two hundred artists. Reminiscent of the old automobile shows, the Antique Car Club of America brought a large collection of classic cars to the Boardwalk in 1972. And the Boardwalk Chapel celebrated its fiftieth anniversary in 1994 with a series of events at the chapel and at the band shell.

Upper: The Douglass Fudge store...a perennial favorite with millions of resort visitors.
– Wildwood Historical Society

Middle: The Original Hot Spot, a well known Boardwalk eatery located at the site of the Starlight Ballroom. – Wildwood Historical Society

Left: Kohr Bros., the most famous frozen custard maker in the world, at Cedar Avenue on the Boardwalk. – Kohr Bros. Collection

The famous Kohr Bros. frozen custard stand at 26th Avenue.
– Kohr Bros. Collection

The Nut Hut, a popular Boardwalk location for fresh roasted nuts, fudge, taffy, and custard. – Ron Franks Collection

Unfortunately the new era brought an end to many of the Boardwalk's traditional events. Most unfortunate was the demise of the Baby Parade. In 1970, the sixtieth Baby Parade was held on the Boardwalk and drew an estimated 50,000 spectators. After that high point, interest in the event waned. There were only 163 entrants in 1977 and 148 in 1978. Still, the parade committee struggled to keep the event alive. In 1985, the parade sparked some renewed interest when it marked its seventy-fifth birthday. But, by 1989 there were only eighty-six entrants, city financial backing had fallen to a few hundred dollars, and parade spectators were pitifully sparse. With little community interest and even less financial backing, the Baby Parades faded into Wildwood history.

BEACH INVASIONS

Amazingly, the wonderful bathing beach that had drawn visitors for more than a century, continued to widen, even as other New Jersey beaches were eroding. An 1991 engineering survey revealed that the beach had expanded at a rate of about 40 feet per year since 1978, for a total of 520 feet. In some places the beach was now 1500 feet wide. But, as beautiful as the beach was, there was still a major battle being waged to control the pollution. The Wildwood beaches, like those at Cape May, were sometimes closed because of dangerously high levels of bacteria. Most of the waste came from the large cities, but in 1975 a reporter observed an out-of-state truck dumping Wildwood's own sewage sludge directly into the Tuckahoe River. Business people in the Wildwoods became so frustrated that they took matters into their own hands and tried to kill bacteria by pouring chlorine into stagnant pools near rainwater run-off outlets.

The annual pre-season auto show, now including antique vehicles, was still a popular event in 1969-70. Viewing a 1927 Rolls Royce are Lou Wingate, left, and Mayor Charles Masciarella on right. – Wildwood Historical Society

The world famous Boardwalk Chapel.
– Temple University, Urban Archives

Mayor Charles Masciarella and Queen
Oceana at the 60th Baby Parade in 1970.
– Wildwood Historical Society

Mayor Guy Muziani with the National
Marble Tournament champions of 1975.
– Wildwood Historical Society

Wildwood

*Although interest
in the Baby Parade
was waning, it still
drew contestants and
spectators.*
– Wildwood Historical Society

Queen Oceana and her 1970 court
on a float in the Baby Parade.
– Wildwood Historical Society

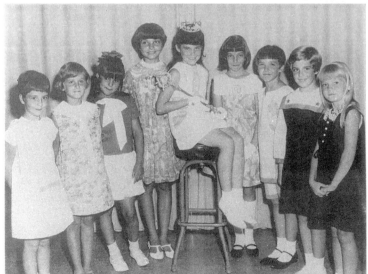

Queen Oceana LVII and her princesses.
– Wildwood Historical Society

The beach in 1975, with Hunt's Pier in the background. – Wildwood Historical Society

Meanwhile, the City of Wildwood was having difficulty coping with the annual expenditure of $400,000 to maintain and operate the beach. Once again, the city proposed beach fees, and once again, protests from residents ended the discussion. Although Cape May and other communities charged for the use of their beaches, the sands of Five Mile Beach would remain free to all who cared to use them.

While many families stayed away from ocean beaches during the years of dangerous pollution, the crowds on the Wildwood beaches were still huge. In 1971 the Wildwood Beach Patrol opened a new facility at Taylor Avenue that housed medic and first aid rooms, a patrol lieutenant, and lockers for twenty-six lifeguards. The expenditure was justified; that season the Wildwood Beach Patrol made 102 rescues, reunited 953 lost children with their families, and treated 1747 cases of illness and injury. On the North Wildwood Beach, where 2,571,400 people used the strand in 1971, the beach patrol handled 95 rescues, 451 lost children, and 1005 first aid cases.

A National Marble Tournament event of the 1990s. – Cape May County Department of Tourism

Modern Boardwalk stores at the Convention Hall, 1990. – Wildwood Historical Society

With the involvement of federal and state governments in ecological matters, the condition of the water off Cape May County began to improve. It is hoped that within a few years the ocean will be cleaner than it was in the 1890s when the beaches first became popular.

"ROOM"-INATIONS AND A NEW CONVENTION HALL

The hospitality industry was less troubled than the beach and the Boardwalk during most of the 1970s and 1980s. The rush to build motels continued, and by June, 1970, two thousand new motel rooms were ready to greet guests. In 1972, the Wildwoods offered 600 fairly modern motels as well as 150 hotels, the majority of which were showing their age. Some of the older hotels were modernized, such as the Ocean Crest in 1992, but overall, especially since 1970, many of the resort's best known historic hotels have been destroyed. The Hotel Cromwell was lost to a fire in 1973, while the Sheldon, the Arcadia, the Hof Brau, and the grand dame of Wildwood hotels, the Dayton, were lost to the progress of urban renewal projects. In the 1990s, Greater Wildwood offered about 13,000 lodging rooms of all types, ranging from the first-class seaside hotels to low-priced efficiency units. A survey conducted in relation to the convention business stated that about half of the Wildwood area's hotels were below the standard expected by most conventioneers.

But, depending on one's point of view, these older motel rooms could either be considered hopelessly outdated or classic examples of well-preserved 1950s popular culture. In fact, it was not until the 1990s that serious architectural historians and university students began to realize that the Wildwoods possessed the finest collection of 1950s motels in the world. What Cape May is to Victorian architecture, the Wildwoods are to post-war motel design. In fact, many believe the future of the Wildwoods lies in preserving and exploiting these wonderfully colorful examples, complete with pink walls, plastic donkeys, fake palm trees, and neon signs.

The convention trade had always been closely aligned with the hotel and motel business. There was no question that Wildwood had lost its edge in this market and, although many conventions still used the Wildwood facilities, Atlantic City, Asbury Park, and even Cape May were able to offer better meeting facilities. The absence of a good, modern convention hall was painfully obvious to every business in the community. It was especially evident in 1970 when the Elks announced that their 1971 convention would be held in Atlantic City instead of Wildwood. Although many cited a lack of cooperation from hotels and motels, the fact that a new convention facility was not yet available had to be a major factor in the loss of the Elks convention. When Charles

Wildwood's new Convention Hall.
– Wildwood Historical Society

Masciarella was elected mayor of Wildwood in 1968, he had pledged to build a new convention hall and appointed Max Gershman chairperson of the Convention Hall Committee. Plans moved ahead swiftly, and by early 1969 a number of construction bids were in hand. Deciding that the low bid of $1,497,000 was too high, architects began finding methods of reducing costs. By late in the year, bids totalling $1,019,677 were accepted. The hall was finally completed in late 1970 at a cost of $1,200,000. The grand new structure boasted seating for 4,200, banquet facilities for 2,800, and included 10 Boardwalk stores.

About three thousand people attended the Convention Hall dedication on January 10, 1971, although its first event, the South Jersey convention of the Jehovah's Witnesses, had been held about three weeks earlier. The new hall became a center of activity, hosting the Miss New Jersey Pageant and various other beauty pageants, roller derby games, rock concerts, string band festivals, basketball, club dances, free children's festivals and, of course, conventions.

Within two years of opening, it was announced that the hall was losing money, but it more than paid for itself by helping to attract new conventions to Wildwood. Starting in 1969, Wildwood had aggressively tried to capture the New Jersey Firemen's Association annual September convention from Atlantic City. Although they failed to sign a contract for the 1974 convention, the firemen agreed to hold their 1975 convention in Wildwood. To sweeten the deal Wildwood permitted the firemen to hold a giant parade, something that Atlantic City had forbidden. Gradually other conventions moved from Atlantic City to Wildwood,

including the New Jersey Lions Clubs in 1974. In fact, the two competitive resorts actually cooperated in order to win the 1974 National Imperial Shriners conclave away from Los Vegas. Although Atlantic City was the official host, Wildwood happily agreed to provide 4,000 hotel rooms for 10,000 Shriners. After gambling was legalized in Atlantic City, convention accommodations at the glamorous casinos were sometimes difficult to obtain. Thus, a number of conventions actually abandoned Atlantic City in favor of Wildwood in order to secure an adequate number of hotel and motel rooms.

DERAILED

By this time, of course, the automobile was by far the most popular way to reach the resort. In fact, the Cape May-Lewes Ferry was so successful because it ferried cars as well as people. Over the Memorial Day weekend of 1969, the ferry line set a new record, carrying 3,237 vehicles and 10,898 people in three days. The line's four original, oil-fired vessels could not be operated efficiently and resulted in a $1,500,000 deficit. Therefore, the Delaware River and Bay Authority announced in 1972 that it would spend $12,000,000 to replace the older vessels with three new, diesel-powered ships. The line continued to modernize its ships for the next two decades, becoming as popular with motorists heading for Florida in the wintertime as it was with tourists destined for the coast in summer.

Keeping pace with the demands of tourism, the Delaware River and Bay Authority now operates ultra-modern ships on the ferry route from Lewes, Delaware, to Cape May. – Delaware River and Bay Authority

Meanwhile, the Pennsylvania-Reading Seashore Line was in no position to think about new equipment and could barely maintain what it had. Twenty years of declining patronage had the railroad's management pleading for the right to abandon passenger service to the seaside resorts. In 1968 the line suffered a deficit of $1,285,000, despite a state subsidy of $200,000. Early in the spring of 1973, the railroad finally terminated all passenger service to the Wildwoods. There was quite an outcry over the suspension of service, coming as it did in the midst of a recession and a gasoline shortage. As a result, service was temporarily restored on a reduced basis, but was soon dropped permanently. Three years after Wildwood service ended, the Pennsylvania-Reading Seashore Lines were conveyed to Conrail and ceased to exist. The railroad that had been a cornerstone in the development of the Five Mile Beach resorts, and that had served the area so faithfully for decades was finally gone. With its passing, the resorts lost a significant tie with their past.

PIER RENAISSANCE

For the railroad, the night club owners, the operators of the older hotels, and the army of seasonally unemployed people, the years that followed the glorious 1960s were dismal. Their only hope rested with the amusement piers that protruded from the Boardwalk. While several of the piers had experienced economic difficulties after the mid-1970s, it was the piers and the adjacent Boardwalk properties that would launch the Wildwood renaissance of the 1990s. Just as the center of resort activity had once shifted from the hotels to the Boardwalk during the early 1900s, then later shifted away from the Boardwalk to the night clubs, the Boardwalk amusement piers were once again the core of the modern resort. Atlantic City, at one time the reigning queen of great amusement piers, had lost most of those old institutions with the advent of gambling.

The second Crest Pier was razed in 1987 and a new, modern Crest Pier opened in 1989.
– Wildwood Crest Historical Society

Promoting the pier on the marquee of Hunt's Shore Theatre. – Mark Wyatt Collection

In Wildwood, however, it was a different story. Beginning in the mid-1970s a slow, expensive, and sometimes painful renaissance was begun by the pier owners. Gradually, older piers were expanded and new ones built. This process, while it took some twenty years, eventually helped to pull the community out of the doldrums and at the same time earned Wildwood a reputation as the World Capital of Amusement Piers.

Hunt's Pier retained its position as the nation's premier amusement pier, and was even declared to be a "miniature Disney World" by a 1972 trade publication. Despite Bill Hunt's death, the Hunt enterprises including the pier, the theatres, and the Starlight Ballroom, were maintained and

The entrance to Hunt's Pier.
– Photograph by Charles J. Jacques, Jr.

201

In the face of competition from new, all-steel roller coasters, Hunt's Flyer remained a popular attraction.
– Photograph by Charles J. Jacques, Jr.

Hunt's Whacky Shack dark ride.
– Photograph by Charles J. Jacques, Jr.

202

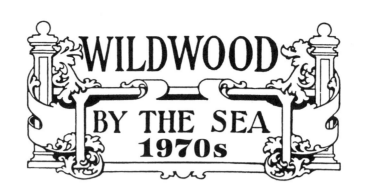

WILDWOOD
BY THE SEA
1970s

The Log Flume on Hunt's Pier. At the time, the Log Flume was one of the most outstanding rides on the Jersey Shore.
– Photograph by Charles J. Jacques, Jr.

In 1982, Hunt's Pier added a costly Ranger ride. – Photograph by Charles J. Jacques, Jr.

Hunt's new Monster ride and the Toyland Circus. – Photograph by Charles J. Jacques, Jr.

operated according to traditional Hunt family standards. In 1970, they spent $400,000 for a log flume, in which riders in log-shaped boats were propelled by a fast-moving current through 806 feet of troughs. They also added the Whacky Shack walk through and a new miniature railroad. These investments were well justified for even on the last day of the season in late September, 36,800 people rode the amusements on Hunt's Pier. The Hunts continued adding smaller attractions for a number of years, then in 1979 spent another $400,000 for a giant slide at the end of the 700 foot pier. Three years later, Bud Hunt invested $600,000 in the Ranger, a massive 40-ton ride that required a $53,000 concrete pad to support its weight. The new rides were very successful and the pier reported an eight percent increase in income in 1982.

In the meantime, Bud Hunt had decided to sell off some of the Hunt interests, and in 1978 the old Starlight Ballroom building was sold to Martin Schwartz. The new owner converted the ballroom into an arcade complex with a dozen different operations under one roof. The ballroom's new career was short lived, however. In August, 1981, the worst fire in Wildwood's history started in the Hot Spot Restaurant which stood adjacent to the ballroom. The blaze soon spread to the drafty old ballroom, to Mariner's

Above: Like all amusement piers, Hunt's Pier was forced to take advantage of every available foot of space. – Mark Wyatt Collection

Below: Hunt's Jungleland continued to be a well patronized attraction throughout the 1980s. – Mark Wyatt Collection

Landing (the new name for the Marine Pier), and destroyed 17 stores, while doing $25,000 in damage to the Boardwalk itself. It took 250 firemen to fight the huge blaze, which did more than $4,000,000 in damage. The totally-destroyed ballroom building was valued at $1,500,000, and Mariner's Landing suffered another $1,000,000 in loses.

After a solid 1985 season, Bud Hunt sold Hunt's Pier to a group of investors for $2,000,000. At the time, it included twenty-five rides, three games, and a food concession. Soon after, he sold the ten theatres owned by Hunt Theatres, Inc. to the Frank Company, the largest independent theatre operator in New Jersey and the owner of forty-three other theatres. By late winter, 1986, all of the Hunts' amusements had been sold, and for the first time in 80 years, the Hunt family was not a major player on the Boardwalk.

The new owners of Hunt's Pier were fortunate that Bud Hunt had installed the new Rapids ride in 1985, for the million dollar ride kept income high at the pier for a few years. The Flyer roller coaster, the last wooden roller coaster on the Jersey Shore, was razed in 1989 to make space for new rides and the new all-steel Kamikaze roller coaster debuted that season. All was not well at Hunt's Pier, however. Declining business and $100,000 in unpaid taxes forced Hunt's Pier Associates to sell the pier. Before the 1991 season opened, the pier was purchased for an undisclosed amount by Conklin

Shows, Canada's highly respected carnival company and long-time affiliate of the Canadian National Exposition. The Hunt name was eliminated, and the pier opened in 1991 as Conko's Party Pier. The new owners planned to redevelop the pier with as many as thirty new rides, twenty games, and four food operations, and so the Conklin managers sold the Kamikaze coaster to Six Flags Over Georgia, and razed Jungleland, the Skua Pirate Ship and many of the other attractions that had made Hunt's Pier famous. Either the new venture was not successful, or Conklin Shows elected not to invest further money in the operation. For whatever reason, the pier closed and stood idle until it opened again in 1995 as the Atlantic Pier. Then, in 1996, the former Hunt's Pier experienced a rebirth at the hands of the Catanoso brothers, Charles, William, and Joseph.

The Catanoso family had been in Wildwood for many years, and in 1994 entered into an agreement with Donald Trump to reopen Atlantic City's fabled Steel Pier across the Boardwalk from the Trump Taj Mahal Casino. Their ability to take on such a major financial investment, as well as the reconstruction of Hunt's Pier, was probably due in large part to the fact that the Catanoso family had won the $9,500,000 New Jersey Lottery in 1993. Using their own funds in combination with bank financing, the Catanosos were able to invest $10,000,000 to renovate the old Hunt's Pier.

Skyline Golf at Hunt's Pier, a favorite diversion on warm evenings.
– Mark Wyatt Collection

Ramagosa's Sportland Pier in 1978.
– Photograph by Charles J. Jacques, Jr.

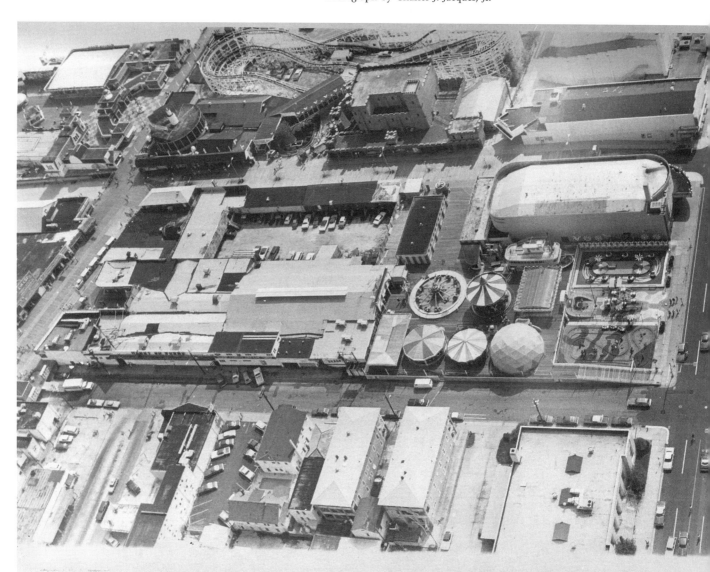

Beach, the aggressive reconstruction of Hunt's Pier by the Catanoso family.
– Dinosaur Beach

The entrance to Escape from Dinosaur Beach, one of the new attractions at Dinosaur Beach. – Dinosaur Beach

The Golden Nugget Mine ride in 1985.
– Mark Wyatt Collection

Left:
Ramagosa's Casino Arcade Park in the late 1970s. The Casino's neighbor is Nickels Midway Pier, with Mariner's Landing in the upper left. – Richard Ramagosa Collection

Every penny of that amount was needed, for the Catanosos were left with only a concrete skeleton of the once bustling pier. Of the many excellent and unique rides that had attracted large crowds in the 1960s and 1970s, only the Golden Nugget and the Log Flume remained. The pier was renamed Dinosaur Beach Adventure, and the two remaining rides were reworked to fit in with the new dinosaur theme. To these rides the Catanosos added a fossil dig for children, a dinosaur adventure with life-sized prehistoric reptiles, a 700-seat amphitheater and other attractions. The new Dinosaur Beach Adventure made its successful Boardwalk debut in 1996. The Catanoso family also took over management of eighteen Boardwalk stores and six theatres, which placed them among the major contributors to Wildwood's renaissance.

In the early 1970s Gilbert Ramagosa had inherited from his father the unofficial title of King of the Boardwalk. He operated twenty-three rides at Sportland Pier and another nine at the Casino Arcade. His varied business interests included new home construction on the Jersey Cape, an amusement center in Miami, importing amusement rides, the Wildwood bus line, and the Sightseer trams, among others. At Sportland, the Aqua Thrill Circus of the 1970s was advertised as, "The World's Largest Water Show Circus," and it became so well-known that the Aquamaniacs appeared on Ed Sullivan's television show.

Although Ramagosa continued to operate his ride importing business, the fire that destroyed the Casino Arcade persuaded him that it was time to divest himself of his local amusement holdings. Ramagosa conservatively estimated that the combined value of Sportland Pier and the Casino Arcade was about a million dollars. The Casino Arcade was rebuilt with a concrete structure and was soon sold. Then, in the mid-1980s, he found a buyer for the Sportland Pier, sold the bus company, and, finally, in 1994, completed the sale of the Sightseer trams. Any future plans he may have had for new operations in the Wildwoods ended with his untimely death in 1995. His son and third generation Wildwood amusement entrepreneur, Richard, continued the company's ride importing business and embarked on a plan to install carousels in shopping malls. Even though the Ramagosas were no longer on the Boardwalk, they maintain a solid presence in the amusement industry.

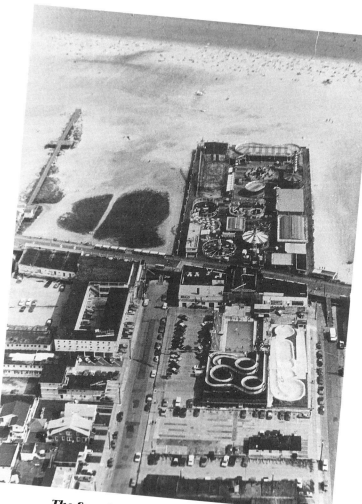

The Sportland Pier of the 1970s.
– Richard Ramagosa Collection

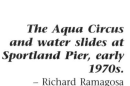

The Aqua Circus and water slides at Sportland Pier, early 1970s.
– Richard Ramagosa Collection

The entrance to Sportland Pier, 1978.
– Photograph by Charles J. Jacques, Jr.

One of the elaborate, European-built dark rides that appeared at the resort in the 1970s and 1980s.
– Photograph by Charles J. Jacques, Jr.

Horror House dark ride on Sportland Pier.
– Photograph by Charles J. Jacques, Jr.

The Marine Pier never lost its prominent place as one of the Wildwoods' best amusement centers, an honor it had enjoyed since 1919. During the early 1970s, under the direction of Helen Coombs Kelly, the pier boasted an array of twenty-four rides and an arcade. Included among the rides were the aging Jack Rabbit roller coaster, the glittering Philadelphia Toboggan carousel that Ed Rhoads brought to Wildwood in 1918, and a new imported scooter ride purchased from Gil Ramagosa. The Marine Pier was still a very profitable venture, but the owners of the Cedar-Schellenger Corporation were busy with their own careers and most of them considered the Marine Pier to be a secondary investment. In 1976 Helen Coombs Kelly, Kenneth Coombs, Palmer M. Way, Jr., and Robert Kay felt the time was right to put the Marine Pier on the market. With an estimated value of about four million dollars, the pier proved too expensive for a single investor to purchase, so they divided the areas east and west of the Boardwalk into two parcels with a selling price of $1,800,000 each. The Morey family purchased the seaward section, while the Nickels family acquired the western section that had once been known as Playland.

A maintenance employee inspects the Jack Rabbit roller coaster before the opening of the 1974 season.
– Temple University, Urban Archives

Marine Pier as it appeared just a few years before its sale to the Morey Organization.
– David W. Francis Collection

211

The front of Playland after it was sold to the Nickels family. – Wildwood Historical Society

Demolition of the venerable Jack Rabbit roller coaster in October, 1984, – Wildwood Historical Society

The Scream Machine, formerly the Jack Rabbit, rolls into the station during the 1984 season, its last year of operation.
– Richard F. Hershey Collection

After four generations in the amusement industry and with thirty years' experience on the Boardwalk, the Nickels family was well qualified to redevelop their portion of the old Marine Pier. Renamed the Nickels Midway Pier, they rebuilt the Jack Rabbit coaster and dubbed it the Scream Machine. They also built Dracula's Castle, a combination walk-through/ride-through attraction. Before long, the Nickels family was operating a popular amusement center that included some twenty rides.

Of course, progress inevitably brings some changes that prove unpopular with old timers. The hand-carved carousel was dismantled and sold. Then, in 1984, after eight years and more than $500,000 spent on maintenance and repairs it became clear

that the Scream Machine coaster was no longer a viable operation. Despite the fact that the cost of a ticket to ride the former Jack Rabbit coaster had risen from five cents in 1920 to $1.20 in 1984, the ride could not be profitably operated. Finally, on September 23, 1984, the company offered the public free rides on the old coaster and then closed it permanently. That fall, it was razed and the last of Wildwood's historic amusement attractions was gone. In 1992, a fire damaged parts of the Midway Pier and another of Wildwood's old structures, Blaker's carousel building, but the Nickels family continued to expand their pier each season and, like the Catanoso family, embraced their role as one of the groups leading the rebirth of the Wildwoods.

All that remained of Kohr Bros. frozen custard stand and part of Nickels Midway Pier after the fire of 1992. Castle Dracula (background) was undamaged.
– Mark Wyatt Collection

THE MOREY ORGANIZATION

While it's true that the resurrection of the Wildwood resorts throughout the 1980s and 1990s was the result of a combined effort, the Morey family must be acknowledged as the fountainhead of Boardwalk transformation. With careful planning, large investments, devoted management, a deep love of the Wildwoods and, on occasion, the willingness to take some chances, the Moreys successfully converted old worn-out piers into exciting, glittering entertainment centers that have become the envy of the international amusement industry.

Brothers Bill and Will Morey had never intended to enter the amusement business. Their background was in construction, and they had become well-respected in the motel industry, eventually building and operating their own hotels. But the course of the Morey's future, and indeed, that of Wildwood, would be altered dramatically in the late 1960s. Enjoying the winter of 1968 in Florida, the brothers spotted a giant slide for sale in a shopping mall. The Morey brothers bought it and searched the coast from Atlantic City to Cape May for a suitable location in which to operate their new slide for the 1969 season. In North Wildwood, between 25th and 26th Street, they found two Boardwalk lots that were available. Separated by city-owned land, one lot was home to Odger's Restaurant and Beach Grille, while the other sported a miniature golf course. The Moreys were considering a lease, but Odger insisted on selling, and for $345,000 the Morey family obtained the two plots of land and riparian rights that would later become extremely important as the beach continued to widen. The Wipe Out, as

the giant slide was called, was installed above the miniature golf course. For just twenty-five cents sliders got a great view of the ocean and the Boardwalk while taking the fast plunge back to Boardwalk level.

The Wipe Out was an instant success, prompting two other Boardwalk operators to install giant slides in 1970. The popularity of their slide inspired the Moreys to expand what was now known as Surfside Pier. A 1972 report from the major amusement industry trade journal noted that the newcomer was "...not viewed favorably, for aesthetic reasons, by veteran pier owners." The Moreys were criticized for inefficient use of the land, and established pier operators did not consider the Moreys to be serious competition. As it turned out they had greatly underestimated the abilities of the Morey family, for within a few seasons Surfside Pier was attracting large crowds with a Moon Bounce, Scrambler, Merry-Go-Round, Round-up, Zipper, and other popular amusement rides.

As more and more rides were installed by the Moreys, Surfside Pier began to expand eastward toward the ocean. New installations included kiddie rides as well as a number of large, and noisy rides for the teenagers. There was also The Haunted House funhouse, and a Go Kart track. Where the old restaurant and grille had been there now stood an imposing 40-foot fiberglass figure of King Kong, earning Surfside the nickname, "King Kong Pier."

Throughout the early years the two sections of Surfside Pier were bisected by city-owned land. Two years after the giant slide was erected, the Moreys attempted to buy the intersecting land and combine the two

Morey's Pier in 1982. The original 1969 attraction, the Wipe Out giant slide, remained an important part of the pier. – The Morey Organization

By 1978, Wildwood's piers offered an impressive array of modern thrill rides. In the distance (upper left of photo), the spiraling incline of the Jumbo Jet on Morey's Pier can be seen. – Photograph by Charles J. Jacques, Jr.

The Haunted House on Morey's Pier was a first-class walk-thru attraction.
– Mark Wyatt Collection

pier sections into one operation. The owners of Sportland Pier and others managed to block the purchase by taking legal action. Four years of court battles ensued. The court's final decision permitted the property to be sold at public auction, and, in order to ensure that no one else could purchase the land and block access to the pier, the Moreys were forced to pay $756,000 to acquire 160 feet of Boardwalk frontage. It was a steep price to pay, but now the Moreys owned a total of 200 feet of Boardwalk in front of what was now named Morey's Pier. The way was cleared for the family to move ahead with major plans for expansion. And move ahead they did, at an incredible clip! Custom-built rides were purchased, an electronic shooting gallery was installed, new

offices were constructed beneath the big slide, and a soon-to-be-famous food concession, Curley's Fries, was opened. While preparing for the 1976 season, both Will and Bill Morey travelled to Europe to inspect new ride innovations at Oktoberfest. There they saw the all-steel Jumbo Jet roller coaster and brought the $400,000 thrill ride to their pier. Installation of the Jumbo Jet required a 250-foot extension of the pier, but it was well worth the effort and the expense, for this single ride became the premier amusement attraction of the entire Jersey Shore. With the great success of rides like the Jumbo Jet, it took only eight seasons for Morey's Pier to evolve from a single giant slide into a major amusement center. Now competitors were forced to admit they had been wrong to underestimate the Moreys. Clearly, they had become major players in the amusement industry. The Moreys were on the Boardwalk to stay.

Nineteen seventy-six turned out to be a pivotal year for the Morey family and for the future of Wildwood. That year the old Marine Pier was divided into two properties, one was purchased by the Nickels family and Will Morey bought the pier section located

The Morey Organization eliminated all of the old Marine Pier attractions and replaced aging rides with the latest amusement devices. – Wildwood Historical Society

east of the Boardwalk. At the time of purchase, the old pier was only 500-feet long and contained just twelve rides and a miniature golf course. Some of the rides, like the Ferris wheel, were hopelessly old and outdated, and only seven of the original rides were retained. Renamed Mariner's Landing, the revitalized pier was opened the 1977 season with three new European rides. The Pirate Ship, the Wave Swinger, and the Enterprise represented an investment of more than a one-and-a-half million dollars. Soon there appeared a succession of great new rides and attractions culminating with the $1,400,000, 115-foot high Sea Serpent boomerang roller coaster in 1984. And, just a year later, the Morey's unveiled a new 146-foot Ferris wheel. Another new attraction was the Raging Waters Waterpark located at the ocean end of the pier. Raging Waters offered an exciting array of water slides and aquatic events that beckoned daytime visitors from the beach and onto the pier. The new waterpark also lured the World Waterslide Speed Championship contests to the resort. Possibly the most spectacular aspect of the waterpark was the Sky Pond Journey, the nation's first elevated river ride. High above the crowds on the pier, patrons of Sky Pond floated down a flume in inner tubes. The next great attraction to appear was Ship Wreck Shoals, a 5,000-square foot pool area featuring a sailing ship with five water slides descending from her deck. Thanks in large part to the beneficial central location of Mariner's Landing, business at the new pier was even better than at Morey's Pier. By 1994, as the Morey family celebrated its twenty-fifth year on the Boardwalk, Mariner's Landing was attracting 1,400,000 visitors.

For several years the Morey family was content to operate their two thriving amusement piers, but when Fun Pier became available in the mid-1980s, it also was acquired by the family. Fun Pier had not produced solid profits during the early 1980s, then, on November 24, 1984, the 600-foot-long pier was totally engulfed in flames. The property was ripe for redevelopment and the Moreys were able and willing to tackle their third pier operation. Renamed Wild Wheels, the newest addition to the Morey empire would be operated a little differently than either Morey's Pier or Mariner's Landing. Wild Wheels was termed an interactive amusement center, where sports-related activities allowed patrons to become a part of the action rather than just spectators. Leading the attractions at Wild Wheels was an actual raceway with down-sized vehicles in which drivers could experience what it was like to race on a NASCAR track, at the Grand Prix

Raging Waters, the waterpark attraction at the end of Mariner's Landing.
– The Morey Organization

or on a traditional Go-Kart track. Other interactive attractions included wall climbing and the Ejection Seat, a form of bungee jumping introduced in 1993.

By the late 1980s The Morey Organization had accomplished something unique along the Jersey Shore; they had established and successfully operated three major amusement piers. Even the legendary John Lake Young, the dean of Atlantic City amusement pier developers, could not match the Morey's record. In addition to their three Wildwood piers, The Morey Organization owned and operated the Park Place Family Entertainment Center on Park Boulevard, the Port Royal Hotel, the Pan American Hotel, and Seapointe Village, a residential community on Diamond Beach in Wildwood Crest. To help manage their huge enterprise, Bill and Will Morey enlisted their children and their spouses into the business and established a policy-making board to oversee operations. And, while the piers are actually owned by different sectors of the family, the Moreys have centralized the marketing, pricing, and group sales efforts of all of their facilities under the umbrella of The Morey Organization.

217

A Modern funhouse at Mariner's Landing.
– The Morey Organization

The Giant Wheel and the Sea Serpent roller coaster, Mariner's Landing.
– The Morey Organization

Mariner's Landing after almost twenty years of investment and development by the Morey family. – The Morey Organization

Bill Morey, Sr. (left) and the late Will Morey, Sr. take the first ride at the dedication of the Great Nor'easter. – The Morey Organization

Even though they were kept busy with the creation of Mariner's Landing and Wild Wheels, the Moreys did not neglect their flagship installation, Morey's Pier. There was no question that amusement rides were the drawing card of Morey's Pier and each season the pier introduced new, exciting, and expen-

sive rides. In 1979, Morey's Pier was extended by another 200 feet. A year later it was expanded again, this time to the south. One of the highest and longest log flumes in the country, the Zoom Phloom, was installed at Morey's Pier, along with several other new rides and shows. The late 1980s brought a number of new attractions to Morey's Pier. Nearly five million dollars was spent to develop a major waterpark on the pier. Both waterparks (at Morey's Pier and at Mariner's Landing) were named Raging Waters. They

The Pan American Hotel, one of the new luxury hotel developments. – The Morey Organization

he Port Royal Hotel, an attractive Wildwood Crest facility with an ocean view. – The Morey Organization

The Zoom Phloom at Morey's Pier.
– Mark Wyatt Collection

Morey family members officially christen the Great Nor'easter, June, 1995. – Mark Wyatt Collection

were so well designed and well-outfitted that they were generally regarded as two of the best waterparks in North America. In 1988, Will Morey again travelled to Europe in search of exciting new rides with which to thrill his customers. In 1989 Morey's Surfside Golf was introduced, a $475,000 project that included five waterfalls, rock formations, and extensive landscaping.

The Seapointe Village development is the island's most luxurious resort complex.
– The Morey Organization

Morey's Pier in the 1990s.
– The Morey Organization

220

Perhaps the most impressive addition to Morey's Pier was the installation of the Great Nor'easter, installed in 1995. The idea for the ultimate coaster experience originated in 1992 when the Moreys began searching for a ride company capable of building a suspended roller coaster with cars hanging below the tracks. Three years later, the Great Nor'easter made its debut. Costing about six million dollars, the new ride measured 2,100 feet long, rose 115 feet into the air, then plummeted 95 feet downward. At speeds of 55 miles per hour, the Great Nor'easter propelled its screaming passengers through diving loops, corkscrews, and breathtaking vertical drops. Needless to say, the Great Nor'easter was an immediate success!

The enthusiastic reception for the Great Nor'easter in 1995 led to the construction of the first major wooden roller coaster in Greater Wildwood since 1919. This time, the Moreys turned to Custom Coasters, Inc. to design and build a fantastic wooden coaster on Wild Wheels Raceway and Adventure Pier. The result was the Great White, a 3,300-foot-long ride reminiscent of the thrilling coasters of the 1920s. With an initial vertical drop of 100 feet, the Great White was among the finest roller coasters built since the Second

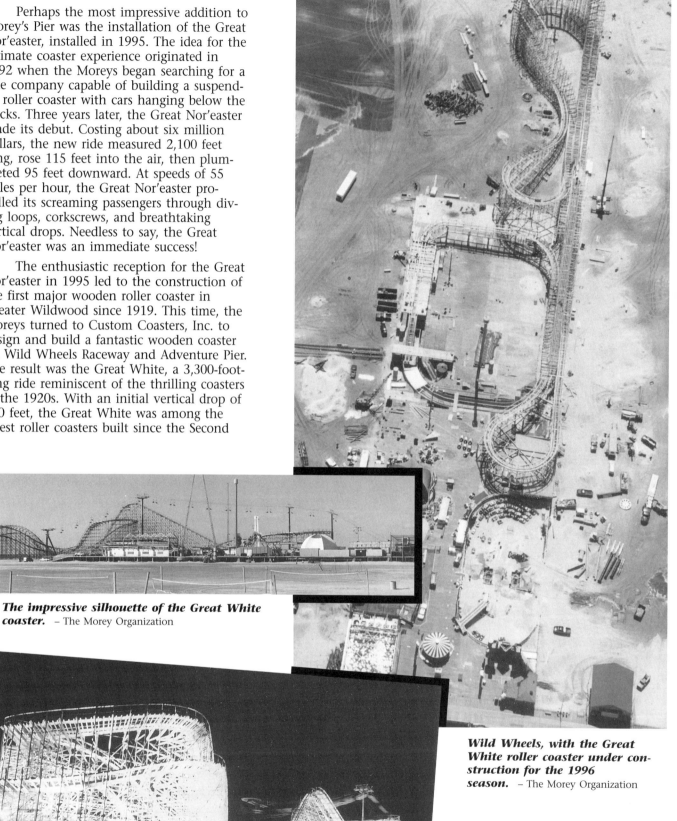

The impressive silhouette of the Great White coaster. – The Morey Organization

Wild Wheels, with the Great White roller coaster under construction for the 1996 season. – The Morey Organization

White sand, white light, the Great White... against the night sky.
– Amusement Park Books

221

Unlike sprawling theme parks, amusement piers utilize every square foot of space. Here the Great White is in the middle of the action surrounded by pier attractions. – Richard F. Hershey Collection

In 1994, crowds still lined Magnolia Avenue and waited for seats at Groff's legendary restaurant. – Earl A. Groff Collection

World War. The introduction of the new coaster in 1996 attracted media attention from all over the East Coast. Twenty thousand spectators attended the unveiling ceremony which included a 1950s-style dance, a party on the pier, and the Flying Elvi, a ten-member parachute team who performed their feats in Elvis Presley costumes. Symbolizing the rebirth of the Wildwoods, it seemed as though the entire community was in some way involved in the promotion and celebration of the opening of the Great White.

"PIERING" INTO THE FUTURE

While no one can predict the future, the fact that the Wildwoods continue to attract nearly four million people each summer should ensure the resort's success well into the new millennium. Obviously, the Atlantic Ocean, the broad stretches of sandy beach, and the revitalized Boardwalk, still beckon vacationers as they have since the early 1900s. Moreover, the island's elected officials, civic leaders, and businesspeople are united in their dedication to ensure that Wildwood's future will be as bright as its past. To that end, amusement operators have pledged to continue making significant investments in new rides and attractions on the piers and along the Boardwalk. The fact that the beach continues to widen at the rate of approximately 35 feet per year has prompted discussion about constructing another amusement pier and a gambling casino. More immediate plans call for a new convention hall, a minor league baseball team and stadium, and improved island-wide transportation systems. And, although there is still concern regarding the redevelopment of areas west of the Boardwalk, major efforts are now underway to renovate the entire island.

Once referred to as the New Atlantic City, the Gem of the Jersey Coast, and even the Rogue of Resorts, the Wildwoods always seemed to rank behind Atlantic City and Asbury Park in both popularity and prosperity. Today, after a decline of more than two decades, Asbury Park is merely a shadow of a once-great resort. And, while Atlantic City has experienced an amazing rebirth thanks to gambling casinos, it is no longer considered a true summer resort. Only the Wildwoods are left to remind us of what summer at the shore really means. Developments that began taking shape in the 1970s have finally put the Wildwoods where they belong: at the very top of the Jersey Shore summer resorts. For more than one hundred years the communities of Five Mile Beach have ridden the roller coaster of fate from prosperity to near poverty and back again. They have weathered hurricanes, fires, Prohibition, two world wars, ocean pollution, devastating publicity, and a host of other traumatic events only to reemerge as one of America's most beloved summer resorts. Today, thanks to the recent rebirth of the Wildwoods and the extensive redevelopment of the Boardwalk, Five Mile Beach stands unchallenged as the "Queen of the Jersey Shore Resorts."

The look of the 1950s is preserved and imitated in numerous motels at the Wildwoods.
– Amusement Park Books

Part of Wildwood's urban re-development program included a pedestrian shopping mall. – Cape May County Department of Tourism

Above:
The Wildwood Crest fishing pier, a private sportsman's retreat with a long history.
– David W. Francis Collection

The amusement piers of the Wildwoods in 1996. From bottom, Wild Wheels Pier, Mariner' Landing, Morey' Pier, Dinosaur Beach Adventure Park. – The Morey Organization

Wildwood

Curiosities in Living Wood.

Ocean Pier.

"Watch the tram car please!" The Sightseer trams are still the convenience that they were when first operated in 1949.
– Cape May County Department of Tourism

226

**Wildwood pier scenes from the camera eye of Walter
Choroszewski.** – Walter Choroszewski Photography

Wildwood pier scenes from the camera eye of Walter Choroszewski. – Walter Choroszewski Photography

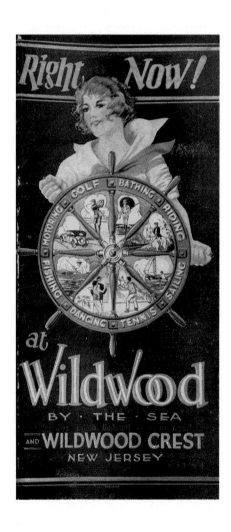

A whirl of color.
– Cape May County Department of Tourism

Int
- M

After coming up for air the Great White makes a steep, long plunge into the swirl of its dramatic track design.
- Lee O. Bush Collection

233

he station on Hunt's Flyer, 1985.
Collection

What goes up, must come down. The 115 foot
Sea Serpent. – Richard F. Hershey Collection

Sportland was a showcase for European amusement rides imported by Gilbert Ramagosa.
– Photograph by Charles J. Jacques, Jr.

Sailboats on the beach in 1992.
– Cape May County Department of Tourism

Where the ocean and the land meet, there is a magical atmosphere that makes seaside resorts possible.

The commercial fishing fleet of the Wildwoods is smaller than it once was, but remains an important part of the resort heritage.
– Cape May County Department of Tourism

Morning strollers and bicyclers on the Boardwalk.
– David W. Francis Collection

Kite flying is just one way to enjoy the great beaches of the Wildwoods.
– Cape May County Department of Tourism

The carousel on Sportland Pier included horses carved by the early New York craftsmen, Stein & Goldstein. – Photograph by Charles J. Jacques, Jr.

Dante's Inferno on Morey's Pier.
– The Morey Organization

Boo - Hisss!
– Cape May County Department of Tourism

The Great White dives under the pier in its approach to the chain lift.
– Richard F. Hershey Collection

The Great White coaster, Aerial Skyride, and Doo Wop Diner at Wild Wheels.
– The Morey Organization

Right: The excitement of the Wildwoods on a hot summer day.
– Cape May County Department of Tourism

The Great Nor'easter at Morey's Pier, 1995.
– Mark Wyatt Collection

Wildwood

Painted white and well illuminated, Hunt's Flyer stands out against a night sky.
– Mark Wyatt Collection

A birds eye view of
Wildwood piers, beach,
and neon.
— AC Photo

240

The modern Wildwood Boardwalk, with the Municipal Band Shell (left).
– David W. Francis Collection

The glow of dusk on the beach at Wildwood. – Amusement Park Books

Since the 1880s, children of all ages have come to the Wildwoods and the Jersey Shore for one purpose...to enjoy a summer vacation experience that cannot be duplicated anywhere else in the world.
– David W. Francis Collection

INDEX

Unless otherwise noted, all indexed subject material is in reference to the Wildwoods.

References to illustrations are in boldface type.

Kay, Robert, 211
Kay, Robert E., 150
Kay, Robert J., 92
Kay and Karol's juggling act, 133
Keating, Harry, 83
Keim, Jacob, 4
Keiter, Reverend, 59
Keith vaudeville circuit, 83
Kelly, Helen Coombs, 211
Kelly Slide (ride), 115
Kenmore Hotel, 124
Kentucky Derby (game), 78
Keystone Leather Company, 41
Kiddie's Theatre, 133
King Edward (hotel), 144
King Kong (fiberglass figure), 214
Kirkwood, Philip, 130
Klienz, Anna, 22
Kline's Restaurant, 58
Kloss, Bill, 128
Knee-Hi (trained lifeguard dog), 112
Knight, Gladys, and the Pips, 193
Knoll's Motel, 143
Koester, Julius, 136
Kohr Bros. Frozen Custard, 146, 194,
    194, **195**, **214**
Kotton Kandy Kitchen, 79
Kotz, Ed, 81
Krause, Cleon, 81
Krogman, George, 111
Ku Klux Klan, 74-75
Kuchi Oishi, 130

Lachappelle, Maurice, 133
Laff Theatre, **118**
Lake Hopatcong, N.J., 20, 194-95
Landis, Charles, 13
Lane, Frankie, 163
Lanoce, Valentino, 144
Lanza, Mario.
    see Cocozza, Alfredo "Freddy"
Lapatina's Orchestra, Professor, 28
LaRosa, Julius, 162, 193
Larson, Morgan, 81
Lasky, Jesse, 153
Latern Lane (motel), 143
Laughing Sal, 117, **118**
Laura, Joe, 79
Laura, Kate, 79
Laura's Fudge, 79, 194, **172**
Lauterbach, Ed, 91
Lawnside, N.J., 80
Lawyer, Jack "Old Shoe", 161, 181
Leaming, Aaron, 13
Lee, Peggy, 163
Lennon Sisters, 182

Lewes, Del., 57, 61, 99, 167, 184
Lewis, Jerry, 163
Liberace, 163
Liberty Root Beer, 79
Liddell, Dee, 106
lifeguards, 104, 109, 113, 133, 152,
    167, **113**, **118**, **134**, **152**
    first female, 113
    first hired by municipality, 55
    first use of, 18, 25,
    labor disputes of, 171.
    see also United States Lifesaving
        Services; Wildwood Beach Patrol
Lilley, Sam, University of Pennsylvania
    Sextette, 87
Lingerman, Sam and Lucy, 48
Lipkin, William, 86, 87-90, 99
Lit Brothers Department Store, 123
Little, Little Jack, 109
Little Miss North American
    Hemishpere Pageant, 181
Little Richard, 163
lodging
    1890s-1900, 20-21
    1910s, 45, 63-65
    1920s, 97-98
    1930s, 124
    World War II, 133
    postwar-1950s, 141-45
    1960s, 182-83
    1970s-90s, 190-91, 198, **223**
    motels, advent of, 141-43
    safety regulations and, 143-44.
    see also specific hotels and motels
Log Flume, 208, **203**
Lombardo, Guy, 109
Long, N.B., 33
Long, R. Arthur, 58-59.
    see also R. Arthur Long and Son
Long Beach, Calif., **9**
Long Branch, 8, 9-10, 143
Lopez, Vincent, 108
Lord Jim, 163
Loreto Hotel, 105
Louisiana Praline Store, 52
Louisiana Purchase Exposition (St.
Louis, 1904), 10
Lowe, Clayton, 23, 79.
    see also Lowe's (candy shops)
Lowe's (candy shops), 23, 45, 52, 53,
    58, 66, 68, 74, 79, **25**
Lowe's Restaurant, 124
Lower Villa (hotel), 21
Loyal's Dogs, Alf, 133
Ludlam, Charles, 31
Ludlam's Beach, 12, 13
Luff, Edward, 83

Luff, F.H., 83
Luff, F.H., Jr., 83
Luff's Pier, 83-85, **84**.
    see also Allison's Pier
Lund, Art, 163
Lyndhurst Bar, 162

McDaniel, Tex, 114
Mace, Charles, 16, 25, 31
Mace's Hotel, 31
Mace's Pavilion, 31, 37
McGarry, Edward, 97
McGuigan, Madeline, 43
MacHarg, Ed, 109
Mack's & Joe's, 146
Mack's Pizza, 194
McKeesport, Pa., 80
Mackey, Harry, 81
McKinney's Cotton Pickers, 109
McMahon, Ed, 186
Madara, George, 19
Magic Mountain (Valencia, Calif.), 190
Magid, Larry, 193
Magnolia Lake, 23, 31, **24**
Maguire Sisters, 163
Malkin, Warren, 152
Mangels, William, 84
Manhattan Beach (Coney Island, N.Y.), 57
Manhattan Player (theatre), 56
Manor Super Club, 163, 181, 182
maps, **33**, **63**, **167**
Marble Tournament.
    see National Marble Tournament
Mariana and her marionettes, 133
Marine Hall, 21, 22, 23
Marine Pier, 92, 119, 120, 121, 159,
    180, 193, 211, 216, **119**, **120**,
    148, **179**, **180**, **211**, **238**.
    see also Amusement Center;
Mariner's Landing; Nickel's
    Midway Pier; Rhoads-Blaker
    Amusement Center
Mariner's Landing, 206, 217-19, **207**,
    216, **217**, **218**, **224**, **226**, **238**
    see also Marine Pier
Mars (ride), 180
Marshall, Slim, 108
Marten's (novelty shop), 52
Martindale, Thomas, 15
Martino, Al, 163, 182
Martino, Vincent, 182
Maryland Hall, 124
Masciarella, Charles, 193, 198-99,
    154, **195**, **196**
Masked Marvel (wrestler), 133
Mathew's Photo Studio, 48, **34**

streetcars and electric railways, 37-38, 61, 105, 132, **38**, **73**, **131**
  see also Five Mile Beach Electric Railway
Strickler, H.L., 47
Sturmer, John, 16
Suez, Eddie, 163
Sullivan, Ed, 168, 209
Sun Deck (motel), **141**
Sun Dial (motel), **141**
Sunday closing laws, 35-36, 58-59, 122, 168
Sunrise Hotel, 16
Surf Club, 163, 181, 182, 193
Surf House (Atlantic City), 10
Surfside Golf, 220
Surfside Hotel, 136, **77**
Surfside Pier, 193, 214
Sweet, Joseph, 55, 73
Sweet's Baths, 52, 55, 93, 100, **92**
Sweeten, Frank B., 38
swim wear, changing fashion and controversies of, 25, 54, 93-94, 112, 149-50
Swooper (ride), 159
Swope, Frederick E., 13

T. Sotto Company, 48
Taj Mahal Casino (Atlantic City), 206
Takamuri's (Japanese goods), 52
Tall Cedars of Lebanon convention, **58**
Tauber ("The Waffle King"), 124
Taylor's Pork Roll Sandwich Shop, 146
Teagarden, Jack, 163
Tempest, John, 136
Temple, Shirley, 123
Tempo (motel), 182
Terminal Cafe, 105
Texas Lunch, 78
theatres.
  see motion pictures; vaudeville; *specific theatres*
Thomas, W.W., 25
Three Stooges, 135
Three Suns, 163
Thriller, (ride), 120
Tilt-A-Whirl (ride), 180, **179**
Tilyou, George C., 9
Tomalino, Andre, 81
Torme, Mel, 163
Tourist Information Center, 163
Tower Villa (hotel), 21
Toyland Circus, **203**
Tracey, Bill, 178
Tram Car Amusement Company, 147
tram cars.

  see Sightseer trams
Traymore Hotel (Atlantic City), 190
Trenton (hotel), 21
Trenton, N.J., 15, 63
Troilo's Royal Italian Band, 43, 65.
  see also Cianfoni, Signor; Cianfoni's Band
Trump, Donald, 206
Tuffy (lion), 111, **112**
Tunis, Dr., 23
Turtle Gut Inlet, 69
20th Century Fox Studios, 153
Two Mile Beach, 12, 99.
  see also Wildwood Crest
Two Moons (Indian chief), 60

U.S.S.*Wisconsin*, 69
"Uncle Wip" (radio personality), 117
Underwood Hotel, 124
Union Trust, 194
United States Army Field Band, 160
United States District Court (Camden, N.J.), 114
United States Lifesaving Services, 25, **25**
United Spanish War Vererans, 166
Uno (dog act), 43
Unwanted Child, The, (play), 80
USO canteen, **130**

Vale, Jerry, 182
vaudeville, 48, 59, 83
  and Blaker, Gib, 28
  at Blaker's Theatre, **27**
  at Casino Arcade, 30
  and motion pictures, competition from, 56-57, 80, 103
  at Ocean Pier, 42, 43
Vaughn, Sarah, 163
Versaggi Brothers Construction Company, 77
Veterans of Foreign Wars, 187
Vineland, 13, 19, 26
Vineland Grape Juice Company, 52
Volstead Act, 74
Vorhees Act, 36.
  see also Sunday closing laws; Bishop's Law

"W" tree, **14**
Walkaway Malties, 78
War Price and Rationing Board, 132
War Prohibition Act, 74
Ward, Ed, 83
Ward, Pat, 81
Ware, J.H., 27, 31

Warren, Allen, 167
Warren, Charles, 67
Warrick, Ruth, 153
Warrington, Phil, 105
Washburn, Rosalie, 30
Washburn and D'Alma Trained Animal Show, 55
Washington, D.C., 2, 22, 33, 166, 194
Washington, Dinah, 182
Water Dodgem, 121
Water Follies, 159
Watercade, 133
Wave Swinger (ride), 217
Way, Palmer M., 92, 113, 122
Way, Palmer M., Jr., 183, 211
Weiner, William, 147
Weiner's Ice Cream Parlor, 70
Welch's Grape Juice Parlor, 52, 69
Wenonah Military Academy, 60
Wenzel, Gwen, 163
West Jersey and Seashore Railroad, 60, 104
West Jersey Electric Company, 29, 56, 91
West Jersey Railroad, 13, 19, 37
West Wildwood, 3, 188
Westinghouse Electric and Manufacturing Company, 94
Whacky Shack (fun house), 204, **202**
What Price Glory, 153
Whip (ride)
  Amusement Center, 90
  Luff's Pier, 84
  Ocean Pier, 117
Whirlwind.
  see under roller coasters
Whitcomb's Honey Chewing Candy, 52
White City Park (Chicago, Ill), 135
Wicks, John, 55
Wild Mouse.
  see under roller coasters
Wild Wheels Pier, 217, **221**, **224**
Wild Wheels Raceway and Adventure Pier, 221
"Wildwood" (song), **110**
Wildwood (steamer), 37, 61
"Wildwood, Beauteous Wildwood", 58
Wildwood, Borough of, 13, 38, 50, 59.
  see also Wildwood, City of
Wildwood, City of, 3, 12, 112, 121, 129, 191, 192, 197
  basketball team, 30, 43
  curfew established by, 171
  and Depression, 104, 110
  founding of, 13
  and gambling, 75
  growth of, early, 13-14, 17-18, **41**
  merges with Holly Beach, 40
  motels and, 187

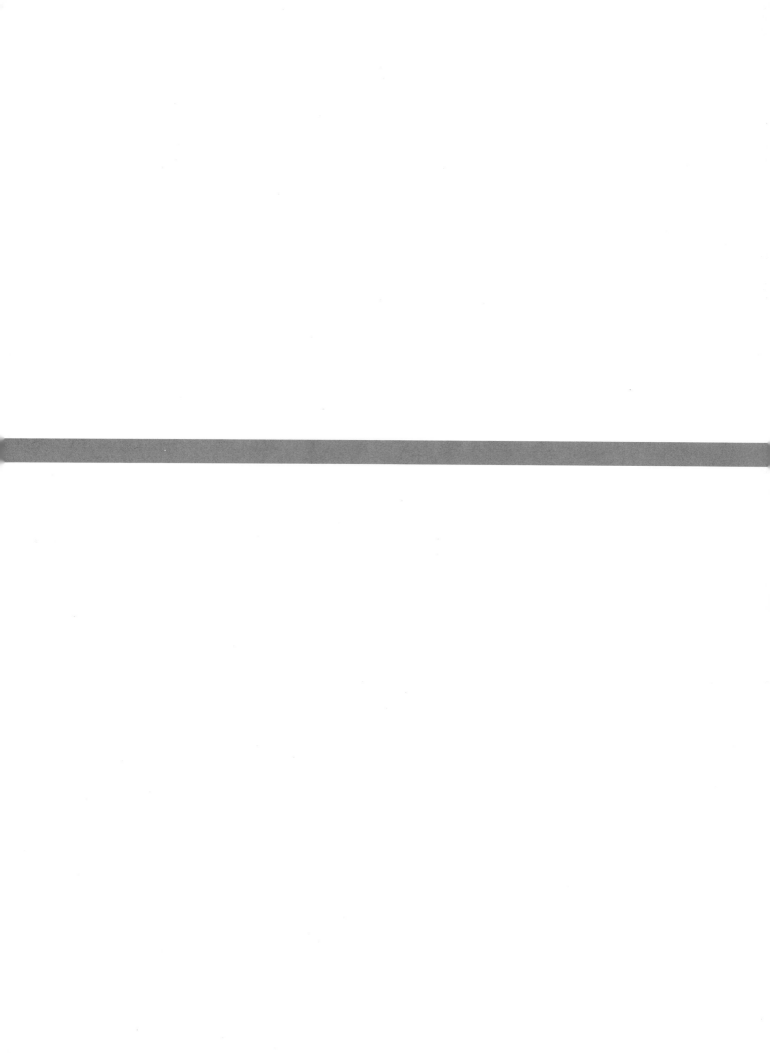

ABOUT THE AUTHORS:

David W. Francis and Diane DeMali Francis

A graduate of Baldwin-wallace College, David Francis has written more than two dozen magazine and journal articles and has been a contributor to *The Encyclopedia of Southern History*. Diane Francis majored in English at the University of Akron before pursuing a career as an advertising copywriter in Akron and New York.

The Francis' collaboration began in the mid-1980s when they began to research the first edition of *Cedar Point: The Queen of American Watering Places*. Since the publication of their first book, they have co-authored three additional works and are currently working on their fourth.

Building on more than 20 years experience in the advertising business, the Francis' founded their own advertising company in Wadsworth, Ohio, in 1990. Maried since 1981, David and Diane share their home with several dogs and cats.

Robert J. Scully, Sr.

Living in Wildwood his entire 64 years, Bob has a deep interest in the community. He attended St. Ann's Elementary School, Wildwood High School for a year and then Wildwood Catholic High School where he graduated in 1951.

In 1955 he graduated from Villanova University with a degree in economics. From 1955 to 1957 he served in the U.S. Army. For the next 10 years he was in lumber, hardware and construction business and for the past 30 years he has been in construction and development. Active in the community, Bob has served on the Wildwood Planning Board and the North Wildwood Zoning Board, the County Park Commission, the Holly Beach Fire Co., the Wildwood Builders Association and as president of the Greater Wildwood Jaycees and as Director of the Union Bank.

In addition, he is a member of the Lions Club, the Community Advisory Board of Burdette Memorial Hospital and was the historian for the St. Ann's centennial committee. Bob and his wife Kitty have four children and 13 grandchildren.

For many years Bob has been the curator of the Wildwood Historical Society and has tirelessly and meticulously helped to document, preserve, and chronicle all aspects of the history of the Wildwoods. Bob devotes many hours to the museum and because of his dedication and the contributions of the Scully family over the past century, future generations will be able to know more about the earliest days of Wildwood and its colorful and unique history.

WILDWOOD
BY-THE-SEA
NEW JERSEY